Understanding People

Alan Millar examines our understanding of why people th
theme is that normative considerations form an indispensable part of the explanatory framework in terms of which we seek to understand each other. Millar defends the idea that normativity is linked to reasons. On this basis he examines the structure of certain normative commitments incurred by having propositional attitudes. Controversially, he argues that ascriptions of beliefs and intentions in and of themselves attribute normative commitments and that this has implications for the psychology of believing and intending. Indeed, all propositional attitudes of the sort we ascribe to people have a normative dimension, since possessing the concepts that the attitudes implicate is of its very nature commitment-incurring. The ramifications of these views for our understanding of people is explored. Millar offers illuminating discussions of reasons for belief and reasons for action; the explanation of beliefs and actions in terms of the subject's reasons; the idea that simulations has a key role in understanding people; and the limits of explanation in terms of propositional attitudes. He compares and contrasts the commitments incurred by propositional attitudes with those incurred by participating in practices, arguing that the former should not be assimilated to the later.

Alan Millar is Professor of Philosophy at the University of Stirling.

Understanding People

Normativity and Rationalizing Explanation

ALAN MILLAR

CLARENDON PRESS · OXFORD

OXFORD
UNIVERSITY PRESS

Great Clarendon Street, Oxford OX2 6DP

Oxford University Press is a department of the University of Oxford
It furthers the University's objective of excellence in research, scholarship,
and education by publishing worldwide in

Oxford New York

Auckland Cape Town Dar es Salaam Hong Kong Karachi
Kuala Lumpur Madrid Melbourne Mexico City Nairobi
New Delhi Shanghai Taipei Toronto

With offices in

Argentina Austria Brazil Chile Czech Republic France Greece
Guatemala Hungary Italy Japan Poland Portugal Singapore
South Korea Switzerland Thailand Turkey Ukraine Vietnam

Oxford is a registered trade mark of Oxford University Press
in the UK and in certain other countries

Published in the United States
by Oxford University Press Inc., New York

© Alan Millar 2004

The moral rights of the author have been asserted
Database right Oxford University Press (maker)

First published 2004
First published in paperback 2008

All rights reserved. No part of this publication may be reproduced,
stored in a retrieval system, or transmitted, in any form or by any means,
without the prior permission in writing of Oxford University Press,
or as expressly permitted by law, or under terms agreed with the appropriate
reprographics rights organization. Enquiries concerning reproduction
outside the scope of the above should be sent to the Rights Department,
Oxford University Press, at the address above

You must not circulate this book in any other binding or cover
and you must impose this same condition on any acquirer

British Library Cataloging in Publication Data
Data available

Library of Congress Cataloging in Publication Data
Data available

Typeset by SPI Publisher Services, Pondicherry, India
Printed in Great Britain
on acid-free paper by
Biddles Ltd, Kings Lynn, Norfolk

ISBN 978–0–19–955672–4

For Rose-Mary and Stéphane

Preface

When I first read Saul Kripke's book, *Wittgenstein: On Rules and Private Language*, it struck me forcibly that something was right about the idea that meaning something by a word is not simply a matter of how one is disposed to use the word. That one means *plus* by 'plus' seems to have implications concerning how one *should* use the word. But it is hard to see how merely being disposed to use a word in certain ways can, by itself, have such implications. A similar issue arises in connection with concepts. It looks plausible that possessing a concept has implications for how it should be employed. If possessing a concept is simply a matter of having certain dispositions, including belief-forming dispositions, then it is hard to see how that can, by itself, have such implications. These thoughts bring others in their train. Beliefs and intentions are psychological states in some way linked to dispositions to thought or action. Yet they seem to incur certain commitments. Having an intention, for instance, seems to commit us to doing whatever is necessary to carry it out. To be so committed is a normative matter—it relates, somehow, to what one should do. But that one has an intention is generally supposed to be a non-normative consideration. So how does the supposedly non-normative consideration relate to the consideration about commitment?

Some philosophers have addressed related matters in terms of the idea that subjects who think and who use language meaningfully operate within the 'logical space of reasons'. The phrase is from Wilfred Sellars (1956) but has been given recent currency by Robert Brandom (1994; 1995) and John McDowell (1994b; 1995). Here is Brandom illustrating a key idea:

A typical twenty-month-old child who toddles into the livingroom and in bell-like tones utters the sentence 'The house is on fire', is doing something quite different from what his seven-year-old sister would be doing by making the same noises. The young child is not claiming that the house is on fire, for the simple reason that he does not know what he would be committing himself to by that claim, what he would be making himself responsible for. He does not know what follows from it, what would be evidence for it, what would be incompatible with it, and so on. He does not know his way around the space of reasons well enough yet for anything he does to count as adopting a standing in that space. (Brandom 1995: 897–8)

According to Brandom, to count as claiming that the house is on fire the child would have to be operating within the space of reasons, and that would require it to have reflective capacities that it lacks. In particular, it would need to have the capacity to think about its own claims, beliefs, etc., and about the commitments and responsibilities that they incur. This is a *high* conception of the space of reasons. An implication of the view is that the concept of making a claim is normative: to view a person as falling under the concept is to view that person as being subject to, and able to appreciate, certain normative constraints.

As it stands, Brandom's illustrative example is under-described. Plausibly, if the child had merely parroted words it had heard on television, no claim would have been made. But suppose that the child had uttered the words having seen a fire start up in the kitchen. Thus far, it is too easy for opposing theorists to dispute the idea that, simply on account of his lacking the resources for thinking about certain types of commitment and responsibility, the child would not count as having made a claim. Granted that a subject who had such resources would think differently from one who did not, it is open to dispute whether the latter would fail to satisfy a necessary condition for making a claim.

For Brandom, making a claim, forming a belief, and so on, take place within the space of reasons. But it is important to ask at this point why we should accept a high conception of that space. One might think that to operate within the space of reasons is, for instance, to believe things and do things *for reasons*. Suppose that, as many have thought, reasons for beliefs are other beliefs, and reasons for action are desires and associated beliefs. Then to believe P for a reason would be to believe P because one has other beliefs that constitute one's reason for believing P. Similarly, to Φ for a reason would be to Φ because one has a belief and desire that constitute one's reason for Φing. Given acceptance of these assumptions, it might well seem baffling that operating in the space of reasons should be thought to require one to have the reflective capacities that Brandom takes to be inextricable from any such operation.

If beliefs and intentions are inextricably tied to normative *commitments*, then, on a natural reading of what such commitments involve, it would follow that subjects who have beliefs and intentions have appropriate reflective capacities. We would be right not to describe a subject as having made a promise if that subject lacked the resources for thinking about promises and the commitments they incur. Likewise, subjects who lacked the resources for thinking about intentions, and the commitments they incur, could not properly be said to have incurred a commitment to doing what is necessary to Φ in virtue of intending to Φ. But that does not settle the substantive matter. Theorists who wish to ascribe intentions to those who lack the requisite reflective capacities will deny that there is any inextricable tie between intending and incurring commitments, so understood. It is open to such theorists to speak of what it would make sense for a creature to do, given that it has a certain intention, but to refuse to cash this out in the language of commitments. On this way of thinking, explanations of what subjects are led to do by an intention would make no reference to an understanding on their part of what makes sense since, under the operative assumptions, they have no such understanding.

It is widely held to be implausible that subjects who lack the resources to think about commitments and other normative matters are unable to make meaningful utterances or form beliefs or other propositional attitudes. This scepticism might be bolstered by appeal to the plausibility of ascribing beliefs and desires to non-human animals that clearly lack the supposedly requisite resources. That said, the course ahead for such theorists is by no means downhill all the way. Suppose it is conceded that a solid case has yet to be made for the view that, in order to make claims and have propositional attitudes, a subject has to be operating within the space of reasons, conceived in line with Brandom's high conception. An implication of such a view is that the subject so operating must have the reflective capacities required for thinking about reasons, commitments, and the like. Even so, such a view is not open to straightforward refutation by appeal to considerations about very young children and non-human animals. There might be a difference in kind between, for instance, the believing of subjects operating within the space of reasons and some analogue of believing of which very young children and non-human animals are capable. (Whether the latter should be described as a species of believing or something else is as may be.) Those who take this possibility seriously owe us an account of why we should think that there is this difference in kind. But, taken by itself, the fact that there are subjects who do something like believing, yet lack the resources for operating within the space of reasons (on the high conception), does not tell against the prospect of providing such an account.

To place my own cards on the table, I take seriously the idea that the beliefs and intentions that figure in our thinking about each other are inextricable from reflective capacities, including those necessary for appreciating the normative commitments incurred by beliefs and intentions. I also take seriously the idea that using words meaningfully implicates reflective capacities, including those necessary for appreciating the normative commitments incurred in virtue of meaning something by a word. But I regard these as problematic ideas. The main aim of the book is to develop a picture on which they emerge as being clear and plausible, and as having interesting implications for the character of our understanding of people. *En route* I highlight problems for opposing views. On the one hand, we have ascriptions of beliefs and intentions and claims about what people mean by words. On the other hand, we have normative considerations about the commitments people incur because of what they believe or intend, or because of what they mean by a word. The problem for the opposition is to explain how the supposedly non-normative ascriptions and claims relate to the normative considerations. Believing and intending, and meaning something by a word, do seem to incur commitments. Believing one thing, for instance, seems to commit us to believing others. At any rate (so as not to beg important questions), with respect to subjects with appropriate resources, believing P seems to incur a commitment to believing what follows from P. (Refinements will be introduced in Chapter 3.) Analogous claims are plausible in connection with intending and meaning something by a word. This requires some explanation. What do believing and intending, and meaning something by a word, have to be such that they always or sometimes give rise to normative commitments? Some theorists think it is easy to account for how meaning something by a word determines how one should use the word. The explanation, they think, lies with aims that are extrinsic to meaning. The aim might be that one believe only what is true, or that one communicate with others, but the important point is that any normativity attached to meaning something by a word is not intrinsic to meaning. This is the approach taken by Paul Horwich (1998). A similar strategy concerning propositional attitudes is pursued by David Papineau (1999) and by Fred Dretske (2000a). I touch on these matters explicitly in Chapter 6. The entire book, however, may be seen as an attempt to meet the challenge from the sceptics to show why we should acknowledge a normative dimension in thought and action and why we should conceive of that dimension in the way I do.

It is not easy to find a clear path through these thickets. One reason for the difficulty is that the very idea of the normative is unclear. Another widely held view—one that I share—is that there is a constitutive link between propositional attitudes and rationality, so that any creature that has propositional attitudes must exhibit some degree of rationality. Rationality surely implicates standards or norms of rationality. So, one might think, if it is constitutive of having propositional attitudes that a subject having such attitudes is to some degree rational, it follows that having them is an intrinsically normative matter. Maybe so, but sometimes, for instance in Kripke's discussion, talk about the normative is about what subjects ought to do. On a natural interpretation, the relevant kind of ought is such that claims about what a creature ought to think or do are true only of creatures with the resources for thinking about reasons bearing upon what they think and do. (The ought of expectation, as in 'The hammer ought to be on the bench', is a different matter.) Those who accept that propositional attitudes are inextricably tied to rationality, and accordingly accept that there is, in some sense, a normative dimension to the attitudes, may yet balk at the idea that the relevant kind of normativity is to be understood in terms of this type of ought. The issue here is evidently closely related to what is a stake in the choice between high and low conceptions of the space of reasons.

I think it would benefit the philosophy of mind if this and related issues were to be moved closer to centre stage. It should not be taken for granted that the reflective capacities that we have are an overlay on a belief–desire psychology that we share with creatures who lack those capacities. The upshot might be a philosophy that, far from ignoring intentionality in non-human animals, enables us to focus more sharply on the shape of such intentionality and its differences from our own. A project in that direction is, however, beyond the scope of this book. Recent work by José Bermúdez (2003) is highly relevant to such a project.

Mainstream philosophers of mind, used to focusing on psychological explanation and the metaphysics of mental causation, might find it frustrating that so much of the space in this book is devoted to discussions of normativity, normative reasons, and normative commitments. Some parts of the discussion might look more at home in a work about practical reason. Other parts would not be out of place in a work on epistemology. What I have already said provides a rationale for the attention paid to such matters. We can hardly avoid them if we are to become clear about what is in dispute between those who think there is rich normative dimension to human thought and action and those who think otherwise.

In writing this book I have been much helped by friends and colleagues at Stirling and elsewhere. Among those who have in some way contributed to the project, sometimes just by raising a question that prompted clarification or forced revision, are José Bermúdez, Andrew Brennan, John Broome, Michael Brady, Peter Carruthers, Tim Chappel, Fred Dretske, Antony Duff, Alan Gibbard, Jane Heal, Christopher Hookway, Martin Kusch, Isaac Levi, Gideon Makin, Hugh Mellor, David Owens, David Papineau, Christian Pillar, Huw Price, Duncan Pritchard, Gideon Rosen, John Skorupski, Michael Smith, Peter Sullivan, Neil Tennant, Suzanne Uniacke, Ralph Wedgwood, and Timothy Williamson. Audiences at Aberdeen, Edinburgh, Genoa, Leeds, Nottingham, St Andrews, York, and Birkbeck College London provided useful feedback and encouragement. Points raised by anonymous readers of Oxford University Press led to improvements.

Work on the book has been made possible by sabbatical leaves from the University of Stirling and by leaves made possible by a Mind Association Research Fellowship and an award under the Research Leave Scheme of the Arts and Humanities Research Board. I have also benefited from the receipt of grants from the Carnegie Trust for the Universities of Scotland. In 1997 I enjoyed a short period as a Visiting Fellow at Clare Hall, Cambridge. I am grateful to the college and to the Cambridge Philosophy Faculty for facilities generously provided during that stay and to all of the individuals and institutions that have provided me with support.

Portions of this work draw upon and develop material that has previously been published. I am grateful to Antony O'Hear, Director of the Royal Institute of Philosophy, for inviting me to give a lecture in the Institute's 2000–1 annual lecture series. The published version is 'The Normativity of Meaning', in O'Hear (2002: 57–73). Much of this forms part of Chapter 6 of this book. I have also drawn upon 'Rationality and Higher-Order Intentionality', in Walsh (2001: 179–98). This is the published version of a talk given at a Royal Institute of Philosophy conference in Edinburgh in 1998. I am grateful to Denis Walsh for inviting me and to the Institute for its support. I am also grateful to Oxford University Press for permission to use material from 'Reasons for Action and Instrumental Rationality', in Bermúdez and Millar (2002: 113–32).

Last but not least, I owe an immense debt to Rose-Mary and Stéphane for their forbearance.

A.M.

Stirling, September 2003

Contents

1 **Introduction**   1
  1. Personal understanding   1
  2. Propositional attitudes and rationality   3
  3. Rationalizing explanation   9
  4. Propositional attitudes and generalizations   16
  5. Understanding and the normative dimension of the mental   21
  6. The way ahead   39

2 **Reasons for Belief and for Action**   41
  1. Introduction   41
  2. Reasons for belief   42
  3. Reasons for action   57
  4. The constitutive aim of intentional action   63
  5. Motivating reasons   68

3 **Normative Commitments and the Very Idea of Normativity**   72
  1. The topic   72
  2. Beliefs, intentions, and commitments   72
  3. Commitments and justification   79
  4. Normative commitments and practices   83
  5. Can practices give rise to reasons in the way proposed?   89
  6. Differences between kinds of commitments   91
  7. Normativity, normative concepts, and normative import   92

4 **Explaining Normative Import**   100
  1. The way ahead   100
  2. Dispositionalism   103
  3. Dispositionalism and the explanation of normative import   108
  4. How we relate to our current intentions and beliefs   110
  5. Intentions, beliefs, and psychological commitment   118
  6. The problem of representing the dispositions characteristic of beliefs and intentions   125
  7. Back to explanatory irrelevance   131

xvi CONTENTS

5 The Reflexivity of Intention and Belief ... 133
   1. The high conception of beliefs and intentions ... 133
   2. Reflexivity ... 138
   3. Intention and reflexivity ... 139
   4. Precarious intentions ... 146
   5. Unreflective intention ... 148
   6. The reflexivity of belief ... 149
   7. Self-deception ... 151

6 Meaning and Intentional Content ... 159
   1. The topic ... 159
   2. Normativity, correctness, and use ... 160
   3. Normativity and truth ... 166
   4. How meaning can be normative ... 167
   5. Deflationist tendencies ... 175
   6. Words and concepts ... 178
   7. Content and psychological explanation ... 186
   8. Normativity and truth again ... 188
   9. Reflexivity in relation to concept-use ... 190

7 The Problem of Explanatory Relevance ... 192
   1. The character of the problem ... 192
   2. The messiness of rationalization ... 203

8 Rationality and Simulation ... 213
   1. Simulation theory versus the theory-theory ... 213
   2. Rationality and 'being like us' ... 225

9 Limits ... 230
   1. Taking stock ... 230
   2. Limitations of available explanations ... 235
   3. Limitations to the availability of explanations ... 237
   4. Expectations ... 241

Bibliography ... 248
Index ... 259

CHAPTER 1

Introduction

1. Personal understanding

You might understand why a colleague is seeking information about jobs in terms of her beliefs about and feelings towards her current job. That is an example of the kind of understanding of people that is the topic of this book. I shall call it *personal understanding*. Other examples are understanding why a teenager wants to study at a university some distance from home in terms of his desire to be independent, and understanding why some experts think that the country's economy is in trouble in terms of their beliefs about relevant economic indicators.

Our attempts at personal understanding are of more than theoretical interest. They affect how we react to people in the interactions of everyday life—what we feel about them, how we act towards them, how we evaluate what they think and do. They affect our reactions to those who govern us, or who influence political or cultural events and movements. And, of course, how we understand our own feelings, decisions, and so forth, is important too and can obviously affect how we judge ourselves, and what we do as a result.

Not all personal understanding goes deep. Sometimes we want to understand the simplest things, for instance why someone is heading in a particular direction. We gain understanding by learning of an intention, like meeting someone, or returning home from work. This often puts an end to enquiry because the intention is of a familiar sort and fits into the patterns of life of the agent. Sometimes knowing of the intention provides little understanding because the intention itself is puzzling. When I am told that an able student who has not been turning up at classes intends to drop out, I have some explanation for his absences but I am left wondering why he should wish to drop out. One thing is clear. There is no simple pattern to the explanations that provide personal understanding. In the case of actions, an explanation may home in on a desire behind the action, or an intention, or an anxiety, or on beliefs relevant to why the action seemed a good idea. It may specify a combination of such factors. If what is to be explained is why a person comes to think that something is so, there may be an explanation in terms of other beliefs of the agent or something the agent knows. Even then, feelings can be important factors. Resentment, for instance, can contribute to the explanation of negatively evaluative judgements of a person. Being infatuated can lead to overly optimistic judgements about the object of infatuation.

Personal understanding takes us into the realm of propositional attitudes—that is to say, the realm of beliefs, intentions, desires, wishes, hopes, fears, and the like. These are psychological states that have *contents* specifiable in terms of a proposition. The content of my belief that interest rates will fall further is simply *that interest rates will fall further*. My belief is true if and only if *that* is true. Similarly, if I wish to travel around the world, the content of my wish is *that I travel around the world*. My wish will be fulfilled if and only if it comes to be true that I travel around the world. This way of thinking brings out two important points. (i) Differences between attitudes in different categories (believing, wishing, etc.) are differences in stance towards what would be the case if the content of the attitude were true. If I believe that interest rates will fall, then my stance towards the content that interest rates will fall is such that my subsequent thought and action are liable to be guided by a picture of the course of events on which this content will turn out to be true. If I wish that interest rates will fall, then my stance towards the content that interest rates will fall is such that I will regret it if this does not turn out to be true. (ii) Any subject who possesses a propositional attitude must have the conceptual resources for entertaining the content of that attitude. Unless I have some grasp of the concept of a thermometer, I cannot have beliefs that involve my thinking of thermometers as thermometers. Lacking the concept, I could believe of something that is a thermometer that it is, say, kept in a certain drawer, but I could not believe that it is a thermometer. The same applies *mutatis mutandis* to all the other attitudes. These considerations place an important constraint upon plausible ascriptions of propositional attitudes: it must be plausible that the subject has the concepts that the attitudes implicate.

Because it deals with propositional attitudes, personal understanding has a distinctive subject-matter. To say this is not to say much, however. The subject-matter of chemistry differs from that of physics; the subject-matter of biology differs from that of chemistry. Yet these different sciences are all of a piece; they all deal in empirically based theories about the forces, fields, mechanisms, or processes that account for discernible regularities in nature. A central philosophical issue about personal understanding is whether its distinctive subject-matter calls for a distinctive kind of understanding—a kind of understanding that differs in some marked way from the theoretical understanding of science.[1] Is there any reason to think that understanding why someone wishes to change job in terms of her dissatisfaction with her current job differs *qua* understanding, and not just in subject-matter, from, say, understanding why a muscle contracts in terms of electrical signals conducted along the nerves from the brain?

In the light of the philosophy of mind of recent decades, a natural starting point for reflection on such matters is the connection between propositional attitudes and rationality. For one might think that it is some link between rationality and the attitudes that makes personal understanding differ, *qua* understanding, from understanding of the sort characteristic of natural science. This is the view that I take, but it needs some working out.

2. Propositional attitudes and rationality

Much of the impetus to think about the connection between propositonal attitudes and rationality has come from the work of Donald Davidson. Everybody agrees that propositional attitudes can be *evaluated* in terms of whether or not they are rational or reasonable. That goes for hopes, fears, and desires, as well as beliefs and intentions. Davidson makes the stronger claim that the having of propositional

---

[1] For scepticism on this score, see R. Miller (1987: 126 ff.).

attitudes is inextricably tied to rationality.[2] This *rationality assumption*, as I shall call it, lies behind the following passage:

[W]hen we use the concepts of belief, desire, and the rest, we must stand prepared, as the evidence accumulates, to adjust our theory in the light of considerations of overall cogency: the constitutive ideal of rationality partly controls each phase in the evolution of what must be an evolving theory. (Davidson 1970/1980: 223)

There is clearly an epistemological claim here: ascriptions of attitudes are warranted only if appropriately constrained by the constitutive ideal of rationality. But what is this ideal, and why should it be thought to constrain ascriptions of attitudes? Much of Davidson's thinking on these matters is worked out in the context of a theory of radical interpretation. Such a theory concerns how we can interpret the utterances of others, without a pre-existing translation scheme, by connecting the utterances to each other and to the subjects' behaviour and surroundings. However, the fundamentals of Davidson's thinking on the link between propositional attitudes and rationality are independent of considerations about radical interpretation. The following passage, from the article just quoted, makes it explicit that there are limits to irrationality that are bound up with the requirements of concept-possession:

Global confusion, like universal mistake, is unthinkable, not because imagination boggles, but because too much confusion leaves nothing to be confused about and massive error erodes the background of true belief against which alone failure can be construed. To appreciate the limits to the kind and amount of blunder and bad thinking we can intelligibly pin on others is to see once more the inseparability of the question what concepts a person commands and the question what he does with those concepts in the way of belief, desire and intention. To the extent that we fail to discover a coherent and plausible pattern in the attitudes and actions of others we simply forgo the chance of treating them as persons. (Davidson 1970/ 1980: 221–2)

In the closing stage of this passage there seems to be an implicit argument to the effect that, since the people we seek to understand would be persons only if their attitudes and actions exhibited coherent

---

[2] Analogous views have been advanced by Dennett (1978; 1987).

and plausible patterns, it follows that, so long as we view them as persons, we are committed to making them out to exhibit such patterns. But what is more significant, I think, is the explanation of why persons must exhibit coherent and plausible patterns among their attitudes and actions. The explanation Davidson has in mind is only hinted at, but clearly has to do with what is involved in possessing, and thus having some command or mastery, of the concepts that one's attitudes bring into play. The key idea, I take it, is that if we possess certain concepts we must be able to exploit them in forming, considering, and abandoning attitudes. Exploiting the concepts necessarily goes with respecting their logical roles—their potential to contribute to fixing the logical powers of the contents of beliefs and other attitudes that bring them into play.

An ascription of attitudes that represented a subject as having attitudes that are incoherent in certain ways would be at odds with a presupposition of that very ascription—that the subject has enough grasp of the relevant concepts to have the attitudes that the ascription attributes. For an illustrative example, consider Fred who, in the course of a short stretch of conversation, utters the sentences 'Edinburgh is to the east of Glasgow' and 'Glasgow is to the east of Edinburgh'. (Davidson uses a similar example in Davidson 1990: 24.) Were we to take these sentences at face value, then, assuming that Fred spoke sincerely, we would ascribe to him both the belief that Edinburgh is to the east of Glasgow and the belief that Glasgow is to the east of Edinburgh. In view of this, a natural reaction would be that Fred had made some slip of the tongue. Perhaps instead of saying, 'Glasgow is to the east of Edinburgh' he really meant to say, 'Glasgow is to the west of Edinburgh.' We might be led to take such a possibility seriously because we would be hard put to make sense of how he could have both the beliefs in question. Here is why. If Fred had both of the beliefs, then he would need to have a grasp of that concept of one place being to the east of another place. But having such a grasp would involve respecting the logical role of the concept. This would involve appreciating that it follows from the assumption that Edinburgh is to the east of Glasgow that it is not the case that Glasgow is to the east of Edinburgh. So, barring some special explanation, it is to be expected that Fred would react appropriately to the obvious inconsistency of the two beliefs.³ To have either of the beliefs he would need to have the concept, but if he had the concept then it is odd that he should have the beliefs. There is no suggestion that the mere having of inconsistent beliefs is problematic.⁴ Believing inconsistent things is easy if, for instance, the inconsistency is not obvious, or goes unnoticed because the relevant contents do not come to mind at the same time. The inconsistencies in belief that are problematic are ones that (a) could hardly escape notice in the circumstances and (b) put a strain on the presumption that the subject is exploiting the concepts that the beliefs in question would bring into play.

Implicit in the above discussion is the idea that one who possesses a concept is able to deploy it in reasoning in ways that respect its logical role. I take cogent reasoning to be reasoning from assumptions that comprise adequate reasons for believing a conclusion to a belief in that conclusion. This being so, cogency concerns not just the transition from certain assumptions to a conclusion, but also the status of the assumptions. The assumptions must constitute an adequate reason to believe the conclusion and this will be so only if they are true.⁵ It is convenient, therefore, to work with a notion of *conditional cogency* for the purposes of characterizing transitions in reasoning, without regard to the status of the relevant assumptions An argument is conditionally cogent if its premises would *if true* provide an adequate reason to believe its conclusion. A stretch of reasoning, in the psychological sense, comprises input beliefs and an output belief based on these. A stretch of reasoning is conditionally cogent if it mirrors a conditionally cogent argument, that is, when the assumptions that form the contents of the input beliefs would, if true, provide an adequate reason to believe the conclusion that forms the content of

---

³ The qualification about special explanation accommodates, perhaps among other things, situations like that of Kripke's Pierre, who is blind to the fact that he believes two propositions, one of which is the negation of the other, since he believes them under articulations in different languages (see Kripke 1979). The fact that a subject has incompatible beliefs may be explicable because the subject is unaware that two different expressions designate the same object or express the same concept. In these cases incompatibility is not at odds with the assumption that the subject has an adequate grasp of the relevant concepts.

⁴ See, further, the discussion of Goldman (1989) in Sect. 4 below.

⁵ This seems to me to be in keeping with common sense. The requirement that the assumptions be true might strike some as too strong on the grounds that one can reasonably believe a conclusion on the basis of assumptions, some of which are false. But accommodating that plausible thought does not require a weaker notion of a cogent reason. One may reasonably believe something on grounds that one mistakenly but reasonably takes to be cogent in the stronger sense.

the output belief. Having propositional attitudes is compatible with being deeply confused and unreasonable on many matters. Even so, the fact that one possesses the concepts that one's attitudes bring into play, and that in virtue of possessing the concepts one would have an ability to exploit them in ways that respect their logical roles, guarantees that there must be limits to the extent to which our reasoning lacks conditional cogency. As Davidson notes, too much confusion leaves nothing to be confused about. If somebody appears to treat dry cracked ground as a sign that it has just rained, then we should doubt whether he has taken in that the ground is dry and cracked or whether he understands what would have been the case if it had just rained. There might be a story to tell that would make sense of the thinking he appears to have gone through—perhaps he has a weird conception of the effects of water in certain unusual circumstances. The point is that there would need to be some explanation of how he could be exploiting the concept of its having just rained.

The *rationality assumption* is sometimes thought to be undermined, or at least made problematic, by the fact that people can be highly confused and can reason badly. (See further in Section 5.) But there is no real tension here because, in the sense intended, rationality is compatible with a lot of bad thinking. In this context rationality has to do with, for instance, limits to bad reasoning and to blindness to bad reasoning, and accordingly with limits to incoherence. At least part of the explanation for the limits is that, since the possession of propositional attitudes involves the possession of relevant concepts, it implicates abilities to exploit these concepts in ways that respect their logical roles. Just as there is no mystery about how people can have incoherent beliefs, so there is no mystery about how people can reason badly. The point is that there are steps in reasoning which would betray a level of confusion about certain concepts that cannot be reconciled with the assumption that the subject is exploiting *those* concepts.

I do not mean to suggest that considerations about concept-possession give the whole story about the rationality that is inextricability tied to the having of propositional attitudes. Consider this passage from a discussion in which Davidson provides an overview of his thinking:

8 INTRODUCTION

Individual beliefs, intentions, doubts and desires owe their identities in part to their position in a large network of further attitudes: the character of a given belief depends on endless other beliefs; beliefs have the role they do because of their relations to desires and intentions and perceptions. These relations among the attitudes are essentially logical: the content of an attitude cannot be divorced from what it entails and what is entailed by it. This places a normative constraint on the correct attribution of attitudes: since an attitude is in part identified by its logical relations, the pattern of attitudes in an individual must exhibit a large degree of coherence. This does not, of course, mean that people may not be irrational. But the possibility of irrationality depends on a background of rationality; to imagine a totally irrational animal is to imagine an animal without thoughts. (Davidson 1995: 232; similar remarks occur in Davidson 1975/1984: 159; 1982/2001: 99)

There is a strand in this passage that links up directly with the considerations about concept-possession that I have been outlining. Attitudes are individuated in part by their contents. A subject who has an attitude with a certain content must possess the relevant concepts. In virtue of possessing those concepts, the subject must be to some degree sensitive to the logical powers of that content. But there is another strand in the passage that is about constraints on how attitudes can hang together, which are imposed by the categories to which attitudes belong—whether they are beliefs, desires, intentions or whatever. Beliefs are beliefs at least in part because they supply assumptions in reasoning that lead to the formation of other beliefs. Desires are desires at least in part because, in tandem with beliefs about how they can be satisfied, they lead to the formation of intentions. The attitudes that it makes sense to ascribe to a person must be compatible not just with the concepts the person has, but also with the causal roles that these attitudes have in virtue of belonging to this or that category of attitude.

There is another dimension to how propositional attitudes connect with rationality that deserves attention before we proceed. Routinely, in attempting to understand people we connect what they do with their current surroundings in ways that make sense, taking it for granted that they have taken in what is happening in those surroundings. We understand why someone ducks while playing tennis when we see that the ball just served was heading straight for her face. At a game of soccer we understand why player A moves away from player B because we see that B is trying to mark A. While crawling along in a queue of traffic we see someone gingerly-approaching the queue from a side street. We see that he wants to be let in. These are cases of people doing things in response to knowledge of their surroundings. They illustrate that facts and events 'external' to agents can help to make sense of their thoughts and actions. But there is a deeper point here. The creatures to whom we routinely ascribe determinate beliefs, desires, and other attitudes are rational agents that respond intelligently to what is going on around them. Such creatures may have lots of false beliefs, and on many matters may reason badly. But they would be unable to respond intelligently to their circumstances unless they had ways of telling what their circumstances are. Further, if their knowledge of their circumstances is to relate to present action—for instance, fleeing from a present danger—it must incorporate a demonstrative knowledge of those surroundings. The knowledge that enables me deliberately to avoid a vehicle heading towards me now must incorporate knowledge that *that* thing is heading towards *me now*. For creatures of the sort I have been discussing, then, an important dimension of rationality is being in touch with reality, that is to say, having knowledge grounded in perception. For my purposes we need not explore whether necessarily any creature having beliefs and desires would exhibit this dimension of rationality, though I am inclined to think that this is so. My concern is with how we understand people who, however severely impaired they may be, acquire beliefs, desires, and other attitudes through perceptual encounters with their surroundings and who act intelligently in and on their surroundings. For such creatures there is no separating rationality from knowledge, and indeed from demonstrative knowledge, of the surroundings.

3. Rationalizing explanation

Often people think things or do things or want things, or feel some way, *for a reason*. I believe my neighbour is at home because her lights are on and they are never on unless she is at home. I seek a loan because I intend to buy a new car and need a loan to do so. I want to go for a long walk because I have not left the house for a couple of days and need some exercise. I feel ashamed because I have just given an ill-prepared lecture and I ought to have given a far better one. In each of these cases there is a *rationalizing explanation* of something—an explanation in terms of my reason for, respectively, believing something, or doing something, or wanting something, or feeling some way.[6] Since people believe, desire, and so on, for reasons, rationalizing explanation has a central role in our attempts to understand people. Indeed, necessarily creatures with beliefs, desires, and intentions think and act in ways that admit of rationalizing explanation, since the roles that are characteristic of these attitudes guarantee that they will sometimes issue in belief or action for reasons. However, the relation between rationalizing explanation and rationality is more complex than is generally made explicit.

Some statements that are made about rationalization suggest that, for instance, belief or action for a reason is rational or reasonable belief or action. In one passage Davidson writes:

A reason is a rational cause. One way rationality is built in [to acting on a reason] is transparent: the cause must be a belief and a desire in the light of which the action is reasonable. (Davidson 1974/1980: 233)[7]

In a similar vein, Louise Anthony, writing specifically about action, states that 'rationalization must display the action as being reasonable in the light of the beliefs and desires attributed' (Anthony 1989: 157).[8] The trouble with these ways of capturing what rationalization amounts to is that, since reasons can be pretty bad, beliefs held or actions done for reasons need not be reasonable or rational in any ordinary sense.[9] Reasons in this context are *motivating* or *explanatory* reasons. It is one thing for something to be *my reason for tidying my room*—a motivating reason—and another for it to be *a reason for me to*

---

[6] The relevant sense of 'rationalization' is close to that in Davidson (1963/1980). Readers unfamiliar with the jargon should note that the notion of rationalization in this context is not the same as that used to characterize self-deceiving accounts given by people of the reasons for their own conduct.

[7] See also the remark in Davidson (1982/2001: 99) that 'an emotion like being pleased that one has stopped smoking must be an emotion that is rational in the light of the beliefs and values that one has'.

[8] Here is another example from Coltheart and Davies (2000: 2): 'If we cannot make any sense at all of how a certain person could reasonably have arrived at a particular belief on the basis of experience and inference then this counts, provisionally even if not decisively, against the attribution of this belief to this person.'

[9] It is only fair to note that Anthony is expounding views of others and that her principal concern in the work cited is not with the detailed character of rationalization, but with the explanatory relevance of rationalization. And, to be fair to Davidson, it should be noted that he sometimes speaks of rationalization as making reasonable or rational *from the agent's point of view*; see Davidson (1963/1980: 9).

tidy my room. A reason in the latter sense is a *normative* reason: it in some way favours or recommends that for which it is a reason. An agent may believe something or do something for a reason and lack an adequate normative reason for believing that thing or doing that thing.[10] The same applies to a person's reasons for wanting something or for feeling some way. None the less, I argue, even when this is so, cogency, or at least some semblance of cogency, must be discernible.

Before exploring this theme more fully, I need to say more about how I conceive of reasons. I take it that a natural view, which is in keeping with commonsense thinking on these matters, is that reasons, whether they be motivating or normative, are constituted by considerations—the sorts of things that people put forward as reasons. When we are giving what we take to be normative reasons for a belief, we present considerations in the light of which we take it that the belief is justified. When we are giving normative reasons for an action, we present considerations in the light of which the action would be justified, or at least have a point.[11] The same applies to normative reasons for wanting something or feeling some way. It is no less natural to regard motivating reasons as being constituted by considerations. My regret at having made some remark might be explained (motivated) by my believing it had offended Bill. But my reason is what I believe, rather than my believing it. It is constituted by the consideration that the remark had caused offence. Of course, the consideration can constitute my (motivating) reason for feeling regret *only if* I believe it. But that does not make the believing the reason. Were I to explain why I feel regret, I might say, 'Because it offended Bill', taking it as read that this mattered to me. This particular explanation would be factive—I would be presenting it as a fact that the remark had offended. If subsequently I discover that the remark had not caused offence, it would then be odd to explain why I had felt regret in exactly the same way. I might say, 'I thought that the remark had offended so-and-so.' But that is no reason to suppose that in this case the reason I am alluding to is a belief, in the sense of a state of believing. In speaking of what I thought, I am merely distancing

---

[10] The distinction between normative and motivating or explanatory reasons has long been recognized; see Baier (1958: ch. 6), T. Nagel (1970: 14–15), Bond (1983: ch. 2), Darwall (1983: ch. 2; 1997), Schueler (1993: 96 ff.), Smith (1994; 1997), Scanlon (1998: 18 ff.), and Dancy (2000).

[11] The difference between an action's being justified and its having a point is a central topic of Ch. 2.

myself from a reason to feel regret that I previously took there to be. There are other locutions that can be used to make the reason explicit while distancing oneself from it. Subsequent to the discovery that I was mistaken, I could give the reason for my ill-founded regret by saying, 'Because, as I thought, the remark offended Bill' (compare Dancy 2000: chapter 6). The same general approach applies to reasons for belief. My believing that it has been freezing may have a rationalizing explanation in terms of my believing that there is frost on the grass and that there would be no frost unless it had been freezing. Here too my reason is constituted by the considerations that make up the contents of the beliefs that figure in the *explanans*. If it turns out that what seemed like frost was a covering of white dust, I can explain my belief that it has been freezing using the 'distancing' locution.

In the cases just discussed my reason is constituted by a consideration that comprises the content of a belief. In the case in which what is rationalized is regret, the consideration is something I take to be true and to make my regret appropriate. In the case in which what is rationalized is a belief, the consideration is something I take to be true and to make it reasonable for me to believe that it has been freezing. The same general approach applies to reasons for action. By way of explaining to you why I went to see what turned out to be a disappointing film last night, I might tell you that a critic, whose judgement I respect, spoke highly of it. Here I indicate a consideration that is relevant to explaining both why I wanted to see the film and why I actually went to see it. What the critic said seemed to make it reasonable to suppose that the film would be worth seeing. It was in the light of the consideration that it would be worth seeing that I wanted to see it. And it was in the light of the consideration that I wanted to see it that I did so. In this case, a belief figures in the rationalizing explanation of my desire to see the film and a belief about that desire figures in the rationalizing explanation of the action. The desire to see the film is, of course, explanatorily relevant to the explanation of my action, since if I did not have the desire I probably would not have believed that I had it. But, on the view I am proposing, the desire figures indirectly in the explanation of my action, via my belief that I want to see the film. (That seems right, because our desires do not lead us to act blindly. We act with a view to satisfying them.) The same applies to intentions. Suppose that I am leaving my office at 3 pm. I am doing so in view of the consideration that I intend to catch a train and believe that if I am to do so I need to leave at 3. The intention contributes to the explanation of my action, but, like the desire in the previous example, it does so indirectly, being mediated by my knowledge that I have this intention. It should not be surprising that when I act on my intention I have the intention in view. The consideration that if I am to catch the train I need to leave at 3 has practical significance for me only to the extent that it bears on an intention I know that I have.

On this view of how desires and intentions contribute to rationalizing explanations of actions, the considerations that constitute the relevant reasons cannot simply be read off from the contents of the desire or intention. The content of my desire to see the film was *that I see the film*. That is not a consideration that counts, or even seemed to me to count, in favour of my seeing the film. Indeed, *qua* content of my desire, it is not a consideration at all but a specification of a state of affairs I desire to bring about. Similarly, the content of my intention to catch the train articulates the state of affairs that, in virtue of having that intention, I am motivated to bring about. As such it is not a consideration in the light of which I leave my office at 3, and not a component of my reason for leaving at 3. This view is by no means the only one in the field. Works by Davidson and Anthony referred to earlier testify to an alternative, still widely held in the philosophy of mind, which has it that motivating reasons for action are belief–desire pairs and motivating reasons for belief are other beliefs. I suspect that this alternative view arises from a conflation of reasons why, that is, causes, with reasons for which an agent believes or does something— a conflation that was encouraged by the project of showing how rationalizing explanation can be causal explanation. But we are not debarred from thinking that rationalizing explanation is causal explanation by thinking of reasons as considerations. For, plausibly, considerations can constitute a person's motivating reasons for a belief, action, or whatever, only if the person not only believes those considerations, but is caused to form that belief or perform that action by so believing. There is a familiar view that beliefs alone cannot motivate action. Maybe so, but a belief to the effect that there is a reason to do something undoubtedly can motivate an agent who is disposed to be moved by what he or she regards as a reason.

Thinking of reasons, both normative and motivating, as considerations does not by itself settle any substantive philosophical matter. None the less, it is a striking that commonsense thinking about reasons in the realm in which such thinking is most at home—that of human thought and action—implicitly treats subjects who have reasons as subjects capable of thinking about considerations as reasons. Philosophers like Brandom (1994; 1995) adopt what I called, in the Preface, a high conception of the space of reasons. That is to say, they think that operating within the space of reasons requires reflective capacities, including the capacity to think about one's own beliefs and assertions. Our ordinary ways of thinking about reasons in connection with people do not belie such a view.[12]

Returning to what for the present is the main theme, the question before us is how rationalizing explanation links up with rationality. What makes the issue complex is (i) that rationalizing explanation is in terms of motivating reasons, and (ii) that motivating reasons need not be adequate normative reasons. In the case of belief, or in the case of an action calling for justification, a reason will be an adequate normative reason only if it justifies the belief or action as the case may be.[13] In the case of a desire, it will be an adequate normative reason only if the reason shows what is desired to be worthy of desire, or shows, at least, that satisfying the desire would have some point. In the case of a feeling, for instance resentment, the reason will be an adequate normative reason only if it shows that the resentment is appropriate, being directed at someone who has in some way injured the person feeling resentment and proportionate to the nature of the injury. Motivating reasons may fail to be adequate normative reasons on either of two counts: they may be constituted by considerations that are false, or they may be constituted by considerations that, even if true, would not supply an adequate normative reason. In a case of belief, for instance, we have an example of the first type of failure when the motivating reason is conditionally cogent though the consideration constituting the reason is false. We have an example of the second type of failure when the motivating reason is not even conditionally cogent.

---

[12] The link between beliefs, intentions, and reflective capacities is more fully explored in Ch. 5.
[13] The qualification that the action calls for justification relates to discussion in Ch. 2 aimed at showing that not all action calls for reasons that supply justification.

Think of an employee, Jones, who believes that a colleague, Perkins, is out to undermine him. Perhaps this belief is based on the following assumptions: that behind Jones's back Perkins takes every opportunity to speak badly of Jones's abilities, the quality of his work, his manner of interacting with his colleagues. In addition, Jones thinks that Perkins has been removing papers from his desk, so as to make him look incompetent. If these assumptions were true they would justify Jones in thinking that Perkins is out to undermine him. So they constitute at least a conditionally cogent reason for Jones's belief in that conclusion. But now consider why Jones believes the operative assumptions. Suppose that he lacks any direct evidence that Perkins has been doing the subversive things that he (Jones) thinks he has been doing. He thinks Perkins has been doing these things because, let's say with good reason, he thinks that Perkins is inordinately ambitious and utterly ruthless. He also knows that some papers that had been on his desk are missing and knows of at least one other colleague to whom Perkins had represented him in an unfavourable light. This evidence, however, does not add up to much of a case for the conclusion that Perkins has actually been doing all the subversive things that Jones attributes to him. Jones's reason for reaching that conclusion is bad because his inference is not conditionally cogent. Yet if, relying on this reason, he believes that Perkins has been doing the subversive things, he must have taken the reason to amount to an adequate reason for so believing; for otherwise there would be no substance to the idea that he believes as he does *for a reason*.[14] This is why there must at least be what I called a semblance of cogency in his thinking. In the first place, it must be possible to see why he should have taken to be true the considerations constituting his reason for thinking that Perkins has been doing the subversive things. This condition is met in this case. In the second place, it must be possible to see why he should have regarded the considerations not only as true, but as justifying the belief in question. In this connection it is significant that Jones's assumptions about Perkins's general character and what he knows of Perkins's bad-mouthing are at least

---

[14] Compare the following passage from Darwall (1983: 32): 'Something may be somebody's reason for having acted without having been a reason for him so to have acted ... but it must none the less be a consideration that *he regarded* (or perhaps would have regarded under certain conditions) as a reason for him so to act. What characterizes explanation of action in terms of the agent's reasons is that it explains it as an expression of the agent's own conception of what reasons there were for him to act.'

circumstantially relevant to his belief that Perkins has been doing the various subversive deeds. If Perkins were inordinately ambitious and utterly ruthless then he would not have qualms about such actions. If he had bad-mouthed Jones once he might well do it again. And if he had taken the papers from Jones's desk there would be an explanation for why they are missing. So, although Jones's thinking is not conditionally cogent at this point, he relies on assumptions that are evidentially relevant to his conclusion. If, further, he is feeling vulnerable as a result of stress, then it is explicable how he could have treated a bad reason as a good one.

Rationalizing explanation does bring considerations about rationality into the understanding of why people come to think things, do things, and so on. But, as I have shown, the link is not straightforward, and it is not such as to make out all belief and action admitting of rationalizing explanation as rational or reasonable in the ordinary sense of these terms. Rationalization is a messy business. I return to this topic in Chapter 7.

4. Propositional attitudes and generalizations

I endorse the rationality assumption—that propositional attitudes are inextricably tied to rationality. I have stressed the importance of considerations about concept-possession for the explanation of why the rationality assumption holds. The question now is whether the link between propositional attitudes and rationality contributes to showing that personal understanding not only has a distinctive subject-matter but is distinctive *qua* understanding. There is a familiar response to this question, which contrasts explanation in terms of an agent's reasons with explanation that appeals to regularities in nature. Here is John McDowell:

> To recognize the ideal status of the constitutive concept [of rationality] is to appreciate that the concepts of the propositional attitudes have their proper home in explanations of a special sort: explanations in which things are made intelligible by being revealed to be, or to approximate to being, as they rationally ought to be. This is to be contrasted with a style of explanation in which one makes things intelligible by representing their coming

into being as a particular instance of how things generally tend to happen. (McDowell 1985/1998b: 328)[15]

In this passage there is a positive view about rationalizing explanation—that it implicates normative considerations—and a negative view—that it is to be contrasted with explanation in terms of regularities and thus in terms of generalizations about what tends to, or is liable to, happen. I agree with the positive view. Here I raise some problems for the negative view. The problems arise in view of considerations that make it plausible that rationalizing explanation is causal.

Suppose that on asking Mary where she is heading we learn that she is going to the cafeteria for lunch. That certainly makes sense of what she is doing by alluding to her motivating reason. But it is not clear why the fact that what she is doing makes sense in the light of her reason should be thought to take us away from considerations as to what generally tends to, or is liable to, happen. For in acting as she does, Mary is doing the sort of thing that anyone is liable to do in view of having the sort of intention and associated belief that she has. People who intend to have lunch and have a belief to the effect that they can obtain lunch in such and such a place are liable to head for that place. Indeed, it is hard to see how the explanatory insight we gain from learning of her reason can be divorced from such generalizations about what people are liable to do under such-and-such conditions. This consideration is reinforced by others that support the view that rationalizing explanations are causal.

Mary could have had the intention to have lunch and the associated belief and not headed in the direction of the cafeteria. She might have forgotten all about lunch, because she was preoccupied by work. Yet, in that case, she might still have had the intention and belief. So merely having the intention and belief is not the whole story about why she heads for the cafeteria. Or she might have retained the intention and belief and headed for the cafeteria, but not to have lunch. Suppose she had received a phone call from a friend who wanted to meet her urgently at the cafeteria. Thinking about what's up, she might have set out for that place to meet her

---

[15] See also McDowell (1994b: 70–2), where we find the idea that the intelligibility appropriate to the realm of propositional attitudes is '*sui generis*, by comparison with the realm of law'.

friend without any thought of lunch. In that case her motivating reason for going towards the cafeteria would not have implicated the intention and belief in question. Since they did not lead to her going to the cateteria. This makes it natural to suppose that, if the intention and belief provide, or at least contribute to, a rationalizing explanation of her action, they must have contributed to the causation of her action.[16] It seems then that the rationalizing explanation of Mary's action depends on an assumption about the causal explanatory role of the relevant intention and belief. The question is whether the insight provided by the explanation can be detached from assumptions about what tends to, or is liable to, happen. There is a strand in Davidson's thinking that might lead one to think that it can.

Davidson is well known for seeking to reconcile the following theses: (i) that causation is nomological (wherever there is causation there are appropriate covering laws); (ii) that there is mental causation; and (iii) that the mental is anomalous in that there are no psychological laws that can serve as a basis upon which mental events, *qua* mental events, can be predicted and explained.[17] The reconciliation is to be effected by treating mental events and actions as particulars that fall under both mentalistic concepts and physicalistic concepts. According to this view, the event that is striking me, that a car is approaching me rapidly, falls under some physicalistic concept. It involves some kind of brain-event and some kind of physical relationship with those surroundings—a relationship that underpins my having a perceptually grounded thought about my current surroundings. It also falls under a mentalistic concept, since it involves my thinking that a car is approaching me rapidly. Similarly, the event that is my quickening my step to avoid the path of the car falls under a physicalistic concept—since it is a bodily movement—and under a mentalistic concept, since it is my (intentionally) avoiding the path of the car. Suppose that my thinking that the car is approaching rapidly and my desire to avoid the path of the car cause me to quicken my step. In that case we have mental causation. The nomological character of causality and the anomalousness of the mental are preserved because the laws covering the transition from the occurrence of the

---

[16] The basic idea here is prominent in Davidson (1963/1980), though he formulates the point with reference to desires.

[17] Davidson (1970/1980). The anomalousness of the mental is anticipated in Davidson (1963/1980).

relevant mental events to the occurrence of the action are couched exclusively in physicalistic terms. The upshot is that it seems that we can hold to the nomological character of causality without bringing laws into our model of rationalizing explanation.[18]

There is a problem for this view. The causes cited in rationalizing explanations are presumably supposed to provide explanatory insight *qua* causes. When we explain Mary's heading for the cafeteria in terms of her intention to have lunch and the associated belief, we represent her as having attitudes that led to (figured in the causation of) her heading in that direction. How does this provide explanatory insight? It does so because it presupposes that those sorts of attitudes are liable to lead to this sort of action and that they did in fact lead to this sort of action on this occasion. With regard to many everyday causal explanations, this is as much insight as we gain. We may know nothing of the processes leading from exposure to rain to the onset of rust, but when we learn that what caused a garden tool to be rusty was its having been left out in the rain, we acquire information which implies that exposure to rain is liable to make garden tools rusty.

Davidson observes that not every correct specification of a cause implicates a specific generalization. By way of illustration, he notes (1963/1980: 17) that the cause of some event reported in Wednesday's *Tribune* might be specified as the event reported on page 5 of Tuesday's *Times*. Specifying the cause in this way does not implicate a generalization to the effect that events reported on page 5 of Tuesday's *Times* cause events reported in Wednesday's *Tribune*. But it is noticeable that the statement about the cause of the event reported in Wednesday's *Tribune* is devoid of explanatory insight. The cause is not described in a way that shows it to be explanatorily relevant to the occurrence of the effect. When specifications of causes provide explanatory insight they pick out those causes via features that figure in generalizations. Accepting the explanation provided by these specifications commits us to accepting the corresponding generalization.

Suppose the vet tells me that a virus caused my cat's death. This is not by any means a sophisticated explanation. It does not state which

---

[18] McDowell goes further, suggesting, though not I think arguing, that 'the Prejudice of the Nomological Character of Causality looks like ... [another] dogma of empiricism' (McDowell 1985/1998b: 340).

virus was involved or the process by which it resulted in death. But it does provide some limited explanatory insight. It is built into the very idea of a cause of an event of a certain kind that the cause is the sort of thing that is at least liable to result in occurrences of events of that kind. So, even if I did not already know that viruses contracted by cats are liable to lead to death (a generalization), I could glean this from what I have been told. The information would enable me to appreciate that the death was at least no great surprise. Davidson's example of a specification that does not implicate a specific generalization is a poor model for thinking about rationalizing explanation just because it is not an example of a specification that provides even limited explanatory insight. It provides no support for the view that the explanatory insight provided by causal explanations can be detached from generalizations. This is not a problem for Davidson. What anomalousness is primarily meant to rule out is not that causal explanatory insight is tied to generalizations, but that rationalizing explanations implicate *laws* in Davidson's strict sense. Davidson acknowledges that the anomalousness of the mental is compatible with there being true, though loose, generalizations in the realm of the propositional attitudes (Davidson 1970/1980: 219; 1993: 11). There is no pressing reason for him to deny that the explanatory insight provided by causal explanations implicates generalizations *of some sort*, be they laws or the looser generalizations implicit in commonsense causal explanations.

The intelligibility of personal understanding is not best illuminated by being contrasted with the intelligibility gained when we learn that something's happening is an instance of what generally tends to, or is liable to, happen. If there is something special about personal understanding, this still needs to be spelled out. There is a further problem that makes this task look difficult. Let us suppose that, since rationalizing explanations are causal, and their specifications of causes are causal-explanatory, they must implicate generalizations. Nothing I shall subsequently argue is meant to dislodge this conclusion. But now, assuming that a rationalizing explanation of an action, say, is causal-explanatory, how is the fact that the relevant attitudes rationalize the action supposed to be relevant to the explanatory insight provided by the rationalizing explanation?

Addressing closely related matters, Louise Anthony observes:

Davidson's causal account of action is meant to underwrite the explanatory value of an appeal to reasons; but we can see that in fact, the model leaves the rational and causal aspects of rationalization radically detached. (Anthony 1989: 168)

The rationalizing and causal aspects of rationalizing explanation would indeed be radically detached under Davidson's theory, if on that theory causal-explanatory insight were tied to the level of physicalistic description. I have argued that there is no reason why Davidson should not link the explanatory insight provided by rationalizing explanations to generalizations couched in the vocabulary of intentional description, provided that the generalizations are not laws in his strict sense. But even if this is granted, there is still a problem of explanatory relevance. If rationalizing explanations are causal, then the attitudes cited in such an explanation explain *qua* causes of the action (or belief, or desire, or feeling). What matters is that the attitudes should be such that someone with those attitudes is liable to perform the action explained (or to have the belief or desire or feeling explained). The challenge then is to show how the fact that the agent's attitudes rationalize what they explain can be relevant to the explanation of what is explained.

I shall return to the problem of explanatory relevance in Chapter 7. The next step is to outline another approach to bringing out the distinctive character of rationalizing explanation, and to highlight some ways in which it might be resisted or deflated.

5. Understanding and the normative dimension of the mental

A few years ago a clever advertisement on British television depicted a young man with closely cropped hair, jeans, and Doc Martin boots running along the pavement (sidewalk) past some shops towards a conventionally dressed middle-aged man carrying a brief case. On reaching the older man the young man grapples with him. The sequence of events is first viewed as if from an upper window of a building opposite. From this point of view it looks as if the young man is trying to mug the older man. The film then cuts back to the moment when the young man started to run. This time the point of view is at pavement level from behind the young man and looking in the direction in which he is running. This reveals something we could not see before—that something is about to crash down on to the older man. Seeing this, the young man runs up and pushes the older man out of the way, preventing him from being struck. As I recall, the advertisement, which was for a national newspaper, urged viewers to look at things from a different angle. The second angle made all the difference. It enabled us to understand why the young man was running towards and grappling with the older man. His benign intention was revealed, and the interpretation that ascribed to him a violent intention shown to be a mistake, encouraged by the stereotype that viewers would be liable to link with a certain mode of dress and appearance. My interest is not so much in the fact that we can easily be wrong about what people are doing. Our reactions to the events depicted in the film strikingly reveal how we go about trying to understanding what people are doing in the absence of information deriving from them about their intentions. We have to work out what the young man is doing from his behaviour and the surrounding circumstances. What especially interests me is the role of normative considerations in our attempts to do this.

Once we know that something is about the fall on to the older man, how do we connect this with what the young man does? What we do is connect the circumstances to a suitable intention and connect that intention with the action of running up to and grappling with the older man. What does the trick is the assumption that the young man intends to prevent injury. But what grounds that assumption is that it would *make sense* for the agent to have such an intention and, in virtue of having such an intention, it would *make sense* to act as this agent does. By formulating things in this way, I mean to indicate loosely and without complication that we are in the realm of the normative. What it would make sense for an agent to think or do is not about what the agent actually does think or do. It makes contact with what there is reason for the agent to think or do in the light of his values and concerns. Not everyone seeing the danger would react as this young man does. But reacting in that way is an intelligible reaction to the perceived danger. Not everyone having the intention would carry it out in the same way. Some might call out a warning.

But the young man's action is an intelligible way of carrying out the intention. So we have two considerations—normative considerations—about what would make sense. One is to the effect that it would make sense for the agent to have the intention; the other is to the effect that it would make sense to act as the agent did in the light of that intention. Taken together, these considerations provide support for the key assumption that the agent had the intention to prevent injury. The example makes the role of the normative considerations especially vivid, because we are given no information about the agent's intentions or beliefs other than what, with the help of those considerations, can be gleaned from his non-verbal behaviour and the facts about his situation. But normative considerations are no less important when agents inform us of their intentions. When this is so, we still need to be able to make sense of their having the intentions they seem to declare themselves to have and to make sense of anything they do by way of carrying out those intentions.

I claim that normative considerations figure crucially in our attempts at personal understanding. They have an epistemological role in that they form part of the basis we have for ascriptions of propositional attitudes and motivating reasons. I shall argue, further, that the very concepts we have of the attitudes—concepts like that of believing this, or intending that—are normative concepts. More specifically, I shall argue that ascriptions of beliefs and intentions represent those to whom the ascriptions are made as incurring certain normative commitments. I shall explore how such commitments link up with reasons.

The subject matter of personal understanding is people conceived as *rational agents*. Rational agents interact with their environment in ways that depend on their acknowledgement of the reasons there are to think this or do that and on their acknowledgement of the normative commitments they incur in virtue of believing and intending as they do. Applied to people, the rationality assumption should be understood accordingly. The rationality of people is not simply a matter of the conformity of their attitudes and actions to certain sense-making patterns. To understand people, we must take account of the fact that they are sometimes aware of what there is reason for them to think and do, and of what they are normatively committed to thinking and doing. And, because they have such awareness, considerations of these sorts can have a role in the explanation of what they think and do. Sometimes people believe there is reason for them to think this or do that, and the explanation for why they so believe is that there *is* reason for them to think this or do that and they have managed to recognize this. Taken by itself, this claim hardly looks like something to write home about. Indeed, it strikes me as a truism. If it is at least true, then the subject-matter of personal understanding is distinctive in that it concerns what there is reason to think or do. This is not just one other difference in subject-matter. It calls for a mode of understanding that is distinct from that which is characteristic of natural science as usually conceived. As usually conceived, natural science engages with the forces and processes involved in the physical changes that occur around us. It addresses, for instance, why rain falls, why cancers grow, or why metal rails develop cracks in terms of empirically supported theories that incorporate generalizations relevant to the forces and processes at work. Such theories do not deal in what there is reason to think or do. Scientific theories comprising a psychology of propositional attitudes might address what people *think* there is reason for them to think or do. But what carries explanatory significance under such theories is the fact that the people under consideration think as they do on such matters. What there *is* reason for them to think or do does not come into the explanatory picture. On the view that I shall develop, they do.

There are various ways in which one might try to play down the significance of normative considerations in personal understanding. I consider three strategies: (a) argue against the claim that I called the rationality assumption—that there is an inextricable link between propositional attitudes and rationality; (b) hold to the rationality assumption but deny that rationality is normative in any sense that need trouble those who hold that personal understanding is essentially the same as scientific theoretical understanding (this is *the deflationary strategy*); (c) adopt an expressivist approach to normativity by analogy with expressivist meta-ethics.

Against the rationality assumption

A number of considerations might be mobilized against the rationality assumption. First, it is not entirely clear what rationality requires of us. What strikes some as being a reason for a belief or action will not strike all in that way. What strikes some as being irrational will not strike all in that way. Given the elusiveness of reasons and rationality, it might seem implausible that in everyday attempts at understanding people we deploy considerations about what is rational. Second, people often violate what are taken to be norms of rationality even though we seem able to make well-grounded ascriptions of propositional attitudes to them. They hold inconsistent beliefs, for instance, or they make incoherent probability judgements.

I concede that what rationality requires of us is not entirely clear, and I do not wish to play down the significance of the many puzzles about rationality that those seeking to work out a developed theory of rationality would need to address.[19] But the rationality assumption does not require us to deploy a developed theory of rationality in order to understand each other. The rationality assumption is shorthand for a number of more specific considerations having to do with coherence, cogency, and being in touch with reality. In this connection, taking a cue from Davidson, I emphasized (in Section 2) that our ability to deploy concepts sets limits to how confused our thinking can be. Ascriptions of attitudes go with ascriptions of concepts, and ascriptions of concepts commit us to supposing that attitudes and actions fall into patterns that make sense in terms of the more specific considerations. The absence of such patterns would undermine the ascriptions. But their presence is compatible with much bad thinking.

It is important, too, that at least some considerations concerning rationality seem tolerably clear. Later, in Chapters 2 and 3, I defend the idea that there is reason for us to avoid having an intention while never getting around to doing what is necessary to carry it out. A requirement of rationality is that we do justice to this reason. There is no good reason to doubt that we are subject to a means–end requirement of some sort, even if there can be reasonable doubts about my formulation of such a requirement. Importantly for my purposes, it is hard to see how we could make sense of the idea that subjects have intentions at all if their thought and action were not shaped by such a requirement.

The second consideration that might be deployed against the rationality assumption invokes evidence of irrationality.[20] There is

---

[19] Examples that have received much discussion include Newcomb's puzzle and Allais's paradox.
[20] Relevant experimental evidence of failures of rationality is conveniently reviewed in Stein (1996).

reason to doubt that the evidence really tells against the assumption, because the assumption is compatible with there being much irrationality in our thinking. None the less, the evidence in question is sometimes taken to be a problem for the views of philosophers like Davidson who treat rationality considerations as a constraint on justified ascriptions of attitudes. In this connection Alvin Goldman, for instance, invokes the paradox of the preface. In his version, an author, Hannah, believes of each thing she has written in a book that it is true, but acknowledges in the preface that she believes, on the grounds of her own fallibility, that at least one thing she has written is false. If this description of her is correct, then Hannah has inconsistent beliefs in that not all of her beliefs can be true. Goldman comments:

> Now if the consistency norm were part of our ordinary interpretation procedure, an interpreter would try, other things equal, to avoid ascribing to Hannah all the beliefs she ostensibly avows. Understood as a description of interpretive practice, the rationality approach 'predicts' that interpreters confronted with Hannah's avowals will try to find a way to assign a slightly different set of beliefs than Hannah seems to endorse. Interpreters will feel some 'pressure', some *prima facie* reason, to revise their belief imputation to be charitable to Hannah.... Speaking as one interpreter, I would feel no temptation to avoid ascribing the inconsistent belief set to Hannah. And I submit that other everyday interpreters would similarly feel no such temptation. (Goldman 1989: 164–5)

Like Goldman, I feel no temptation to avoid ascribing inconsistency to Hannah, or at least none arising from assumptions about good interpretative practice.[21] But those who link the ascription of attitudes to rationality considerations need not be committed to treating the mere presence of inconsistency in an ascription of beliefs as counting to some degree against the ascription. Goldman takes 'the rationality approach' to involve commitment to what he calls *the rationality principle*. This principle is significantly stronger than my rationality assumption, since it dictates that we ascribe beliefs and desires so as to *maximize rationality*. A plausible epistemology of attitude-ascription will not endorse the rationality principle. For one thing, it is obscure what maximizing rationality amounts to. For another, as Goldman

[21] There is an issue as to whether even a conscientious author of a book should be regarded as believing, as opposed to, say, believing to be defensible, or acceptable for the purposes of serious debate, everything assertively stated in the book.

notes, if we apply the principle, then too many inconsistencies will count as being problematic. A more promising approach is to suppose that inconsistencies are problematic in the context of attitude-ascription if they put a strain on a particular ascription of attitudes. They might do so because they make it difficult to see how the subject can be deploying the requisite concepts. There would be an air of paradox about the case of Hannah if she were aware that not all her beliefs regarding the truth-value of what she has written can be true *and* she thought that this is a stable position. Even if she does not think the position is stable, it is unclear what specifically she is supposed to do about the inconsistency. Pending further enquiry, she has no basis for revising her attitude to any particular claim she has made. Giving up all of the beliefs in the inconsistent set, when each strikes her as being true, seems far less sensible than holding fire, while being open to making revisions in the face of objections targeted at particular beliefs. If she appeared determined, come what may, to stand by everything she had written in the body of the book and in the preface, then we might wonder about our ascription of attitudes to her. Is it belief rather than some other attitude that she has regarding what she has written? But as things stand there would be no reason to take her current refusal to withdraw any particular claim as reason to think she does not believe everything she seems to believe.

Goldman also makes use of much-cited observations about probability judgements by Tversky and Kahneman (1983). Subjects are told various things about a character, Linda, including that she has majored in philosophy, cares about issues of social justice, and has participated in protests against nuclear weapons. They are then asked to rate the probabilities that Linda has certain occupations and interests. A large proportion of subjects rate the probability of Linda being both a bank teller and a feminist higher than the probability of her being a bank teller, despite the fact that the probability of the conjunction cannot be more than the probability of each of its conjuncts. Goldman notes that, if avoiding incoherence in assignments of probabilities is a norm of rationality, then these subjects do not respond rationality. He takes this to be an objection to the adoption of the rationality principle. As I have indicated, I am not concerned to defend that principle. My interest is in the weaker rationality assumption. That said, there is a real question whether Tversky and

Kahneman's observations tell even against the rationality principle. For this might well be a case in which the subjects do not understand the subject-matter of the judgements they are being asked to make, or at any rate do not understand them in the way the experimenters do.[22] Be that as it may, the more interesting point is that, even if the case does present a problem for the rationality principle, it does not show that well-founded ascriptions of beliefs are not constrained rationality considerations. As I observed above, the problem with the rationality principle is that it counts too many incoherences as problematic.

Making sense of a person's thought or action does not require making it out to be warranted or justified or rational. What it requires is that the thought or action should fit into a body of attitudes and actions of which we can make some kind of sense. There are limits to how incoherent such a body of attitudes and actions can be, limits to the extent to which a subject's reasoning can be bad, and limits to the extent to which it can be out of touch with reality. It remains an open possibility that some of the attitudes an agent appears to have are deeply problematic.[23] But such cases do not undermine the general point about limits.

The deflationary strategy

The deflationary strategy is to stick with the rationality assumption but attack the idea that rationality is in any interesting sense normative. This strategy is suggested by lines of thought in Churchland (1979: 100–7; 1981: section 4; 1989: 228–30). I think it is best construed as involving four claims. The first claim is that for a subject's propositional attitudes and actions to exhibit rationality is nothing other than for those attitudes and actions to conform to certain patterns. The second claim is that, at least so far as our commonsense psychology is concerned, there are laws governing the functioning of propositional attitudes, some of which pick out

---

[22] The subject-matter is probabilities as defined by the probability axioms. There is little reason to expect people to have a mastery of that subject-matter without special training, and so little reason to expect them to make sensible judgements in the absence of such training.

[23] See Coltheart and Davies (2000) for intriguing cases.

rationality-exhibiting patterns. An example, from Churchland (1981), might be

> (x) (p) (q) [((x believes that p) & (x believes that (if p then q))) ⊃ (barring confusion, distraction, etc., x believes that q)]

The third claim is that laws such as these are entirely on a par with laws of physical theory which relate physical magnitudes. An example of such a law (also from Churchland 1981) would be the classical gas law:

> (x) (P) (V) (μ) [((x has pressure P) & (x has volume V) & (x has quantity μ)) ⊃ (barring very high pressure or density, x has temperature PV/μR)

We are to think of the values of content variables in the psychological law as having the same sort of status as the values of the physical magnitude variables in the gas law. According to the gas law, the temperature of a gas under certain conditions is a function of its pressure, volume, and quantity. The functional dependence is captured by the formula, $T = PV/\mu R$. The formula expresses an arithmetical relationship between values of the specified physical magnitudes, which represents a physical relationship between those magnitudes. Similarly, we are to suppose, according to the psychological law, a belief in a conditional and in its antecedent will, under certain conditions, be accompanied by a belief in the consequent of the conditional. The formula, 'p. If p then q. So q', is supposed to expresses a relationship of logical consequence between propositions that represents a psychological relationship between beliefs.

The fourth claim is that, just as there is nothing interestingly normative about the gas law, so there is nothing interestingly normative about the psychological law. Both laws incorporate (at least implicitly) a formula dealing with relationships between abstract entitles—numbers in one case and propositions in the other. But in the context of the laws, these relationships are supposed to serve as representations of real-world relationships between, in the one case, physical magnitudes and, in the other case, beliefs. If we think of the regularity described by the psychological law as being normative, that, according to this strategy, is only because we value conformity to that regularity.

It would be question-begging to object that to bring rationality into the picture *is* to bring normativity into it. The strategy presupposes that there is nothing intrinsically normative about the rational order. It invites us to take this view via the assumption that the rational order can be captured at the level of the order of logical relationships between propositions. Logical relationships are taken to be like arithmetical relationships. They are useful in theory because they enable us to represent real-world relationships. But since there is nothing intrinsically normative about the arithmetical relationships, it is assumed that there is nothing intrinsically normative about the logical relationships. It is concluded that there is nothing intrinsically normative about rationality. This last step is open to question, however, on the grounds that it conflates logic with rationality. It might be conceded that logic deals with non-normative abstract relationships, but denied that we can capture rationality purely in terms of such relationships. One way of developing this thought is in terms of the idea that rationality is an ideal that we *ought* to respect.

Faced with this sort of intuition Georges Rey, in a discussion very much in the spirit of Churchland's, urges us to take note of an ambiguity in talk of ideals:

> [T]here are genuinely *normative* ideals, such as one finds in ethics and aesthetics, ideals of goodness and beauty which ... are the standards by which we judge things. These are to be distinguished from *descriptive, explanatory idealizations*, which seem to arise essentially *throughout the sciences* ... [for example] Boyle's and Kepler's Laws, Bernoulli's Principle, and even ... the fundamental laws of electromagnetism and gravitation, which must idealize away from interactions among themselves. (Rey 1997: 276)

Rey suggests that we think of ideals of rationality as idealizations in the descriptive, explanatory sense, rather than the normative sense. On this reading,

> idealizations to rationality need make no more claim to how people *ought* to speak, think, or act, than do Boyle's idealizations about gases make some sort of moral claim about how gases morally *ought* to behave, or Kepler's laws about how planets morally *ought* to move. (Rey 1997: 276)

The reference to *moral* oughts is a red herring, since those who think that rationality is a normative ideal do not in general think of it as a moral ideal. So let us leave that aside. What matters for my purposes is that we have here an attempt to explain away intuitions about the normativity of rationality in terms of a conflation of two quite different senses of 'ideal'.

It is implicit in Rey's discussion that, in the realm of thought and action, normativity worthy of the name must in some way hook up with how people ought to regulate their thought or conduct. Notions of what ought to be done or ought to happen are notoriously tricky. An anxious parent may think that her child ought to be home from school by now. The 'ought' in play here could just be the 'ought' of expectation, signalling that in the usual course of events the child would be home by now, and thus that there is reason to think she would be home by now, if the course of events were as usual. If that is so, the 'ought' does not capture anything that is normative *for the child*. It relates to what is to be expected of the child, but not necessarily to what the child ought to be doing. Even when it is said that a subject ought to do this or think that, it does not always follow that we have normativity in any interesting sense. Explaining the notion of an intentional system, Dennett speaks of the beliefs and desires that a system ought to have. He means to pick out those beliefs and desires the system 'would have if it were *ideally* ensconced in its environmental niche' (Dennett 1981/1987: 49). 'Ideally' has the ring of normativity about it, and Dennett explicitly regards considerations about what creatures would ideally do as normative (1981/1987: 52). But it turns out that the system's being ideally ensconced is a matter of its being aware of everything that is in its interests and having goals that are in keeping with those interests. One might wonder, then, whether this imports normativity in any interesting sense.[24]

I touch on these matters only to highlight how slippery the notion of the normative is and to make clear that I shall be focusing on normativity which relates to normative reasons for subjects to think things, do things, and so on. Given the fluidity in the use some philosophers make of the term 'reason', even this characterization does not, without qualification, pick out my favoured notion (see e.g.

---

[24] This emphasizes disagreement with Dennett. However, Dennett seems to me to be entirely right to stress the importance of rationality considerations in understanding creatures. It is how this is worked out in detail that is the issue.

Dennett 1984: 23). So, to be quite explicit: I take normative reasons to be constituted by considerations, and I take normative reasons to apply only to creatures with the capacity to treat considerations as reasons. Such creatures need not possess a sophisticated concept of a reason. What is required is a capacity for thoughts like: 'Since this is so, we must conclude that this is so (is likely to be so)'; 'This seems unlikely in view of that'; 'I think this because such-and-such'; 'This being so we had better do that'; and so on. This is not to say that a subject for whom there is a normative reason to do something must be aware of this reason. Nor is it to say that, faced with the considerations that constitute the reason to do something, the subject must see, or would with suitable help be brought to see, that they constitute a reason to do that thing. The point is that the subject must be in the business of thinking about considerations that constitute reasons and treating them as reasons. Owing to limitations of understanding or pigheadedness, such subjects may sometimes fail to treat a consideration that is a reason as a reason.

With reason-linked normativity as the operative conception, Rey and Churchland seem to me to be right at least to this extent: *if* rationality is simply conformity to certain patterns, then there is nothing intrinsically normative about it. There are contexts in which this looks like the right way to think about the matter. Suppose it is a condition of rationality that one not continue in pursuit of a goal while never aiming to do what is necessary to achieve that goal. Call this the means–end condition. Now suppose that a dog, eager to fetch a stick that has been thrown by its owner, runs to catch it. Assume that the dog is led to do this by intentional states that track the location of the stick and intentional states that represent fetching the stick as a goal. The dog satisfies the means–end condition. It maintains its goal, and its behaviour is directed at achieving the goal. Maybe at other times the dog loses track of the stick and ceases to maintain the goal. Here too it satisfies the means–end condition, though this time it does so because the goal is abandoned, rather than because it aims to do what is necessary to achieve it. In general, we may expect the dog to exhibit behaviour that tends to conform to certain patterns, including patterns that satisfy the means–end condition. But this provides no ground for thinking that the means–end condition, or any other rationality condition, generates reasons for the dog to do anything. Indeed, it provides no ground for thinking that the idea of a (normative) reason even applies to the dog. On the picture under discussion there is, we could say, a rational order, comprising patterns of intentional states and intentionally characterized behaviours. It is arguable that to have any kind of intentional psychology a creature must behave in ways that, to a significant degree, conform to the rational order, so conceived. If that is as far as we need go, then Rey and Churchland are right: there is nothing intrinsically normative about rationality. It is one thing to link intentional psychology to rationality and another to show that rational patterns are normative in that they are about what there is reason for a creature to think or do.

It is just as clear, however, that there is a richer conception of rationality that applies to what earlier I called *rational agents*. As I have already noted, rational agents not only think and act in conformity with the sorts of patterns that might be thought to make up the rational order. They sometimes think things and do things because they see, or assume, that there is reason to think these things and do these things. This happens in contexts in which they engage in *deliberative thinking*—that is, when they reflect on what is to be said for or against this or that view or course of action. But it also happens when people react spontaneously to situations. Again, the young man running illustrates the point. He has no time to engage in deliberation. He takes stock of what is about to happen and acts. Yet his reaction is not like ducking to avoid a missile hurtling towards one's head or ramming on the brakes of one's car in an emergency stop. These are situations in which the agent's body takes over—a perception prompts a bodily reaction in a fairly direct way, leaving little if any time for thoughtful shaping of what one does. By contrast, though the young man reacts quickly, without weighing up the merits of pushing the older man out of the way as against calling out a warning, his pace and path are shaped by his understanding of what he is doing and his estimate of what he needs to do to carry out his intention. He has values and concerns in the light of which, in this situation, it would make sense for him to try to shove the older man out of the way of the falling structure, and he acts accordingly. When we try to understand what he is about we do so with reference to what must have struck him as the thing to do. Whether or not we share his values and concerns, we can see that there are values and concerns in the light of which it would make sense to do what he did. This is how things are with matters of personal understanding. We aim to understand others so far as we can in terms of their understanding. But our route to their understanding will draw on assumptions about what it would make sense for them to think or do and thus ultimately on assumptions about what there is reason for them to think or do. The upshot is that, even if in some contexts there is a notion of rationality in play that is not intrinsically normative in my favoured sense, the kinds of considerations that enter into our attempts to understand people *qua* rational agents are normative in that sense.

Those who adopt the deflationary strategy might concede that rational agents are more sophisticated creatures than cats, dogs, and other non-human animals which, it is plausible to assume, have an intentional psychology. But they will deny that the layers of sophistication exhibited by rational agents are essential for having propositional attitudes simply as such. On this basis, they will contest the claim that propositional attitudes are inextricably tied to the kind of normativity that is my main concern. I have already touched on this matter in the Preface and I shall return to it at various points throughout the book. The main arguments for thinking that the propositional attitudes that form the subject-matter of personal understanding are inextricably tied to normativity, and to the reflective capacities that go with normativity, are set out in Chapters 4 to 6. As I remarked in the Preface, to accommodate the intentionality of non-human animals lacking the reflective capacities, it is not necessary to deny to those animals an intentional psychology. There is the option of arguing that there is a distinction in kind between their intentional states and ours.

Expressivism

To be expressivist about rationality is to treat judgements to the effect that a belief or action is rational as expressive of endorsement of a system of norms of rationality that permits the formation of the belief or the performance of the action. This is a position that has been worked out with considerable sophistication by Allan Gibbard

(1990). There seem to be two principle motivations. The first is naturalism. This comes out in the following passage:

> In my own picture, all strict facts will be naturalistic. Facts of meaning will come out as genuine facts, and so as naturalistic. Apparent normative facts will come out, strictly, as no real facts at all; instead, there will be facts of what we are doing when we make normative judgements. It does make sense to do some things and not others, but that will not be part of a systematic picture of nature. Our thinking about these things will. (Gibbard 1990: 23)

From this standpoint, to claim objectivity—a kind of factual status—for norms of rationality, and judgements made in conformity with these norms, seems to commit us to weird facts and weird means of gaining knowledge of these facts (Gibbard 1990: 154). The second motivation arises from consideration of puzzles about what rationality demands, some of which I alluded to earlier in discussing objections to the rationality assumption. They are puzzles about what is rational in some situation on which different people take different views, and it is not clear how the matter should be settled. The expressivist thinks that, because the issues to which the puzzles give rise seem intractable, it is plausible that people operate with different norms of rationality and that their thinking on these matters is not answerable to facts or truths about rationality. So the motivation here is rather like one motivation for expressivist meta-ethics: the seeming intractability of differences in judgement is taken to be at odds with the notion that there is a truth or fact of the matter (see especially Gibbard 1990: chapter 1).

The expressivist strategy denies objective status to normative considerations. Such considerations are conceived as being located in the mind of the person who deploys them in evaluating or making sense of people's thoughts or actions. On such a view there is an obligation to account for why it strikes us that normative considerations about rationality, or at least some such considerations, have an objective status, but no such account will vindicate objectivity.

I shall not attempt to refute this position.[25] Our judgements about rationality and reasonableness are very various. For all I shall argue, it could be that the expressivist approach is right for some of these judgements. For instance, sometimes what we judge as making sense

---

[25] For some critical discussion, see Boghossian (2002).

or as being crazy reflects well-entrenched values and beliefs that we have, rather than an assessment of what would make sense if we accepted the rather different values and beliefs of those we seek to understand or evaluate. Perhaps in these cases it is not plausible to suppose that the judgements are made in terms of norms to which all rational agents are indisputably subject. By the same token, it would be correspondingly implausible to suppose that the norms that are implicated would figure in a framework for understanding people in general. I shall in any case be focusing on requirements of reason, including a means–end requirement, which seem to be objective requirements and would, I think, be hard to accommodate within an expressivist framework.

Expressivism is incompatible with the view that normative considerations have the kind of explanatory role that I take them to have.[26] It might be thought that, independently of expressivism, there is good reason to deny that normative considerations about reasons can have this sort of explanatory role. I now consider a line of thought in this direction that is suggested by a discussion by Gilbert Harman (1977) of moral judgements and principles.

Harman aimed to show that the role of moral observations—non-inferential moral judgements about particular situations made in response to an encounter with those situations—is both similar to, and importantly different from, the role of observations in science.[27] Moral principles can be tested against moral 'observations' since, conjoined with assumptions about particular situations, they yield moral claims pertaining to those situations. If the moral observations we actually make do not cohere with our principles, then we have a clash. If revising the observational judgement is not an option we are prepared to tolerate, then we are committed to rejecting the principle. In these respects testing moral principles is somewhat like testing scientific theories. But, Harman argued, there is a crucial difference between moral principles and scientific theories.

The difference is that you need to make assumptions about certain physical facts to explain the occurrence of the observations that support a scientific theory, but you do not seem to need to make

---

[26] For some subtle and interesting twists to the debate, so far as it concerns explanation, see Gibbard (2002).
[27] For a discussion dealing with aspects of the kind of epistemology of observation that Harman assumes, see Millar (2000).

assumptions about any moral facts to explain the occurrence of the so-called moral observations I have been talking about. In the moral case, it would seem that you need only make assumptions about the psychology or moral sensibility of the person making the moral observation.

In the scientific case, the theory is tested against the world. As Harman views the matter, observing a proton passing through a cloud chamber confirms the theory of sub-atomic particles because the theory is the best explanation of the making of the observation. The theory posits particles that leave a vapour trail when passing through a gas. It explains the phenomenon we observe, and the existence of the phenomenon explains our making the observational judgement that a proton is passing through. By contrast,

[a] moral observation does not seem, in the same sense, to be observational evidence for or against any moral theory [i.e. body of moral principles], since the truth or falsity of the moral observation seems to be completely irrelevant to any reasonable explanation of why that observation was made. (Harman 1977: 7)

To take Harman's example, suppose that someone observing children torturing a cat judges: 'That is wrong'. According to Harman, nothing in the process gives us reason to regard the making of such an observation as providing anything like evidential support for some moral principle.

It appears to be true that there can be no explanatory chain between moral principles and particular observings in the way that there can be such a chain between scientific principles and particular observings. Conceived as an explanatory theory, morality, unlike science, seems to be cut off from observation. (Harman 1977: 9)

The strictly moral philosophical issues that Harman discusses are not my concern.[28] The ideas I want to highlight are:

(a) that those of us seeking to understand the thinking of a person making a moral judgement about a particular situation need not endorse either the judgement or moral perspective of the person making the judgement; and

---

[28] For a detailed critique of Harman focusing on these issues, see Sturgeon (1985).

(b) that the explanation of the making of the judgement can be done in terms of non-normative principles connecting non-normatively specifiable facts, ordinary perceptual judgements, dispositions to make moral judgements about particular situations, and, no doubt sometimes, the acceptance of explicitly held general moral principles.

I shall use another example to connect these themes more closely to the considerations about reasons. Suppose my neighbour appears at my front door in some distress and calls on me for help. You are not surprised when I do help. Let us suppose that you know that I accept a general moral principle to the effect that the fact that one's neighbour is in distress and is calling on one's help is a reason to help. You see that I believe that my neighbour is in distress and calling on me for help, and you expect that, since I hold to the general principle, I shall treat what I believe as a reason to help. If made explicit, your explanation for my actually offering help would refer to my awareness of the non-normatively specifiable facts of the situation, my acceptance of the general moral principle, the implication of the principle for the particular case, and the fact that I am liable to act on what I take to be a reason to do something, at least in the absence of countervailing considerations. Normative reasons need not figure in the explanatory story you tell. You will have assumed that I treated my neighbour's situation as providing me with a normative reason to help, and that I acted accordingly. But that there is such a reason need not be part of your story. Nor need *you* assume the principle that you attribute to me.

I draw attention to this way of thinking about understanding why people make moral judgements because it provides a clear illustration of the idea that moral facts and principles are explanatorily irrelevant. Whether or not this is right, my concern is with the extension of the idea to rationality considerations, conceived as being normative. Is it the case that normative considerations bearing on what it would make sense for agents to think or do have no indispensable role in the explanation of belief and action other than as ingredients of the contents of the beliefs of those we seek to understand? In view of my remarks at the beginning of this section, it will come as no surprise that my own answer is 'No'. I take it that normative considerations can have a genuinely explanatory role. I hold that, for instance, sometimes people believe that they incur certain normative commitments in part because they do incur those commitments. If this is right, then it is not open to us to invoke the explanatory irrelevance of considerations to the effect that agents incur such commitments in defence of an expressivist analysis of such considerations.

6. The way ahead

As I have been indicating, the overarching theme of this book is that the subject-matter of personal understanding is *people considered as rational agents that, as such, sometimes recognize what there is reason for them to think or do and what they are normatively committed to thinking and doing*. Our understanding of why people think or act as they do is inseparable from normative considerations bearing on coherence and cogency of their thinking and on their being in touch with reality. Such considerations constrain justified ascriptions of attitudes and of motivating reasons, and therefore also constrain what counts as a rationalizing explanation for a belief or action. I shall argue that the very concepts we have of propositional attitudes—concepts of believing this, desiring that, and the rest—are normative, because they represent those who fall under them as incurring normative commitments. The arguments in support of this view in Chapters 4–6 make up the core of the book. In these chapters I proceed in two stages. I take believing and intending to be distinctive among the attitudes, in virtue of the kind of normative commitments that believing and intending incur. The case for thinking that the concepts of believing and intending are normative is made in Chapter 4. Further arguments relevant to a defence of the view are set out in Chapter 5. In Chapter 6 I consider the normativity of semantic meaning and conceptual content and argue that concepts of any attitudes with conceptual content are normative.

The notion of the normative is slippery, as we have seen. For this reason I devote Chapters 2 and 3 to clarifying the reason-linked conception of normativity that figures in this book and the conception of normative commitment, which has a key role in Chapters 4–6. Chapter 2 deals with some tricky matters concerning normative reasons for belief and action. Chapter 3 focuses on the shape of normative commitments and includes discussion of commitments incurred by participating in practice as well as those incurred by beliefs and intentions. It is important that the commitments incurred by beliefs and intentions are not to be explained in terms of practices.

Throughout the book I am concerned with epistemological constraints on the ascription of attitudes. But I also consider how the attitudes figure in explanations. In Chapter 7 I address the problem of explanatory relevance on which I touched in Section 4 of this chapter and relate it to the issue of explanatory irrelevance discussed in the previous section. In Chapter 8 I examine recent debates about the significance of simulation for understanding people. In Chapter 9 I draw attention to the limits to the explanatory insight available to us at the level of personal understanding.

CHAPTER 2

Reasons for Belief and for Action

1. Introduction

A *rationalizing* explanation for a belief, action, or whatever is an explanation in terms of the agent's (motivating) reason. The two most straightforward cases are these:

(a) The considerations constituting the reason provide the agent with an adequate normative reason.
(b) The considerations constituting the reason do not provide the agent with an adequate normative reason, but would do if they were true.

As I observed in the previous chapter, these do not exhaust the cases. There are cases of the following sort:

(c) The considerations constituting the agent's reason would not provide the agent with an adequate normative reason even if they were true.

The notion of a rationalizing explanation would be hopelessly restricted if it did not accommodate case (c). The reasons for which people believe things or do things can be bad reasons, and the badness of the reason is not always explicable simply in terms of the falsity of the reason-constituting considerations. Sometimes it is due to bad thinking. What makes it the case that the explanation in such cases is a *rationalizing* explanation? I touched on the answer to this towards the end of Chapter 1, Section 3. A constraint on an adequate rationalizing explanation is that it should be possible to see how the subject could have taken the considerations in question to provide an adequate normative reason. In case (a) this will often be straightforward. In case (b) it will often be possible to see how the subject could have thought that the considerations in question were true. Cases of type (c) are more messy. If we are to think of the considerations in these cases as making up the agent's reasons, we must be able to make sense of how the subject could have mistaken them for adequate normative reasons. For this it is not enough to see why the subject took the relevant reason-constituting considerations to be true. We need to see why the considerations should have been taken to recommend the conclusion drawn, the decision reached, or whatever. These points suggest that, in making sense of people's reasons, we work with the following principle connecting motivating with normative reasons:

> *The Motivation Principle*: For any agent x, x's motivating reasons for a belief, action, etc., are reasons that x takes (rightly or wrongly) to be an adequate normative reason for that belief, action, etc.

The 'taking' need not be a matter of (consciously) thinking to oneself that such-and-such considerations are adequate normative reasons for this or that. It is a matter of being aware of what one's reasons are, and presupposing that they are good reasons.

I shall say more about the connection between motivating and normative reasons in Section 5 of this chapter and again in Chapter 7. The main focus of this chapter is on normative reasons for belief and action. This topic is crucial for the aims of this book. The conception of normativity with which I shall be working links normativity to normative reasons. Since the notion of a normative reason is not problem-free, I need to take stock of where the problems lie. In later chapters I shall invoke normatively characterized relations between believing P and believing things implied by P, and between intending to Φ and doing what is necessary in order to Φ. In this connection I shall make use of the notion of a normative commitment and draw attention to links between such commitments and normative reasons. What follows here prepares the ground for that discussion.

2. Reasons for belief

The idea of a (normative) reason for belief is tolerably clear by comparison with the idea of (normative) reasons for action. There are many difficult philosophical problems about reasons for belief, most of which I shall ignore. My concern is with the comparative obscurity of the notion of a reason for action by contrast with the notion of a reason for belief. There are two reasons for this obscurity.

(i) If there is an adequate normative reason (a sufficient reason) for me to believe P, it must justify my believing P. We sometimes speak of reasons in a weaker sense, as when we say that a consideration gives one *some* reason to believe P, suggesting that the reason falls short of sufficient reason to believe P. In such cases the consideration constituting the reason must still be positively relevant to a justification for believing that P—its being true must raise the chance that P is true. Of course, there are philosophical problems about justification—for instance about inductive justification, about the structure of justification, and about how justification should figure in an account of perceptual knowledge. None of these problems affect the fundamental point that reasons for belief must be positively relevant to justification. As I shall be arguing in Section 3, when we turn to the sorts of considerations that count as reasons to do something (whether or not we actually do it), it is not at all obvious that there is an analogous condition of positive relevance to justification.

(ii) Despite the fact that there are problems about the justification of belief, it is relatively clear why normative reasons for a belief must provide, or contribute to, its justification. Belief constitutively aims at truth.[29] So belief needs justification, and the measure of the adequacy of a reason for believing must therefore be that the reason supplies justification. There is no other measure by which the adequacy of a reason for belief can be evaluated. If there is a constitutive aim of action, it is far less clear what it is, and thus far less clear what reasons for action are required to be. Normative reasons for an action must in some way favour that action. But there are different ways in which they can do this. I shall be arguing that not all such reasons are relevant to justification in any sense that is the analogue of justification for belief. Some do, of course.

---

[29] The notion that belief aims at truth is discussed in Williams (1970). It is developed in different ways in Railton (1994), Velleman (2000a), and Wedgwood (2002).

One might wonder whether something like believing can have any constitutive aim at all. Believing is not normally regarded as an action. If it is not an action, how can it have an aim? I take it that speaking of belief as having an aim is a shorthand way of speaking of a goal that governs the believing of subjects. Whether the aim can be properly ascribed to the agent, as opposed to some component of the agent's cognitive system functioning below the level of intention, is another matter, to which I turn shortly.

How exactly does belief's aiming at truth explain the need for belief to be justified? The answer, I suggest, is that the goal of believing only what is true will be achieved only if one's beliefs are safe, in the sense that they could not easily be false.[30] Having adequate justification for a belief renders it safe. This has implications for what reasons must be. An adequate reason to believe P must be such that one could not easily believe falsely in believing P for that reason.

The idea that belief constitutively aims at truth serves to distinguish believing from some other propositional attitudes, for example imagining, and supposing. Neither imagining nor supposing is governed by the goal of imagining or supposing only what is true. Without qualification, however, it does not distinguish believing from guessing and conjecturing, both of which aim at—are directed towards—the truth.[31] One guesses that something is so in the hope that it is so, but in the absence of sufficient reason to think it is so. Despite the absence of sufficient reasons, one wants to end up having guessed correctly (= truly). Because guessing aims at truth, a person guessing, when there is relevant evidence to hand, will not be indifferent to this evidence. But there can be pure guesses, as when one guesses as part of a game in which there is no relevant evidence available. A guess can also be made even when one knows that enquiry might discover relevant evidence that is not currently available. In a situation in which this is so there might be practical reasons for guessing, and acting on one's guess, without further enquiry. (A fugitive fleeing along the sewers of Vienna might guess that taking some particular turn gives the best chance of escape, and act on that, without delaying to make further investigations that might settle the matter.) Conjec-

---

[30] On the notion of safety, see Williamson (2000).
[31] A paper in typescript by David Owens prompted the remarks that follow in this paragraph. I have not attempted to address all of the issues raised in his paper.

turing is like guessing in that a conjecture is made when there is insufficient reason for believing what is conjectured. But, whereas a guess can be wholly unconstrained by evidential considerations, a conjecture must be so constrained. It is not a shot in the dark, but something like a guess guided by what one takes to be considerations lending some plausibility to the proposition in question.

This is where the project of explaining what adequate normative reasons for belief must be is not entirely straightforward. Guessing, conjecturing, and believing all aim at truth. So the question arises as to how to distinguish the different ways in which the goal—holding the attitude in question only if its content is true—governs the attitude. Guessing is of less interest to the present discussion because guessing does not always call for a reason. I shall focus on conjecturing and believing.

A natural suggestion is that the difference between conjecturing and believing depends on differences in how one who believes and one who conjectures are liable to think about the evidence they take themselves to have. Belief aspires to be based on adequate evidence for the truth of what is believed. Conjecture aspires to be grounded on evidence that shows what is conjectured to be plausible (such that it might well be true). If this is right, the difference in aspiration should be reflected by differences in presumptions about the nature of the available evidence. Those who believe P would not do so unless they presumed that they had evidence supplying a sufficient reason for thinking that P is true, and would be prepared to give up believing P if they came to think that there was evidence showing that P is false, or at least casting doubt on whether it is true. Those who merely conjecture that P is true would not do so unless they presumed that they had evidence that falls short of supplying a sufficient reason to think that P is true, but did show it to be plausible.

This is fine so far as it goes, but it raises a problem. The project is to shed light on reasons for believing in terms of the idea that belief aims at truth. It should yield an explanation of why adequate normative reasons for belief must justify belief. But in thinking about what it is for belief to aim at truth, we find ourselves having to explain the distinction between believing and other attitudes that are directed at the truth. So far as belief and conjecture are concerned, the natural way to do this is in terms of the distinction between evidence needed for a conjecture and evidence needed for a belief. The trouble is that evidence needed for a conjecture that p is, in effect, evidence providing a sufficient reason for conjecturing that p, and evidence needed for a belief that p is evidence supplying a sufficient reason for believing that p. So we end up trading on the very notion—that of a reason for belief—that the project is meant to illuminate. Still, something can be gleaned from these reflections which will suffice for present purposes.

There is a spectrum of attitudes that are truth-directed and are tied to what the subject regards as evidence. The spectrum stretches from firm and settled belief through lesser degrees of confidence and down to attitudes, like conjecture, which intuitively seem to be distinguished from belief.[32] There seems to be little prospect of distinguishing between the kinds of evidence appropriate to each truth-directed attitude in the spectrum without relying on a prior understanding of what it is to have that attitude. We distinguish, for instance, between *taking something to be true beyond reasonable doubt*, and *thinking it very likely to be true, though not beyond reasonable doubt*. We know that the latter attitude calls for weaker evidence than the former. We have to explain the different ways in which these truth-directed attitudes are governed by the goal that the attitude be held only if its content is true in terms of differences in the strength of evidence that each attitude calls for. These differences are reflected in differences in the psychology of the different attitudes. In adopting the bolder attitude, one presumes that one has compelling evidence. In adopting the more cautious attitude, one presumes that one has weaker evidence. This approach relies upon a prior grasp of intuitive distinctions among the attitudes—distinctions that have to do with differences in the subject's level of confidence in the truth or plausibility of the proposition in question. To approach the matter in this way is to give up any prospect of fixing the character of each attitude in terms of independently intelligible distinctions between the ways in which the goal of truth governs the attitude. But for the purposes of the present project, this does not matter. The important point is that, because each attitude in the spectrum is truth-directed, normative reasons for that attitude must justify the kind of confidence in which that attitude

---

[32] It will not affect the main line of argument in this book if conjecture is conceived as a low degree of partial belief.

consists. So, despite the complications presented by there being a range of truth-directed attitudes, the fact that an attitude is truth-directed dictates that reasons for that attitude should justify the kind of confidence characteristic of the attitude. I shall argue in due course that nothing comparable holds for reasons for action; there is no constitutive aim of action that demands that adequate normative reasons for action should always justify the action.

Some might think that the view of belief I have adopted imposes too stringent a requirement on believing. In matters of opinion and personal conviction it is not uncommon for people to suppose, or talk as if they supposed, that it is open to them to think whatever they like. And sometimes—in matters of religious conviction, for instance—it may seem that the degree of conviction is independent of, or even inversely proportional to, the strength of evidence possessed.

It is true that in matters of personal conviction people often display little interest in testing what they think, or in responding to reasons adduced against it, and may even make a virtue out of believing in the absence of evidence, or in the face of apparently contrary evidence. Even so, those adopting such attitudes are not best represented as lacking the kind of sensitivity to evidential considerations which I claim to be characteristic of belief. They presuppose that their beliefs are well founded, even if they recognize that they do not pass muster by canons of evidence dictated by REASON or THE WORLD'S WISDOM. They think of these canons as having limited applicability—as being applicable to some areas of enquiry, say natural science, but not to the truths of their faith.[33] They presuppose that they have grounds for what they believe, provided by, for instance, the testimony of the faithful and their own personal experiences, though they recognize that non-believers do not regard these as providing compelling evidence for their convictions. If they really did think their convictions were being put under pressure by contrary evidence, they would not be indifferent to this matter. If they are complacent in this respect it is because they do not think their beliefs are really being put under pressure.

---

[33] Perhaps this is what Pascal had in mind when he said that the heart has its reasons, of which reason (= REASON) knows nothing.

It needs to be borne in mind that the topic is not the ethics of belief—what is required for intellectually virtuous believing. I am trying to shed light on what reasons for belief have to be, in terms of the idea that believing constitutively aims at truth. How the goal of believing only what is true controls believing varies depending on the degree of confidence characteristic of the believing. Correspondingly, being really convinced that something is so depends on *presuming* that one has evidence of suitable strength. But the considerations on which one relies to provide evidence (one's evidential considerations) may be inadequate to the purpose. They may be quite out of line, even crazily out of line, with what intellectual virtue requires.

I have been addressing a concern as to whether the view of belief I have been advancing places too stringent a constraint on believing. Other considerations might motivate such a concern. What should we say about beliefs involved in perceptual knowledge? A novel I have been reading is on the coffee table. I see, and so believe, that the novel is there. In so believing, do I at least implicitly take myself to have evidence that the book is there? One might reasonably think that seeing that the novel is there is not a matter of having evidence that it is there—that to have evidence would be to believe something else on the basis of which I believe that the novel is there. And what about the multitude of background beliefs that we exploit? Are there not items of information that we rely upon though we have forgotten what reason there is to think them true? These are tricky matters which I hope to address more fully elsewhere. Here I shall briefly outline what I take to be promising responses. The main arguments of the book do not depend on whether these responses are correct.

A fairly standard response to the problem about perception makes use of the idea that perceiving that the novel is on the coffee table implicates perceptual experiences of a sort that I might have had even if there had been no novel on the table and it had merely seemed to me that there was. One way of making use of this idea is in terms of the view that the consideration that one has such experiences might be evidence that the novel is on the coffee table. Another is to treat the experiences themselves as non-propositional evidence that the novel is there. On both of these approaches, to see that p is to believe that p based on some prior evidence—either propositional evidence constituted by some consideration other than that p, or non-propositional evidence in the form of perceptual experience. A quite different approach, which I favour, has it that my seeing that the novel is on the table is my forming a belief that the novel is on the table before me, not as a response to prior evidence, but as direct result of seeing it there. Although the belief is not formed in response to prior evidence, in having it I presuppose that I have reason to think that the novel is on the table. In the absence of reasons independent of my seeing the book, the belief would be sustained only so long as I take it for granted that I do indeed see the book on the table. Likewise, if the belief survives in the form of a belief that the novel *was* on the table back then, it will persist, in the absence of independent evidential considerations, only so long as it is sustained by the consideration that I saw the book on the table.[34] What about my belief that I see, or saw, the book on the table? Like my belief that it is on the table, this belief is itself a direct response to the fact of the matter, rather than being based on prior evidence. Just as the book's being on the table can cause me to believe that it is there in such a way that I know that it is, so my seeing the book on the table can cause me to believe that I see it on the table in such a way that I know that I see it. The seeing can make available to me the consideration that the book is on the table as well as the consideration that I see that it is.

The problem of background belief was posed by the thought that we retain lots of beliefs while being unaware of the evidence or seeming evidence on which they were based. I do not recall when I last checked that La Paz is the capital of Bolivia, though I believe that it is. Of course, if when I next look in the atlas I were to find that La Paz is not the capital of Bolivia, I would abandon the belief that it is. There is no problem about my believing being sensitive to evidential considerations to that extent. But what about the idea that my believing presupposes that I have sufficient reason to do so? One response is to suppose that my having such evidence does not require me to be to be able to produce it. (For this response, see Owens 2000: 148.) But there is another option, very much in the spirit of the previous discussion about perceptual knowledge. My evidence for thinking that La Paz is the capital of Bolivia may be that I remember that it is. This evidence is not the evidence on which I originally

---

[34] There are affinities at this point with McDowell (1994a/1998a; 1995/1998a), and Williamson (2000).

formed the belief, or evidence that might subsequently have reminded me that La Paz is the capital of Bolivia. Evidence of these sorts might have been supplied by what a teacher said, or by my looking at a map of South America, or by my hearing a comment on a news broadcast. The situation I am considering is one in which I have forgotten about all such evidence. But having forgotten is compatible with knowing that I know, in virtue of remembering, that La Paz is the capital of Bolivia. Knowing that I remember, I would have reason for thinking that what I remember is so. Note that the consideration in play here is not about whether I seem to remember that La Paz is the capital of Bolivia, but about whether I do so remember. If I do, then the consideration that I do can be my reason for believing that La Paz is the capital of Bolivia. Obviously, I could falsely take myself to have a reason of this sort, because, though I seem to remember, I do not actually remember.

I shall take it that belief aims at truth in a sense that implies that believing depends upon one's presuming one has sufficient reason to do so. It must be conceded, however, that the boundaries between believing, in its various forms, and other truth-directed attitudes are not sharp. In a recent discussion of belief, David Owens gives the following example:

I am wondering whether to purchase a house this year and that decision largely depends on whether I think prices will rise. I carefully read the property pages, listen to the pundits on television, determine that the house market will remain flat and plan an expensive holiday instead of a house purchase. Just before I form this view, a newspaper article by a respected columnist appears which purports to show that house prices will rise. I don't read the article and don't let it worry me. Having insufficient time to assimilate and weigh this testimony against that of other experts, I stick to my view that prices will not rise.... Were I an economist specialising in the housing market and about to give a paper on future price rises to a conference of estate agents, I probably would not be entitled to have a belief on the matter that did not take account of the article. (Owens 2000: 26)

Owens uses the example to illustrate a claim he makes about belief and justification: that whether evidence is adequate to justify a claim depends in part on pragmatic considerations. In the example, the pragmatic considerations have to do with the time available for enquiry and what is at stake in being wrong. It does seem plausible that such considerations are relevant in the way Owens suggests.[35] There is a question, though, as to whether the attitude described in this case is best regarded as belief. Often when we make practical decisions we proceed on the supposition that certain things are true. We do our best under the constraints available to ensure that they are true, but, having made a decision on their basis, we may knowingly ignore enquiry that might show them to be false. When Owens decides to ignore the article, he continues to proceed, as we might say, *on the assumption* that the house market will be remain flat. That is an intelligible way to proceed. But if he really thought there was a good chance that what the article suggests is true, then it strikes me as odd to say that his persisting attitude that the market will remain flat is one of belief. I am inclined to think that it is not so much that he believes that the market will remain flat as that he is going to risk proceeding as if it will remain flat. The trouble is that this is pretty much what some theorists call partial belief. Differences in intuitions on such matters suggest that our everyday terminology is vague. Belief shades into other truth-directed attitudes, and people may differ over where to stop talking of believing and start talking of something else, short of believing.

Even so, there are limits to how far the notion of belief should be stretched. Keith Lehrer distinguishes between acceptance out of regard for truth and believing for the sake of felicity. As an example of the latter, he gives believing 'that a loved one is safe because of the pleasure of so believing' (Lehrer 1990: 11). Believing for the sake of felicity seems to be conceived as a kind of believing that involves no presupposition to the effect that one has suitable evidence. There are genuine phenomena that might be thought to match Lehrer's descriptions. There can be genuine belief that implicates the relevant kind of presupposition about evidence, even though what is presumed to be evidence is far from being so. The presumption might be explained by strong motivational bias. There is also indulgence in fantasy, where there is no presupposition about evidence. I would not call this belief even though it may function in some respects like belief and, to the subject, may be indistinguishable from belief.

---

[35] If they are then this suggests that how safe belief needs to be to count as being justified is sensitive to the pragmatic factors.

Suppose it is granted that belief aims at truth and involves the kind of sensitivity to evidential considerations that I have been discussing. Should we think of belief's aiming at truth in terms of a *concern* on the part of believers that they should believe only what is true? If so, then belief's aim is really an aim on the part of the believer, rather than an aim possessed by a component in the believer's cognitive system operating below the level of concerns and intentions. That human believers of sufficient maturity have such an aim should not seem problematic once due allowance is made for ineptitude in how it can be manifested. But this is not the only way to think about what it is for belief to aim at truth. As David Velleman has observed, activities can be goal-directed, even if they are not the expression of an explicit concern that the goal be achieved.[36] Walking along the street, I steer my way through crowds. I do this intentionally, but not every twist and turn I take is an intentional action. I avoid bumping into people and obstacles in my path, or just maintain a comfortable gait, but many of the adjustments I make are like the automatic adjustments made when riding a bicycle or driving a car. I need not, for example, intentionally pass oncoming walkers on one side rather than the other. Or, again, think of picking up a can from a shelf in a supermarket. You may intentionally pick up a can of a particular product, but you need not intentionally pick up the particular can you actually do pick. That is not to say that you picked it unintentionally. The point is rather that picking out that particular can was *sub-intentional*.[37] In situations like these agents engage in various activities in the course of carrying out their intentions. These activities are, arguably, goal-directed in that the way they unfold is sensitive to cues indicating whether or not the goal is being achieved. The adjustments while walking are, roughly speaking, directed to the goal of steering a smooth and comfortable course. More specifically, they are directed at various sub-goals—avoiding a collision, maintaining a regular pace—the effect of achieving which is to maintain a smooth and comfortable course. The activities by means of which an intention to pick up a product in a supermarket is carried out are governed by various sub-goals—raising one's arm, directing one's hand towards a

---

[36] Velleman (2000b: 21, 184–5, 252–4).
[37] The term is used in O'Shaughnessy (1980: vol. 2, ch. 10). Velleman (2000b) speaks of sub-agential activity.

shelf, grasping the product, etc.—the effect of achieving which is to pick up the product. Though in the examples I have given the agent is engaged in intentional action, there are activities involved in carrying out the intention that are goal-directed, even though they are not themselves intentional actions. They occur because capacities are exercised which ensure that, in the absence of countervailing factors, the goal is achieved. It might be thought that belief's constitutive aim should be conceived in the same way, as depending on sub-intentional systems, which work towards ensuring that one believes only what is true. That such activities take place in forming, retaining, and abandoning beliefs is, I think, indisputable. Though we can affect what we believe through intentional enquiry, there is no disputing that beliefs come and go as a result of sub-intentional activity. The question is whether we can make sense of belief's aiming at truth purely in terms of such activity.

The kind of sub-intentional goal-directed activity of which I have been speaking is the activity not of agents, but of systems that are so organized that they maintain a certain goal-state. An example of such a system is that by which the water content of human blood is maintained. The mechanisms that effect this, including the kidneys, respond to imbalances in water content with activity that restores equilibrium.[38] Such systems, by and large, react to indicators that the goal is not being achieved by activity that restores the situation. In their case I shall say that the goal *strongly governs* the way the system behaves. Strong governance does not provide a good model for thinking about the way in which intentional actions are governed by goals. (I am talking here not of any constitutive aim of intention as such, but rather about the particular goals linked to particular intentions.) People intending to be good parents or spouses or teachers may have a seriously inadequate conception of what is required to be so. They are in a sense governed by the goal because they explicitly aim to achieve the goal. What they do to this end is, therefore, affected by their beliefs about how the goal is best achieved and

---

[38] The example is from E. Nagel (1977), which is a penetrating discussion of goal-directedness in the absence of intentions. For my purposes it does not matter greatly whether the systems under discussion are properly regarded as being directed at a goal or as merely displaying the appearance of goal-directedness. If the latter, then talk of the system's aiming at a goal and of the goal's governing its activity can be regarded as metaphorical. Talk of belief's aiming at truth would have to be understood accordingly.

about what works against its being achieved. But this governance cannot be strong governance; it is not a matter of being so disposed that activity that is in fact inimical to the realization of the goal, or inclinations towards such activity, by and large results in some counterbalancing activity. Rather, the agents in question are guided by *what strikes them* as being necessary to achieve the goal. They may be quite mistaken about what contributes to, and what is at odds with, the realization of the goal, and they may be unaware of indicators that the goal is not being achieved. If the governance relevant to belief's aiming at truth were just strong governance, then, by and large, whenever people had false beliefs something would kick in to put things right. Plainly this is too crude a picture of the way things are. Just as the person aspiring to be a good parent does not always respond appropriately to indicators that the aspiration is not satisfied, so the person aiming at truth does not always respond appropriately to indicators that the aim is not being satisfied.

We cannot adequately account for how the believing of human beings is governed by the goal of believing only what is true solely in terms of the notion of strong governance. So if we are to account for belief's aiming at truth purely at the level of sub-intentional activity, we had better not take strong governance as our model for how the goal controls the subject's activity. Is there some sense in which, at this sub-intentional level, activity that is not strongly governed by a goal could none the less be directed towards the goal? It helps to think again about the kidneys. If the kidneys do not reliably reduce the concentration of water in the blood to the right level, then their activity is not strongly governed by the goal of maintaining the right water content. But nor is it governed in any other sense by that goal. Governance by a goal has to do with how a system is actually functioning. There is nothing in the case of the malfunctioning kidneys which corresponds to what at the level of intentional action would be aspiring, but failing, to bring about the intended end. If they are consistently regulating the water content of the blood to some level higher than that achieved when they are functioning properly, then we may think of them as being strongly governed by the goal of maintaining the level of water content to which they are actually working. But that is no reason to suppose that they are doing anything analogous to aspiring to maintain the 'right' water content.

When it comes to the sub-intentional activity *we* engage in, the situation is more complex. Various goals that contribute to maintaining a smooth and comfortable course while walking strongly govern a range of sub-intentional activities. What if your capacities are impaired because you are feeling faint? Is there anything at the sub-intentional level that corresponds to aspiring, but failing, to achieve the goal, and thus aspiring to achieve a goal by which one is not strongly governed? It might seem that there is. If you have not actually fainted or become immobilized, the various capacities that normally enable you to keep your balance, take in information about objects around you, maintain a steady pace, and so forth will not have packed in completely. You walk, but in a less steady way. You still manage for the most part to avoid bumping into people, but less reliably than when you are well. There seems to be some sense in which you retain the capacities that normally enable you to maintain a smooth and comfortable course—it's just that these capacities are impaired. It is the fact that you retain the capacities, and are still being responsive to the cues indicating that you might run the risk of not maintaining a smooth and comfortable course, that gives sense to the idea that in some sense you are governed by the goal. But these reflections do not help in trying to make sense of how, at the level of sub-intentional activity, there can be governance that is not strong governance by a goal. For the governance relevant to the case in which capacities are impaired is just strong governance. The crucial point about strong governance is that by and large the system responds appropriately to cues indicating that the goal is liable not to be achieved. In the situation in which you are faint there is still strong governance, even though in regarding it as such we need to interpret 'by and large' liberally. In such cases we do not have a system aspiring to a goal it does not achieve. We have a system that achieves its goal but less reliably than when all is well. So we do not have an analogue for what at, the level of explicit intention, would be aspiring to achieve a goal by which one is not strongly governed.

This last consideration might seem to show that we should think of belief's aiming at truth solely in intentional terms and leave strong governance out of the picture. This would certainly be an overreaction, for two reasons.

First, *both* sub-intentional activity strongly governed by the goal of believing only what is true *and* explicit concern for believing only what is true have a role in the story of how belief aims at truth, at least in the case of humans. This so because some of our beliefs are strongly governed by the goal and others are governed by the goal via our concern that they should be true. For an example of the former, suppose that I believe that a committee is meeting in a room that I am about to enter. On entering the room I find that no one is there. Because it is well past the time the committee was supposed to begin its meeting, but too soon for it to have concluded its business, I assume that the committee is meeting elsewhere and accordingly cease to believe that it is meeting in this room. In this case the obvious falsity of something I believe triggers appropriate adjustments in my beliefs. This looks like a clear case of strong governance. The falsity of my belief is registered by my taking in a fact that is obviously incompatible with it, and I react accordingly. With respect to such beliefs, there *is* strong governance by the goal of believing only what is true and this governance operates at the sub-intentional level. This fits with the fact that the adjustments of belief resulting most directly from our perceptually taking in facts about our environment are made without deliberation or intentionally directed enquiry. This cannot be the whole story, however, because many of the adjustments we make to our beliefs are mediated by inferences drawing upon existing standing beliefs, not all of which are strongly supported by empirical evidence, and some of which are false. At this level too belief aims at truth, but, as I have remarked already, it is not the case that truth-directed adjustments to belief reflect strong governance. Rather, they are influenced by the believer's styles of reasoning and estimates of the weight of evidence and so on. (Attitudes acquired or abandoned in the course of unreflective responses to encountered facts are, of course, also subject to revision in the light of reflective enquiry, and therefore in the light of the subject's possibly mistaken assumptions and judgements about the balance of reasons.)

Another reason for not leaving strong governance out of the picture is that it would be wrong at this stage of the enquiry to adopt a view of belief that is incompatible with the possibility that non-human animals have beliefs. I shall be arguing for a high conception of belief such that beliefs implicate reflective capacities and an understanding of normative constraints on reasonable believing. I recognize that some theorists will take issue with such a conception. It is open to them to make use of the idea that belief constitutively aims at truth even if believers lack the reflective capacities required for having a concern that their beliefs should be true. For they can think of believing as being strongly governed by the goal of believing only what is true through the operation of sub-intentional systems.

I have dwelt at some length upon the idea that belief aims at truth because, despite some complications which it brings in its train, it feeds into a plausible explanation of what normative reasons for belief must be. Because believing is governed by the goal of believing only what is true, considerations count as adequate normative reasons for believing P only if they justify believing P. In the next section I discuss normative reasons for action and explain why I think that not all such reasons bear on the justification for action. In Section 4 I shall offer further support for the view proposed, drawing upon an idea about the constitutive aim of intentional action.

3. Reasons for action

An assumption routinely made in the literature on reasons for action is that so-called normative reasons for action are reasons that provide the agent with a justification for performing that action. Thus Michael Smith writes, 'Normative reasons are considerations, or facts, that rationally justify certain sorts of choices or actions on an agent's behalf.'[39] This view is deeply embedded in current philosophical thinking about practical reason—so much so that it could easily seem that to challenge it is simply to misunderstand the view. I think it is, at the very least, misleading. It is far less clear what justification amounts to in the case of action than it is in the case of belief.

It is not my aim to challenge the idea that there are reasons that provide a justification for actions. To see what I am challenging, we need to consider some aspects of the wider picture into which the

---

[39] Smith (1997: 87). The passage occurs in a review and defence of Smith (1994). A number of philosophers work with the contrast already noted in Ch. 1 between normative and motivating reasons. In such contexts they more or less explicitly treat normative reasons as providers of justification. Compare Nagel (1970: 14–15), Bond (1983: ch. 2), Darwall (1983: ch. 2; 1997), Schueler (1993: 46 ff.), Cullity and Gaut (1997: 1), and Scanlon (1998: 18 ff.).

concept of a normative reason fits. It is part of that picture that normative reasons are contrasted with motivating reasons along the lines noted in Chapter 1, Section 2. Motivating reasons for actions are reasons for things actually done—they are the reasons for which agents do things. Contrasted with these are the reasons there are for agents to do certain things. It is reasons of this latter sort that the notion of a normative reason is intended to capture.

It is incumbent on anyone who challenges the view that normative reasons for action provide justification to say why reasons for action that do not provide justification should be regarded as normative in any sense. The intuitive answer to this is that, though not all such reasons provide justification worthy of the name, all represent an action as being favoured in some way.[40] Much of this chapter is concerned with different ways in which an action can be favoured. I begin with a couple of examples in which we seem to have reasons for a person to do something, with respect to which talk of justification is out of place. Both concern ways of spending leisure time. In the first example I am considering what to do while in Madrid. Someone tells me that the Prado is worth a visit because it has numerous paintings by the great masters of Spanish art. I think that visiting this museum would be enjoyably edifying and take that to be a reason to visit. Plausibly, this consideration—that visiting the museum would be enjoyably edifying—does indeed provide me with a reason to go. Since having such experiences is a good thing, visiting the museum would be something worth doing. Should we say that this reason provides me with any kind of justification for going? It is not obvious that it does—not, at any rate, if justification is conceived as being analogous to justification in connection with belief. Contrast a situation in which I am considering whether P is true with a view to reaching some verdict on the matter. The options are to believe P, to disbelieve P (believe the negation of P), or to withhold both belief and disbelief from P. An adequate normative reason for believing P must discriminate between these options. It must show that the right verdict is belief. To disbelieve P, or to withhold both belief and disbelief from P, is to fail to appreciate the force of the reason. But a reason for visiting the Prado does not have

---

[40] This is how the idea of a normative reason for action is explained in the glossary to Darwall (1998).

to show that visiting the Prado as opposed to doing something else is the right or appropriate thing to do. The fact that visiting would be enjoyably edifying is a reason to visit, but it does not have to be a reason that justifies visiting as opposed to something else, because the situation need not be one in which there is any right thing to do.

These considerations are relevant to the second example. Suppose that I intend to buy a newspaper and can do so at the corner shop. This consideration, I take it, supplies me with a reason to go to the shop. It recommends going to the shop, but only in that it gives an instrumental point to my going. It seems overblown to speak of this reason as justifying my going to the shop. This is not because it does not provide enough justification. The action need not call for justification, since there need be nothing in the situation that would count as the right thing as between going to the shop and doing something else. It suffices that the reason shows the action to be one that has a point in that it is a means to something I intend. If we like, we can speak of the action as having instrumental value or worth, but that simply repeats the consideration that it is a means to an end; it falls far short of showing that going to the shop is desirable in the sense of being worthy of being desired. Just because it falls short in this respect, some might suggest that the consideration I am alleging to be a reason, taken by itself, is no reason at all to go to the shop. A genuine reason, they might say, would have to be a consideration that shows going to the shop to be something worth doing in some richer sense. This response assumes what I am disputing—that the action in question calls for justification. This assumption may drive some to suggest that there is reason for me to go to the shop because there is reason for me to buy a paper. Perhaps buying a paper is desirable.[41] I shall presently argue that genuine reasons for action need not relate to desirable ends—that a consideration can be a reason for action simply by being a means towards an end that the agent has in fact adopted. But even supposing that all reasons for action must show, or be positively relevant to showing, that the action is worth doing in terms of some desirable end, it is not obvious that this would make it reasonable to think of all such reasons in terms of the provision of justification for the action. Visiting the Prado was

[41] Smith (1997: 87 ff.) has it that normative reasons for actions are propositions of the form, 'Acting in such-and-such a way in so-and-so circumstances is desirable.'

worth doing, but that does not show that it, as opposed to other things I could have done, was in any sense the right or appropriate thing to do.

There are at least two different kinds of context in which it makes sense to evaluate actions as being or failing to be justified. Both are contexts in which something is at stake in such a way that how one acts should have a justification.

In one kind of context, agents are addressing a practical problem and the issue is how best to deal with the problem. In such a context a consideration would justify a given course of action if it showed that it was the best, or an optimal, way of solving the problem. Such contexts may or may not be ones in which moral considerations need to be addressed. In any case, the question faced is, 'What is the best way to achieve an end, having regard to this or that constraint?' The end might be building a bridge over a river. There might be financial, geographical, technological, moral, and political constraints. In such a case the course of action selected ought to be backed by reasons showing it to be at least as good a way of satisfying the relevant constraints as any other. Given the complexity and diversity of the constraints, the difficulties of weighing one kind of relevant factor against another, there is unlikely to be a method for calculating optimality even given unlimited time and resources for enquiry. None the less, the nature of the enterprise dictates that the course of action chosen should be at least defensible as a way of attempting to address the constraints in all their complexity. The course chosen should therefore be backed by reasons establishing it to be defensible in this sense, and to that extent justified. Obviously, not all of the practical problems that agents face are simply concerned with means to ends. Suppose that Nicola has an elderly mother who lives on her own, some distance away, and is becoming increasingly frail. Nicola faces a problem concerning how she should respond to her mother's increasing frailness. Should she live with her mother, or visit more regularly to boost her morale and ensure that there is adequate provision for her care, or have her mother come to live with her? In reflecting on this, Nicola will no doubt take into account what she owes to her mother, as being her mother, as well as her feelings about her mother and the kind of relationship she has with her. She will consider whether adequate care can be arranged at one place or another, the commitments she (Nicola) has to her job, and so on. The kind of reason she needs is one that shows some course of action to be a defensible way of meeting the variety of complex constraints. In this case it will be a reason that takes into account a variety of desirable ends, as well as obligations and commitments.

There is another kind of context in which an agent is not faced with the kind of practical problem I have been considering, but does have particular responsibilities, moral or otherwise, that give rise to issues as to whether a course of action would be justified. The responsibilities might be those involved in being a parent, or occupying some post or office. The issue might be whether a course of action, which an agent has some reason or inclination to pursue, would be compatible with his or her responsibilities. A reason for taking that course must show it to be defensible, from that point of view, and in that sense justified.

Many contexts in which there are reasons for action are unlike either of those just described because there is not anything at stake *in the way* it is at stake in these cases. In the museum example I address the question, 'What is worth doing around here?' I need not be faced with either a practical problem about what is for the best or an issue about whether a course of action is compatible with my responsibilities. Since I am not called upon to aspire to an optimal course of action, or to discharge particular responsibilities, talk of justification is out of place. Other, more culturally driven, souls may face more pressing issues. They may, for instance, be seeking an optimal experience in the time available, in which case for them it becomes a pressing matter whether there might be better places to visit. But the situation need not be like this. Nor need it be one in which I have any particular responsibilities, such that if I failed to discharge them I would be open to criticism. Of course, any situation might develop in a way that could give rise to an issue as to whether the responsibilities one has have been discharged. While thinking about what to do in Madrid, I might be confronted with a road accident at which help is needed. A question could arise as to whether I should have proceeded to visit the Prado as opposed to offering help. A justification for what I do in such a context need not show my action to be right or appropriate. It could just show it to be permissible.[42]

---

[42] Uniacke (1994) emphasizes this kind of justification.

It might be thought that I have been mistakenly assuming that a reason providing justification must provide sufficient justification. I suspect that a common reaction to the museum example is to object that, although the consideration that visiting the museum would be an enjoyably edifying experience does not *justify* going to the museum, in the strong sense of providing a sufficient justification for doing so, it provides justification in some weaker sense. The trouble with this is that it is far from clear that the consideration in question need be so much as positively relevant to the justification of the action. A consideration will be thus relevant if it counts towards the action's being the right or appropriate thing to do. My point is simply that, because not all action calls for justification in this or any other sense, it is wrong to suppose that all reasons for action should be so much as positively relevant to the justification of the action.

Here is another example, which will help to reinforce the line of thought that I have been pursuing. Suppose that you are enjoying a day off work. There is no reason for you not to have taken the day off, and you are under no obligation to spend your time in any particular way. You may do as you please and you intend to do just that. As it turns out, you have an inclination to go for a walk. You go for a walk, as we say, just because you feel like it. But you are not simply borne along by your inclination. You have decided, and so formed the intention, to satisfy your inclination. Do you go for a walk for a reason? I think you do. Your reason is that you intend to satisfy your inclination to go for a walk, and (though it goes without saying) going for a walk would do just that. True, we might say of the action in question that it is done for no reason, but that might mean simply that there is no reason beyond the consideration that you intend to satisfy the inclination.[43] Not only did you act for a reason; there is a reason for you to go for a walk. For it is true that you intend to satisfy your inclination to go for a walk, and true that by going for a walk you can do so. This consideration therefore confers an instrumental point on your going. It provides you with a reason to go, but the reason is not in any way justificatory. Since the situation is not one that calls for you to have a justification for what you do, your reason is not required to be one that even counts towards such a justification.

---

[43] Compare Davidson (1963/1980: 6). Davidson's point is importantly different. He thinks the reason is provided by the inclination. I think it is provided by an intention to satisfy the inclination.

4. The constitutive aim of intentional action

So far I have given some intuitive reasons for resisting the assimilation of normative reasons for action to reasons providing justification for action. In this section I link up these considerations with ideas about the constitutive aim of intentional action which might seem to demand that reasons for action should provide justification.

Much current thinking about reasons for action has been motivated by two factors. The first is a presumption that reasons for action are in an important respect like reasons for belief. Since reasons for belief necessarily provide a justification for belief, it is assumed that reasons for action must provide justification for action.[44] The second is that much of the discussion of reasons for action takes place in the context of moral philosophical discussions in which the justification of actions in the light of moral considerations is at the heart of the enquiry.

There are other, deeper, considerations that can make it seem that reasons for action must provide justification. When discussing reasons for belief, I noted that the way that believing is governed by the goal of believing only what is true dictates that an adequate reason to believe P should justify believing P. That is because the measure of the adequacy of such a reason is whether one could easily believe falsely if one were to believe for that reason. It is natural to ask whether there is a constitutive aim of intentional action dictating that reasons for action must provide justification for those actions.

On one view of the matter—the classical view as it might be called—the analogue of believing only what is true is aiming to bring about or realize what is good in some respect or degree. This view, which has its roots in Aristotle, surfaced in modern philosophy in Elizabeth Anscombe's ground-breaking work *Intention*, in which she claimed that truth stands to judgement as good stands to wanting (Anscombe 1963: 76). The view is motivated by considerations about the intelligibility of desires. In a passage that has received a great deal

---

[44] T. M. Scanlon (1998: 18–22) introduces the idea of a reason, in what he calls 'the standard normative sense', in connection with belief. In this standard sense reasons provide justification. So far as I can see, he takes it for granted that normative reasons for action are always reasons in this 'standard normative sense'.

of attention (1963: 70 ff.), Anscombe pointed out how odd it would be to want a saucer of mud. Wanting a saucer of mud would be intelligible, she suggested, only if obtaining it were viewed by the agent as being in some way desirable (in the sense of being good in some respect). Stated thus baldly, this consideration seems just to defer the problem of intelligibility by pushing it back on to the intelligibility of what strikes the agent as being desirable. But Anscombe added the further consideration that 'the good (perhaps falsely) conceived by the agent to characterise the thing [wanted] must *really* be one of the many forms of good' (Anscombe 1963: 76–7). Given this view about intelligible wanting, one might think that the constitutive aim of intentional action is the realization of the good and, accordingly, that reasons for an action must be reasons for thinking that the action, or what it brings about, is in some respect good. There is an issue about whether this is correct. Even if it is correct, there is a further issue as to whether it supports the view that reasons for action must provide justification for action. I consider the latter first.

Suppose, for the sake of argument, that intelligible ends must be conceived by the agent as being goods and that the constitutive aim of intentional action is the realization of some good. If that were right, then normative reasons for action would always favour an action by relating the action to the realization of some good. But it certainly does not follow that reasons for an action must justify the action in the sense of showing it to be the right thing to do. There need be nothing that would be the right thing to do. For that reason it would be a mistake to retreat at this point to the claim that reasons for action must at least be positively relevant to such justification. As I observed earlier, this claim presupposes that it makes sense to think of the action as one to which considerations of justification, or the lack of it, are pertinent. I see no reason for thinking that this must be so. The fact that an action would result in some transitory pleasure for the agent helps to make sense of the agent's performing that action. Even so, there need be nothing about the circumstances that demands that the action should admit of evaluation with respect to whether or not it is justified in the sense under consideration.

The idea that the constitutive aim of action is the realization of the good does not establish that reasons for action must provide justification. But it might be thought to create a difficulty for the claim that the fact that an action is a means to an end is in itself a reason for performing that action. Earlier I claimed that the mere fact that I intended to buy a newspaper, and could do so at the shop, supplied me with a reason to go to the shop. This might be contested on the grounds that, unless there were a reason to pursue the end, there would be no reason to pursue the means. (For such a view, see Skorupski 2001.) Those who take this line are not committed to denying that I might give the consideration that I can buy a newspaper at the shop as my reason for going. But they may say that this is merely a partial specification of my reason—that I am tacitly presupposing that going to the shop is instrumental to the realization of some good. In this particular case, it might well be that reading the newspaper is desirable. But there are other examples that make it doubtful that all intentional action is directed at such an end—an end that is, at least by the agent's lights, in some way desirable, in the sense of worthy to be desired. This bears on the other issue raised a couple of paragraphs back: whether reasons for action must be reasons for thinking that the action, or what it brings about, is in some respect good.

The view under discussion implies that all intentional action is directed at something the agent in some way values. This gives rise to a serious problem for the classical theory. As Gary Watson has pointed out, there are 'cases in which one in no way values what one desires' (Watson 1975: 210). Since desires for what one in no way values can lead to intentional action aimed at satisfying them, there can be intentional action that is directed at what one in no way values. Watson gives the example of the 'squash player who while suffering an ignominious defeat, desires to smash his opponent in the face with the racquet' (Watson 1975: 210; compare Stocker 1979 and Velleman 1992). It might be wondered whether the squash player *in no way* values smashing the opponent in the face, since he might see this outcome as at least having the value of satisfying a strong urge that he has. In that case the notion of valuing loses any connection with the good. For the squash player need not think that the course of action would realize something that is good—something that deserves to be given weight in his practical thinking.

It is easy to think of other examples. The despairing father who kills his children and then himself might conceivably think of what he is doing as realizing some good, say by preventing the children from suffering in an inhospitable world in which, as he thinks, they have no chance of prospering. Yet it seems just as conceivable that such a father should do the dreadful deed out of spite against his spouse or other relations, or out of bitterness and resentment at having been ignored. Defenders of the classical theory are committed to supposing that the end sought—hurting others, or drawing the attention of others—is conceived as being in some way good or at least as a means to some good. So far as I can see, nothing in logic, or experience of human conduct and feeling, requires this to be so. If the agent in some sense places a value on such ends, this amounts to no more than being drawn towards them. That the agent is thus drawn is compatible with his not being at that point in any way guided by considerations counting for and against the desirability of the ends.

I am assuming that theses about constitutive aims must be psychologically realistic. There must be features of our psychology that make it plausible that belief or intentional action, as the case may be, is directed at the proposed end. For that to be so, it must actually be the case that we are sensitive to whether or not the goal is going to be realized, or at least to considerations that seem to bear on whether or not the goal is going to be realized. In cases of perverse intentional action, it is highly implausible to think that the subject is sensitive to considerations bearing on whether the end is or is not desirable. That gives us reason to doubt that the constitutive aim of intentional action is the realization of some good.

Anscombe was surely perceptive in drawing attention to the issue of what makes desires intelligible. The appearance of trying to obtain a thing would not by itself make it intelligible that the agent desires that thing. But it is not obvious that all desires need be intelligible if by that is meant that it is possible to see why the subject adopts the end in question. In any case, the point I have been most concerned to stress is that there are dark regions of human psychology that just do not fit the classical theory. There are ends that people set themselves, borne from bitterness and resentment, which are intelligible to us only to the extent that they emerge from extreme forms of emotions which most of us have experienced in less extreme forms. We can make some sense of how twisted resentment leads to horrific acts because we know what it is to harbour resentment. It may remain unintelligible to us how the homicidal father could have been so eaten up as to do what he did, but this unintelligibility will only seem philosophically problematic if we expect more from our commonsense psychology than it is ever likely to yield.[45]

Even granted what I have been arguing, there remains the problem of explaining, or at least shedding some light on, what normative reasons for action have to be. I suggest that there is a plausible view of the constitutive aim of action that explains what reasons for action have to be.

Consider first action done as a means to an intended end. Suppose I intend to Φ and believe that if I am to Φ it is necessary that I Ψ. If I then Ψ with a view to Φing, my doing so has an aim—that I Φ. But there is a sense in which, despite its having an aim, my Ψing will be pointless unless it does in fact contribute to my Φing. A sufficient reason for an action to have a point is that it should be a means to an intended end. An action believed to be such a means might not satisfy this condition. Actions can have a point in other ways. They can have a point in that performing those actions would lead to, or amount to, something desirable, whether or not that thing is (as yet) an intended end. Reverting to a previous example, my visiting the Prado would have a point in that it would provide me with an enjoyably edifying experience. It would have such a point even if I am not yet convinced that it would have this outcome. And it would have such a point even if I have not yet decided that being edified is something I want to go in for right now, as opposed to sitting at a pavement café in the shade having a beer and watching the world go by. A natural suggestion, then, is that the constitutive aim of intentional action is that the intended action should in one way or another have a point. An advantage of thinking about the matter in this way is that it is psychologically realistic. It is plausible, for example, that my willingness to persist in Ψing, in the situation in which I believe it to be necessary for me to Φ would be sensitive to considerations bearing on whether or not Ψing is at least *a* means to my Φing. That sensitivity does seem to be constitutive of instrumental action. And if I decide after all to visit the Prado for the reason that, as I think, it would provide me with an enjoyably edifying experience, then, all else

---

[45] The limits of our commonsense psychology form the topic of Ch. 9.

equal, I shall be willing to persist with this activity, rather than curtail it, only if it does provide such an experience.

Assuming that the constitutive aim of intentional action is that the intended action should have a point, it follows that every (normative) reason for action must confer some kind of point on an action. So there is something at stake in all intentional action, but what is at stake need not demand that the action be justified in the sense of showing it to be the right or appropriate thing to do. An action may have a point simply in virtue of being a means to an intended end. In some circumstances in which this is so it is inappropriate to evaluate the action as being or not being justified. In others there may have been overwhelming reasons not to perform the action. But it would still have a point as being a means to an intended end. It needs to be borne in mind that theses about the constitutive aim of intentional action are about what is intrinsic to all intentional action. An action may achieve the constitutive aim while being subject to criticism in all sorts of ways that are not explicable just in terms of the constitutive aim. An action may achieve the constitutive aim while being foolish, or morally wrong, or perverse, or thoughtless.

All this is compatible with the fact that some actions call for justification of the sort that shows the action to be right or appropriate. As I have already said, such justification can be at issue in contexts in which the aim is to do what is for the best and in contexts in which an agent is responsible for ensuring that certain commitments or obligations are discharged.

5. Motivating reasons

In Section 1, I formulated the following plausible principle:

> *The Motivation Principle*: For any agent x, x's motivating reasons for a belief, action, etc., are reasons that x takes (rightly or wrongly) to be an adequate normative reason for that belief or action.

The preceding discussion has shown that an adequate normative reason in the case of belief must be a justifying reason (the strength of the justification reflecting the strength of the kind of belief). In the case of action, the matter is more complicated. Some actions call for justification in a somewhat similar sense and others do not. But even when an action calls for such justification it may be intelligible, as an action done for a reason, even if the agent did not take his or her reason to provide justification. The constitutive aim of action demands only that the action should in some way have a point and that the subject should be sensitive to considerations bearing on whether or not it has a point.

It is of some interest to reflect on the relation between the Motivation Principle and the following principle, which plausibly applies to action:

The Intention Principle: For any agent x, and action ϕ, x ϕs intentionally if and only if x ϕs for a reason.

Conjoining the Motivating Principle with the Intention Principle yields the conclusion that agents who do something intentionally take there to be a reason for them to do that thing. If a reason to do something had to supply justification for doing that thing, then this conclusion would be highly implausible in view of examples of perverse action of the sort I considered earlier. Obviously, we could avoid the unwanted conclusion by rejecting either the Motivation Principle or the Intention Principle. The former seems intuitively plausible because it is hard to see how else motivating and normative reasons could be connected if not as stated by the principle. Should we reject the Intention Principle?

The Intention Principle is linked to the conception of the constitutive aim of intentional action outlined in the previous section. If the constitutive aim of intentional action is that it has a point, then, plausibly, an agent intentionally acting must presuppose that something confers a point upon the action. What the agent takes to confer a point on the action will be the agent's reason for the action. We do sometimes speak of actions as having been done for no reason, for instance in cases in which one does something just because one feels like it. But arguably these are cases in which, although there is no special reason for the action, there is a reason provided by the consideration that doing the thing in question would satisfy one's inclination to do it. Some find this problematic, but the grounds for thinking it to be problematic, I suspect, depend on the assumption that normative reasons for action must be positively relevant to a justification for the action. In the light of the discussion of the previous section, I believe that this assumption should be rejected. That going for a walk would satisfy an inclination to go for a walk is some kind of reason to go for a walk. After all, it confers an instrumental point on going. But it would in no way justify going for a walk rather than, say, grading some essays that ought to be graded without further delay. What about actions like kissing one's children before they go to school? Such actions are intentional, but it seems odd to suppose that each time they are done they are prompted by inclinations. They can be instances of a habitual pattern of actions that express love for the children. But that means that they have a point—to express love for the children. There is a reason for kissing the children, then. The reason is that kissing them is a way to express one's love for them. That does not have to be a reason that figures explicitly in one's thinking each time one kisses them. It is none the less what gives point to the action. If a parent, because of depression, started to feel that the action was sustained only because it was habitual, then he or she might cease to view the action as an expression of love and begin to see it as having a different point—to sustain the children's belief that the love is still there.

Anscombe, who linked the concept of intention to reasons for action, did not herself accept the Intention Principle. Her view was that intentional actions 'are actions to which a certain sense of the question "Why?" is given application; the sense is . . . that in which the answer, if positive, gives a reason for acting' (Anscombe 1963: 9). The idea is that, where it makes sense to ask 'Why', with a view to learning what the agent's reason was, the action was intentional, even though the right answer to the question might be that there was no reason. Anscombe cited doodling as an example of an intentional action done for no reason (Anscombe 1963: section 17). Let us concede that doodling, as when in a daydream, might be done for no reason. In such cases it might be doubted that the action is intentional. Given the view of the constitutive role of intentional adopted here, doodling becomes intentional only when it has a point—for instance satisfying an inclination to develop a pleasing pattern or to find something to do during a boring talk.

Rosalind Hursthouse rejects the Intention Principle, drawing upon examples of what she calls *arational* action (Hursthouse 1991).

Paradigm cases are kicking a car when it will not start, or scratching a photograph of a person that has upset you. Again, let us concede that such actions might sometimes be done for no reason. This might be so in cases in which the agent is completely out of control. But again, to the extent that such actions are done for no reason, it is doubtful that they are intentional. When they are indisputably intentional, reasons are not hard to find. In the car-kicking case, the agent feels an urge to lash out, as if the car deserved a kick, and intentionally gives way to the urge. In the photograph-scratching case, the agent has an urge to damage the photograph by way of venting anger against the person photographed, and intentionally gives way to this urge.

I am inclined to retain the Intention Principle. The point I want to emphasize, however, is that we can retain both it and the Motivation Principle only if we reject the standard view that all normative reasons provide justification. If we stick with that view and retain both of the principles, then we end up with a distorted treatment of these cases. They have to be squeezed into the mould of actions for which the agent thinks that there is a reason providing justification. We can avoid this by rejecting the view. That seems to me to be a further reason for rejecting the standard view.

CHAPTER 3

Normative Commitments and the Very Idea of Normativity

1. The topic

In this chapter I explore the notion of a normative commitment. This notion is by no means unfamiliar. Someone who makes a promise, for instance, incurs a commitment to doing what is promised. The commitment here is normative. It is not a matter of being resolved or determined to do the thing promised. Rather, it relates, in a manner to be explained, to what there is reason for the agent to do. In Sections 2 and 3 I discuss the normative commitments incurred by beliefs and intentions. These commitments will be crucial for the core arguments in Chapters 4 and 6 in support of the claim that our concepts of believing this, intending that, and so forth are normative concepts. In Sections 4 and 5 I consider normative commitments incurred by participating in practices, and then in Section 6 I highlight important differences between the commitments incurred by beliefs and intentions and those incurred by participating in practices. This part of the discussion feeds into the themes of Chapter 6, which concerns semantic normativity and intentional content. In Section 7, I introduce the general notion of normativity that will inform later chapters.

2. Beliefs, intentions, and commitments

Suppose that I believe

(a) Whenever there is frost on the ground it has been freezing.

NORMATIVE COMMITMENTS   73

Since I have this belief, I incur a commitment to accepting whatever is implied by (a) and whatever is implied by (a) taken along with other things I believe. Exactly why such a commitment is incurred is the topic of Chapter 4. Here I am going to assume that it is incurred and explore the nature of the commitment. I shall shortly go through a similar exercise in connection with commitments incurred by intentions.

In the sense intended here, what is implied by assumptions in a set Δ is what follows from those assumptions without further ado, that is, without the help of other assumptions beyond those that merely amplify the content of the assumptions in Δ. It should be borne in mind that my aim in this book is to characterize ordinary everyday personal understanding, not to provide a regimentation of that understanding. I am going to assume that we have at least an inchoate conception of what it is for one thing to follow from another without further ado. It is true that we often pay scant regard to whether something does follow from something else without further ado, as opposed to depending on further assumptions. Even so, we can make some sense of the difference between the cases. For we can sometimes be brought to see that what we wrongly think follows without further ado from a set of assumptions does not really follow, since it could be false even if the assumptions were true.[46]

The basic *implication commitment*, as I shall call it, gives rise to derivative implication commitments, depending on what is implied by (a), and by (a) together with other things I believe. For example, in virtue of believing (a), and believing

(b) There is frost on the ground

I incur a commitment to believing

(c) It has been freezing.

It needs to be stressed that this way of speaking is shorthand for a fuller statement. When fully specified, the commitment to (c) incurred by believing (a) and (b) is a commitment to believing (c) *if one*

---

[46] There are, of course, differences between theorists about the character of logic. Intuitionists do not endorse some rules of inference that classical logicians accept. If there is a fact of the matter as to which logic is correct, then there will be a fact of the matter as to whether we incur all the commitments that classical logicians might suppose we incur. If there is no fact of the matter as to which logic is correct, then there will be no fact of the matter as to who is right about the commitments relating to the disputed territory.

gives any verdict on (c) at all. The verdicts are believing (c), disbelieving (believing the negation of) (c), and withholding both belief and disbelief from (c). The latter is to be understood as a definite verdict—taking a stance on (c)—rather than as simply the absence of both belief and disbelief. One would not be in breach of the commitment if one believed (a) and (b), but gave no verdict on (c). To discharge the commitment I need to ensure that, *so long as* I continue to accept (a) and (b), I also accept (c), if I give any verdict on it. For the sake of brevity I shall sometimes speak simply of being committed to believing such-and-such, taking it to be understood that the commitment has the character I have just explained.

To say that I incur a commitment—am committed—to believing (c) is not to say that there is an adequate normative reason for me to believe (c). As I stressed in the previous chapter, an adequate normative reason for me to believe (c) is a reason that justifies my believing (c). The claim that believing (a) and believing (b) commits me to believing (c) is compatible with my not justifiably believing (c). Though it would be unusual, it could be that there is no good reason for me to believe either (a) or (b). If that were so, the mere fact that my believing them commits me to believing (c) would not confer justification on my doing so.

Whether or not I am committed to believing (c) by believing (a) and (b) is independent of the status of my belief in (a) or my belief in (b). In particular, it is not affected by whether those latter beliefs are justified or reasonably held. There is, even so, a normative reason linked to the commitment under discussion. For there is a reason for me to avoid continuing to believe both (a) and (b), while giving a verdict on (c) other than belief. I can do justice to this reason either by believing (c) or by giving up belief in either (a) or (b). Correspondingly, I can *discharge* the commitment incurred by believing (a) and believing (b) in one of two ways: by ensuring that I do not give a verdict on (c) other than belief, or by giving up belief in either (a) or (b). The first of these options is *carrying out the commitment incurred*. The second is *bringing it about that it is no longer incurred*. But both are ways of discharging the commitment.[47] The fact that there are these

---

[47] The notion of commitment is in some respects similar to what John Broome (1999; 2002) calls a *normative requirement*. Broome's thinking about normative requirements provided me with the initial stimulus to think about the normativity that is related to belief and intention in terms of commitments.

two ways of discharging the commitment makes it misleading to express the commitment to believing (c) incurred by believing (a) and (b) in terms of the claim that since I believe (a) and (b) I ought to believe (c).[48] Maybe what I ought to do instead is give up believing (a) or give up believing (b).

There are commitments incurred by intentions that are analogous to the implication commitments incurred by beliefs. If I intend to do something, then I incur a basic *means–end commitment* to doing whatever is necessary if I am to do that thing. To discharge this commitment, I need to ensure that I do not continue to hold the intention while never doing what is necessary if I am to do the thing intended. I can discharge this commitment in one of two ways: by doing the necessary, or by giving up the intention.

The basic means–end commitment incurred by an intention gives rise to derivative commitments depending on what is in fact necessary to carry out the intention. If I intend to reach Edinburgh by noon, and to do that need to leave my office by 10, I am committed to leaving my office by 10. This is so whether or not I believe that I need to leave my office by 10. The *basic* commitment incurred by an intention is to doing whatever *is* necessary to carry it out, not to doing what one thinks, perhaps falsely, is the means necessary to carry it out. (In a similar way, the *basic* implication commitment incurred by beliefs commits one to accepting what is actually implied by what one believes, not what one merely thinks is implied by it.) None the less, to discharge the basic means–end commitment incurred by an intention I have to rely upon my beliefs about the means to carry out the intention. Intentions combined with relevant, but possibly false, beliefs about means give rise to commitments to doing what, according to those beliefs, is necessary to carry out those intentions. These are *belief-relative means–end commitments*. Similarly, believing P and having beliefs, which may be false, as to what P implies gives rise to *belief-relative implication commitments*. What it takes to carry out a belief-relative commitment incurred by an intention may not serve to carry out the basic commitment incurred by that intention. For instance, walking in an easterly direction as a means of reaching some destination by a certain time might not

---

[48] For similar claims, see Broome (1997; 1999; 2002). Contrast Jackson (1999).

enable me carry out my commitment to doing what is necessary to carry out my intention to reach the destination by that time. It could be that I needed to walk westwards. Likewise, what it takes to carry out a belief-relative commitment incurred by beliefs might not serve to carry out the basic implication commitment incurred by those beliefs.

Means–end commitments, like implication commitments, are commitments incurred by particular individuals. But they are surely grounded in something more general, which applies to all rational agents. How should we think of this grounding? As a first step towards an answer, I suggest that we should think of reason as setting us certain ideals. These ideals specify things that a rational agent, as such, would ideally do. One such ideal is the following *Means–End Ideal*:

> For any ϕ, avoid intending to ϕ while never getting around to doing what is necessary if you are to ϕ.

Another is the *Implication Ideal*:

> For any π, θ, if θ is implied by π, then avoid believing π while giving a verdict on θ other than belief.

These are ideals of reason in that it is constitutive of being a rational agent that one is suitably sensitive to the need to try to avoid failing to conform to them. Note that this builds into the ideals of reason that one should have certain kinds of knowledge—in particular, knowledge of the means necessary to do what one intends and knowledge of what our beliefs imply. But we need to take great care over how the ideals of reason link up with requirements of rationality if the latter are conceived in such a way that failure to satisfy them is *ipso facto* irrational. In this connection it is significant that you satisfy the Means–End Ideal with respect to an intention only if you do whatever is *as a matter of fact* necessary if you are to do the thing intended. Clearly, not every failure to do so is a failure of rationality. For instance, I may fail to do what is necessary to carry out an intention through ignorance that is in no way irrational. For another, I might be prevented from doing what I know is necessary to carry out an intention in a circumstance that gives me no time to abandon the intention. Suppose I intend to switch on some lights at midnight.

A few seconds before midnight I reach out to flick the switch, and just as I am about to do so, when the clock is about to chime, the power cuts. I have the intention right up until the time is due to carry it out. But though I have not done what is necessary to carry it out and have not abandoned the intention, I have not on that account done anything irrational. To abandon an intention is to change one's mind, and I have not done that. (The intention, so to speak, lapses because it relates to a moment that has passed.) If requirements of rationality are such that to fail to satisfy them is to be in some respect irrational, then I need not have failed to satisfy a rationality requirement. Parallel considerations apply to the Implication Ideal. Certainly, a failure to satisfy the Implication Ideal need not be a failure of rationality. I may fail to satisfy the ideal through ignorance that is not irrational.

Implication commitments and means–end commitments, I suggest, are grounded in the corresponding ideals. Intending to Φ incurs a commitment to doing whatever is necessary to Φ. On my account, our having this commitment amounts to there being a reason for us to avoid retaining the intention to Φ while never getting around to doing what is necessary if we are to Φ. The reason is that if we did not to do so we would have failed to satisfy the Means–End Ideal. Requirements of rationality can be readily added to this picture. For, plausibly, there is a requirement of rationality—the *Means–End Requirement*—to the effect that one should do justice to the reason there is to avoid persisting with an intention while failing to do what is necessary to do the thing intended. We do justice to this by ensuring that we act on it, so far as it is in our power to do so. When I am prevented from turning on the lights by the power cut, I have not failed to do justice to the reason there is for me to avoid intending to turn on the lights while never getting around to doing what it is necessary if I am to turn on the lights. It was not in my power either to turn on the lights or to change my mind about doing so. It seems plausible then that ideals of reason give rise to rationality requirements. The implication ideal gives rise to the *Implication Requirement*, to the effect that one should do justice to the reason there is to avoid maintaining beliefs while giving a verdict on any of the implications of the things believed other than belief. The important point is that, while it is a failure of rationality not to satisfy such requirements, not every failure to satisfy the ideals of reason is a failure of rationality.

It might be thought that we could avoid the complication of distinguishing between ideals of reason and the corresponding requirements of rationality by adopting other, more suitable, formulations of rationality requirements. In this connection, it might be suggested that there is a means–end requirement the correct formulation of which is that we should avoid intending to do something while never *intending* to do what is necessary to do that thing. This approach gives rise to a problem in the form of a dilemma. If the suggested formulation is correct, it must be possible to fail to satisfy the requirement. (A requirement that you cannot avoid satisfying is no genuine requirement.) A problem here is that it seems doubtful that one can intend to do something while not intending to do whatever is necessary to do the thing intended. It seems plausible that if one intends to do a certain thing then one intends to embrace whatever means are necessary to do that thing. Of course, one can fail to intend to do particular things that are necessary means to doing something intended, but that is another matter. That is one horn of the dilemma. Suppose now that it is after all possible to fail to satisfy the requirement as formulated. If that is so then there can surely be cases in which one fails to satisfy the requirement without being irrational. If one can be prevented from doing what is necessary to carry out an intention to Φ, in circumstances that give one no chance of abandoning the intention to Φ, then there seems to be no reason to suppose that it is impossible that one should be prevented from intending to do whatever is necessary if one is to Φ, while having no chance of abandoning the intention to Φ. The assumed gap between intending the end and intending the necessary means opens up the possibility of being prevented from satisfying the requirement without being irrational. That is the other horn of the dilemma.

The suggestion, then, is that means–end commitments and implication commitments are grounded in the corresponding ideals of reason. By distinguishing between the ideals of reason and the corresponding rationality requirements, we can accommodate cases in which the ideals are not satisfied without a failure of rationality. I shall return to related issues in Chapter 4, Section 5.

3. Commitments and justification

I have observed that we must distinguish between the claim that one is justified in believing something or doing something and the claim that one is (normatively) committed to believing that thing or doing that thing. Being committed is not sufficient for being justified. Implication commitments and means–end commitments are on a par in this respect. But reasons for action differ from reasons for belief, in keeping with the views on normative reasons for belief and normative reasons for action advanced in the previous chapter. There I argued that, whereas a normative reason for a belief must justify, or at least be positively relevant to the justification of, the belief, a normative reason for action might present the action in a light that recommends it without providing any justification for it. It can do so, by showing the action to be in some way attractive or desirable, or merely by showing that the action is a means to carrying out an intention the agent has. In our ordinary talk we seem to acknowledge that there are such normative reasons. If asked whether I have any reason to go to the library, I can correctly say that I have, citing the fact that I intend to borrow a certain book. Some may claim that, while such an answer may be correct so far as it goes, it presupposes that I have a reason to intend to borrow the book that justifies so intending. In this case I probably would have such a reason—a reason deriving from considerations obliging me to read the book. But I see no reason to suppose that I must have such a reason if it is true that I have reason to go to the library. Someone trying to make sense of what I am doing would have no reason to withdraw the claim that I have reason to go to the library on learning that I intend to borrow the book on a whim. I have a reason to go simply on account of the fact that I have an intention to borrow a book and have to go to the library to do that.[49]

It is clear that, with respect to many actions that admit of a rationalizing explanation—an explanation in terms of the agent's reason for acting—the agent does not have a justificatory reason for the action, i.e. a reason that is at least positively relevant to

---

[49] This is one respect in which my views diverge from those of John Broome (1999; 2002) on reasons and normative requirements.

a justification of the action. Some may think, however, that to explain the normative link between intention and action something stronger is needed than my notion of normative commitment. In this connection it is instructive to reflect on some aspects of an influential discussion of intention by Michael Bratman (1987).

Bratman makes much of the idea that intentions involve commitments. There is a volitional commitment which, he says, 'derives from the fact that intentions are conduct controllers' (Bratman 1987: 16). An agent who intends to Ψ has a volitional commitment to Ψ in the sense that, so long as the intention survives until the time of action, the agent sees that the time has arrived, and nothing interferes the agent will Ψ. Then there is a reasoning-centred commitment, which involves 'a disposition to retain [the] intention without reconsideration, and a disposition to reason from this retained intention to yet further intentions, and to constrain other intentions in the light of this intention' (Bratman 1987: 17). Going by these explanations, commitment in Bratman's sense is a psychological notion. Volitional commitment is resolve to do the thing in question. It is something like this notion that we have in mind when we speak of people being committed to their work. Reasoning-centred commitment is also psychological and naturally follows on from volitional commitment. Because of the volitional commitment involved in my intending to finish a paper soon, my intention will feed into my reasoning about how to organize my time in the near future.

I am entirely in accord with the view that intentions involve commitments in the psychological sense. (The character of those commitments will be a topic of Chapter 4.) Notice, however, that these commitments are very different from the normative commitments incurred by intentions. The psychological notion is about what agents are disposed to do. Normative commitments link up, in the way explained above, with what there is reason for agents to do.[50] There is no reason to suppose that the two notions are in conflict.

---

[50] Bratman does speak of the commitment involved in intention as having both descriptive and normative aspects. The normative aspect, he says, 'consists in the norms and standards of rationality' (Bratman 1987: 109) associated with the dispositions and roles characteristic of intentions. I am not sure why there being norms and standards of rationality should amount to there being a normative aspect to intention. In any case, volitional and reasoning-centred commitments, as initially introduced, seem to be purely psychological, concerning as they do the agent's actual motivational set rather than any normative commitments incurred.

Even so, it might seem that there is a certain tension between the way I explain my normative notion of commitment and the functional role of intention as explained by Bratman. On my view, having an intention commits you to doing what is necessary to carry out the intention in a sense which implies that there is a reason for you either to do what is necessary or abandon the intention. This reason arises from the Means–End Ideal. One would fail to do justice to this reason if one failed to act on it when it was in one's power to do so. Even so, all other considerations aside, having an intention no more justifies carrying it out than it justifies abandoning it. This might seem to be at odds with Bratman's view, for the following reason. It might seem that if intention involves a reasoning-centred commitment in Bratman's sense then agents who intend to do something will not think of abandoning the intention as being on a par with carrying it out. On the contrary, the argument would go, agents for whom having an intention provides an input to practical reasoning must take that intention to provide a justification for doing what is necessary to carry out the intention. The argument proceeds by analogy with belief. Suppose that you believe that p and believe that if p then q. From these assumptions you might conclude that q. In treating the assumptions as inputs to reasoning, you thereby treat them as providing you with justification to believe that q. Similarly, it might be said, if the assumption that you have an intention to Φ, and the assumption that it is necessary for you to Ψ if you are to Φ, feed into practical reasoning, leading you to form an intention to Ψ, then, in effect, you must regard these assumptions as providing you with a justification for Ψing. This might seem to show that in our ordinary thinking we are bound to think of intentions as doing more than just committing us, in my sense, to taking the necessary means.[51]

It is true that, if you accept a conclusion on the basis of certain assumptions, you thereby treat those assumptions as jointly providing you with justification to believe the conclusion drawn from them. But it would beg the question against the view that I am defending to presuppose that a parallel claim holds for action. I have argued (Chapter 2) that there is in any case an important disanalogy between reasons for action and reasons for belief. When we base a belief on

---

[51] I do not suggest that Bratman would draw such a conclusion.

reasons we need the belief to be true and, accordingly, need the assumptions that constitute the reasons to provide adequate justification for the belief. It is different with reasons for action. We certainly need the considerations we regard as reasons for action to be true, and we certainly need them to confer some kind of point on the action. But we do not always need them to provide justification.

There is a clear sense in which, for an agent who has an intention, carrying out the intention, and so doing what is necessary to achieve that end, is not on a par with abandoning the intention. But that is a conceptual point about the psychology of intention, not its normative commitments. It is in the nature of intending that to some degree the agent is psychologically committed to doing the thing intended. This does not imply that agents who intend to Φ must have, or even think they have, a better reason to Φ, and to do what is necessary to that end, than to abandon the intention.

It might be thought that, even if intentions do not provide justifying reasons for doing the thing intended, they must at least be positively relevant to such a justification. An obvious problem with such a view is to explain why a crazy intention should be regarded as satisfying any such condition. In any case, as I argued in the previous chapter, reasons for action should not be too closely modelled on reasons for belief. There are differences between the constitutive aim of belief and the constitutive aim of intentional action that explain why (normative) reasons for action do not have to be even positively relevant to justification. We can still accommodate the idea that having intentions provides some kind of normative reason for doing what is necessary to carry them out. They can recommend actions precisely by showing them to be, for instance, necessary means to carrying out the intention.

It is worth noting before we go any further that the notion of a commitment seems to be needed to provide a satisfying explanation of what has gone wrong when we have an intention but have not taken the necessary means.[52] To revert to a previous example, suppose that I intend to reach Edinburgh by noon. Let us suppose that this intention is linked to a reason as follows:

---

[52] The argument that follows was suggested to me by what I think is a similar argument advanced in discussion by John Broome. He is not responsible for any defects my version may have.

(a) Since I intend to reach Edinburgh by noon there is a reason, which can be overridden, to set off by 10.

Suppose further that, as it happens, it is a bad idea to go to Edinburgh because I am obliged to attend an important meeting, which I have forgotten about. The right thing to do is to attend the meeting. Since that requires that I not set off by 10, I ought, accordingly, to abandon my intention to reach Edinburgh by noon. How precisely are we to explain why I ought to abandon my intention? Suppose we try to do so in terms of (a) and the assumption

(b) I ought, all things considered, not to set off by 10.

Though (a) is supposed to capture the normative connection between intending and taking the necessary means, it is not clear how, along with (b), it can explain why I ought to abandon the intention. Given (b), the reason mentioned in (a) is overridden. But there does not appear to be a valid step from there to the conclusion that I ought to abandon my intention to go to Edinburgh. On the conception of commitments incurred by intentions proposed here, it is easy to see how this conclusion may legitimately be reached. My intention to arrive in Edinburgh by noon commits me to setting off by 10. So there is reason for me to ensure that either I set off by 10 or I abandon the intention. This reason is such that I ought to ensure that either I set off by 10 or I abandon my intention. Given that I ought not to set off by 10, it follows that I ought to abandon the intention.

I have been dwelling on commitments incurred by intentions and beliefs because they will figure in the later argument to show that the concepts of intention and belief are normative. I now turn to another kind of commitment, which is tied to practices.

4. Normative commitments and practices

Normative commitments have the following basic structure.

(a) There is a commitment-incurring condition—a condition such that because it is satisfied the commitment is incurred.
(b) There is something to which one is committed, given that one satisfies the commitment-incurring condition.

(c) Commitments are linked to reasons. Given that one has incurred a commitment to Φing, it follows that there is a (normative) reason for one to ensure that either one Φs or that one brings it about that one no longer satisfies the commitment-incurring condition.

One can discharge the commitment incurred by a belief or intention by giving up the belief or intention as the case may be. In that way one brings it about that one no longer satisfies the commitment-incurring condition. Obviously, one cannot release oneself from the commitment incurred by a promise by making it the case that one no longer promises. A promise is not the sort of thing one can give up. (Deciding not to keep it is not giving it up.) But there is such a thing as being released from a promise. In the case of promising to meet someone at a particular time, one could take steps to be released. This might simply be a matter of securing an understanding on the part of the person to whom the promise has been made that there are good reasons why one cannot keep it. Taking such steps is a way of trying to discharge the commitment without carrying it out.

An important dimension of variation among commitments concerns the strength of the reason with which they are linked. I have suggested that implication commitments and means–end commitments are linked to reasons that derive from certain ideals of reason. If I intend to Φ, and Ψing is necessary if I am to Φ, there is reason for me either to abandon the intention or to ensure that I get around to Ψing. This reason is constituted by the consideration that, were I to retain the intention while never getting around to Ψing, I would fail to satisfy the Means–End Ideal. This is not a reason that it is plausible to suppose could be undermined or overridden by some countervailing consideration. There might be all sorts of reasons not to take the means necessary to carry out an intention. In that case there would be reason to abandon the intention, but the reason to ensure that one either carries out the intention or abandons the intention is not thereby overridden or undermined. The commitments to be considered now arise from participation in what I shall call *practices*. These commitments are weaker than those incurred by beliefs and intentions, being linked to a weaker sort of reason.

Practices are *essentially rule-governed* activities. Not every activity governed by rules is *essentially* rule-governed. Walking in the grounds of a college as a visitor may be governed by certain rules. The rules might prohibit walking on the grass, making inordinate noise and entering certain areas. But walking in college grounds is not *essentially* rule-governed. The same activity could take place even if it were not subject to the college's or any other rules. The case is different with a game of soccer. It is essential to the activity of playing a game that it is governed by rules. Indeed, each variant of the game defines a distinct practice governed by a characteristic set of rules.

Roles and offices are linked to practices. Institutions, like armies, firms, and universities, are spaces of interlocking offices that are defined by duties. Occupying such an office incurs a commitment to carrying out the duties of the office. Deans, acting in their capacity as dean, will do many things subject to rules that could be done in different ways and be subject to different rules. But to be dean is in effect to play a role that is of its very nature subject to a rule prescribing that the duties of the office be carried out. To be dean is therefore to engage in a practice—the practice of carrying out the duties of the office.

Participating in a practice incurs a commitment to following its governing rules. If this is right, then as a player in a game of soccer you incur a commitment to following the rules governing the game, and as a dean of faculty you incur a commitment to following the rule prescribing that its defining duties be carried out. Given the basic structure for commitments identified above, it follows that there is a reason for the player either to follow the rules or withdraw from the game, and there is a reason for the dean of faculty either to follow the rules or resign. It is worth taking care to spell out why this should be so.

Note first that, from the claim that an activity is governed by rules, it follows straightforwardly that anyone engaging in it is *subject* to the rules. This is so irrespective of whether the activity is *essentially* rule-governed. Visitors walking in the college grounds are subject to the college's rules in the sense that they are subject to having the rules applied to them. But walking in the grounds does not, in and of itself, incur a commitment to following the rules. To participate in a practice is to incur a commitment to following its governing rules because the activity in which one engages, in virtue of participating, is the activity of doing the things the rules prescribe. The reason a player has to follow the rules or withdraw from the game is simply that playing the game is the activity defined by those rules. This is not to deny that some games can survive even though players deliberately flout the rules. The claim is not that it is impossible to participate in a practice and flout its rules, but that one cannot participate in a practice without incurring a commitment to following its rules.

It is pretty clear that the commitments incurred by participating in a practice must be weaker than those incurred by intentions or beliefs. The commitment incurred by an intention, for instance, is linked to a reason that cannot be undermined or overridden. The commitment to following the rules incurred by being a participant in a practice is not quite like this. As a player in a game of soccer, one cannot flout the rules with impunity, since breaches are subject to penalties. None the less, there can be good reasons to flout rules. Here are a couple of cases. The first is a situation in which there is a weak referee and the opposing team is getting away with deliberate and gross fouls. There could be reason to repay the opposing team in kind to avoid its having an unfair advantage. The other case relates to a general consideration about practices. Practices are modifiable and can be modified with good reason. One can envisage circumstances in which players have good reason to flout an unpopular rule with a view to having it abandoned or modified. Similar considerations apply to practices associated with institutional offices. If some of the procedures that a chief of police is supposed to implement are manifestly unjust, then there could be reason for someone who is chief of police to remain in office while trying so far as possible to avoid implementing them. So the reason one has to avoid being a participant and yet not follow the rules is a reason that can be overridden.

The commitments I have been discussing arise from the nature of particular practices. Some may feel that we could have reached the conclusion that participating in a practice incurs a commitment to following its governing rules by another route. The idea might be that a player incurs a commitment to following the rules since (a) by joining in the game the player at least tacitly *undertakes* to play by the rules, and (b) there is a principle to the effect that people are committed to doing what they undertake to do. This view assimilates the commitment incurred by participating in a practice to the commitment incurred by making an undertaking. No doubt there are practices in which people are permitted to participate only if they make some explicit undertaking. Occupying a post often requires one to sign a contract in which one agrees to accept the specified terms and conditions of service. In such cases a commitment is incurred by a very formal undertaking. But this approach to explaining the commitments incurred by participating in practices clearly does not apply to all practices. Many have thought that to use a word meaningfully is to participate in a practice. (I shall be defending such a view in Chapter 6.) If there are such practices, they are clearly not such that participation in them requires that an undertaking to follow the rules be made. There are, in any case, other less controversial examples of practices that do not meet the proposed condition, including the practice of making undertakings itself.

Undertakings are of some interest beyond their relevance to the immediate point. They provide an instructive illustration of how informal practices can be by comparison with playing games and the activities associated with well-defined roles and offices. Undertaking differs from promising in that it does not require the use of a particular verbal locution. To undertake you do not need to say 'I promise', or even 'I undertake'. All you need do is let it be understood that you will do something in a manner that counts as having incurred a commitment to doing it. There may be contexts in which the borderline between genuinely undertaking to do something and merely saying that one will do it is not sharp. But there are also contexts in which it is clear enough. Imagine a group of people sharing an apartment. From time to time people in the group may undertake to do something—wash up the dishes, meet somebody at an arranged time, do some shopping, check what films are on, and the like. As often as not, such undertakings are made not by making a promise, but simply by declaring that one will do something in a manner and in a context which gives it to be understood that one is taking on a commitment. For instance, when arrangements are being made, simply saying that you will meet someone at 7, or check what is on at the local cinema, or clean up the kitchen, can be the making of an undertaking.

Given that undertakings can be so informal, what reason is there to think they incur normative commitments? Obviously, people can let it be understood that they will do something without incurring a commitment. Somebody in the apartment, Alf, may say he's going for a walk and then within a few yards of the apartment block he may be lured into a café by the smell of good coffee. If Alf stays in the café, drinks coffee, and reads a newspaper, but does not go on his walk, he need not have failed to carry out any commitment. But nor has he given an undertaking to go for a walk. Undertakings can be given and received only in the context of a practice of giving and receiving them. There must be rules governing what counts as making an undertaking and rules governing what happens as a consequence of having made one. The rules need never have been explicitly formulated. What is crucial is that people act as if there were such rules and that there is mutual expectation of conformity. There must be a rule distinguishing undertakings from mere declarations of intention. Part of such a rule might be that declaring that one will do something in a context in which arrangements are being made counts as an undertaking. Then there must be a rule governing what is expected of a person who has made an undertaking. The rule might be to the effect that if you make an undertaking then you carry it out unless (i) you arrange to be released from it or, (ii) there were factors that prevented you from carrying it out or that made it reasonable for you not to. That people acknowledge such a rule would be manifested by their expectations of conformity and by their reactions to non-conformity. So, for example, they would view failure to do what one undertakes without good reason as open to criticism. Each would be prepared to accept the legitimacy of criticism when he or she fails to discharge the commitment incurred by an undertaking, and would expect the others to do likewise. Each would accept that he or she is open to criticism for not discharging a commitment, and that excuses or apologies are in order when this happens.

From the mere fact that people conduct themselves in a way that always, or by and large, accords with a certain rule formulation, it does not follow that they submit themselves to a rule expressed by that formulation. It could be that, by and large, when people say they will do something, in contexts in which arrangements are being made and so forth, then they do it, unless they give notice that they are unable to, or are prevented from doing it, or it is reasonable for them not to. Even if there is this regularity in behaviour, and even if there is mutual expectation that it will be conformed to, this would not suffice to make it the case that the group submitted to a rule governing the declarations in question. A mark of submission to a rule is treating the sort of behaviour that the rule prescribes as the thing to do and, accordingly, treating behaviour which is not in accord with the rule as open to criticism. The rules are manifested when people make judgements about what someone is, or was, supposed to do, about who has let down whom, and the like. It is these kinds of judgements—implicit applications of rules—that sustain the activity of undertaking and make it a practice. In relation to the community of apartment-sharers, it can be fairly clear that there is a practice because it can be fairly clear that there is submission to implicitly acknowledged rules. But obviously, the practice of undertaking is not confined to groups that constitute communities. Strangers make undertakings in the course of business activities of one kind or another. They make arrangements to meet, for instance. Despite being strangers, they are operating in an environment in which agreeing to meet is not taken lightly and in which much else that is done is governed by implicitly acknowledged rules.

The attempt to invoke undertakings to explain how participating in a practice incurs a commitment to following its rules clearly fails. It will not work for the practice of undertaking itself. If the practice is of the informal kind I described in the case of the apartment-sharers, no undertaking to abide by the rules need come into the picture. Indeed, it could not without the threat of a regress, since any such undertaking would presuppose the existence of a practice of undertaking which one could engage in only if one made an undertaking, and so on.

5. Can practices give rise to reasons in the way proposed?

Some find it puzzling that engaging in certain activities in and of itself incurs a commitment to follow the rules governing those activities. I have heard it said that the occupant of an office in an institution incurs no commitment to following its governing the rules simply on account of occupying the office. This stance perhaps reflects a sense of alienation from institutional life. In any case, it is important to bear in mind that incurring a commitment to following certain rules does not require one to have respect for the rules in any sense that involves approving of them. It is also important recall the distinction between being committed to doing something and being justified in doing that thing. One may not be justified in doing what one is committed to doing.

There is a theme in moral philosophical tradition that might be thought to raise a problem. Moral philosophers have been concerned with whether or not moral obligations that are widely recognized are binding on everyone. The issue would not be settled by there being practices governed by appropriate rules prescribing that this or that be done under such-and-such circumstances. There being such a practice would not by itself explain why any of us has a reason to submit to its rules. In a discussion of rules of etiquette, Philippa Foot writes:

[A]lthough people give as their reason for doing something the fact that it is required by etiquette, we do not take this consideration as *in itself giving us a reason to act*. Considerations of etiquette do not have any automatic reason-giving force, and a man might be right if he denied that he had reason to do 'what's done'. (Foot 1972/1978: 161)

Something very like the point being made here can be made in terms of practices. If there were a practice governed by the rules of etiquette, this would not give anyone who was wondering whether to participate or to continue to participate a reason to do so. So it would not give any such person a reason to follow the rules. But this is entirely consistent with the view about practices that I have been setting out. Indeed, it serves to underline the importance of taking care over the notion of commitment. If there is a practice governed by the rules of etiquette, then those who participate in the practice incur a commitment to following its governing rules. That one incurs such a commitment implies that there is a reason for one *either* to follow the rules *or* to withdraw from the practice. I have been at pains to stress that such a reason would not provide one with a justification for following the rules. An appropriate response to such a reason might be to withdraw from the practice.

Another consideration that might lead one to doubt whether practices give rise to normative reasons is that there might be reason to continue in a practice and flout its rules. I have linked offices in institutions to practices, and thus to commitments and the normative reasons to which, on my view, commitments are linked. Granted that institutions can be corrupt, there clearly could be reason to continue to occupy an office within an institution while attempting to subvert it. There might be reason for a whistle-blower, for instance, to remain in an office while flouting rules against disclosure of information to outsiders. This too is compatible with the view I have been defending because, on that view, the reason to which the relevant commitment is linked can be overridden. Plausibly, it can be overridden by an obligation to disclose information about corrupt practices to appropriate authorities.

6. Differences between kinds of commitments

The commitments incurred by intentions and beliefs and the commitments incurred by participation in practices share a basic structure, though, as I have argued, the former are weaker than the latter because they are linked to a weaker kind of reason than the latter. The differences are not surprising in view of the differences in what grounds the commitments.

The commitments incurred by participating in a practice are explained by the fact that a practice is an essentially rule-governed activity, individuated by the particular rules that govern it. The rules have their status as rules in virtue of being treated as rules. They may be formally instituted or they may attain their status in the informal way I roughly sketched in discussing undertakings in the previous section. Either way, they are humanly created. How can the fact that there is a humanly instituted practice give rise to reasons? Again the details of commitment are crucial. There would be something strange in the idea that invented or conventionally established rules are normative, if that is taken to imply that following the rules is the right thing to do. But the mere existence of a practice does not give anyone a reason to follow the rules that would make doing so the right thing to do. There can, of course, be reasons for participation. There might be reason for a professional player of soccer to play in some particular game provided by the fact that the club has assigned him to the team for that game.

92   NORMATIVE COMMITMENTS

There might be a reason for someone to become a police officer provided by the fact that the job would be interesting and challenging. Whatever the reasons, they will reflect the interests or the obligations of the agent. But we need to distinguish between reasons for participating in a practice and reasons that apply to one given that one is a participant. The reason linked to the commitment to following the rules of the practice is a reason of this latter sort.

The commitments that I have associated with beliefs and intentions are grounded in reasons provided by, respectively, the Implication Ideal and the Means–End Ideal. The Implication Ideal provides a reason to avoid believing P while giving a verdict to any implication of P other than belief. The Means–End Ideal provides a reason to avoid retaining an intention while never getting around to doing whatever is necessary if one is to do the thing intended. It is a requirement of rationality that we do justice to these reasons. This requirement seems to be unavoidable in the way that rules of a game are not. All you need to do to avoid being subject to the rules of a game is to avoid, or stop, playing the game. So there is a contrast between the status of requirements of reason and the status of rules of practices. That said, for a participant in a practice there is no escaping the reason there is either to follow its rules or to withdraw from the practice. It is as much a requirement of reason that one do justice to *this* reason as it is to do justice to the reasons associated with the Means–End and Implication Ideals.

7. Normativity, normative concepts, and normative import

In the chapters that follow I am going to argue that the concepts of believing this and intending that are normative. To prepare the ground for those arguments, I turn now to some clarification of the very idea of normativity.

Normativity, as I understand it, is primarily a feature of, for instance, judgements, beliefs, statements, claims—the sorts of thing that can be true or false.[53] The central case of a normative statement is a statement

---

[53] I shall take it to be unproblematic that normative statements and the like can be true or false in some suitably minimalist sense.

to the effect that there is a reason for some agent or agents to do something. In this context, 'doing something' is to be taken in a very broad sense so that it encompasses not just acting in some way, but believing something, desiring something, feeling some way, and so on. It also encompasses refraining from acting in some way. Sometimes, for the sake of brevity, I shall use the phrase in this broad sense. It should be clear from the context when doings are actions. The normativity of statements other than those that are instances of the central case is to be understood by reference to the relation of those other statements to the central case.[54] So, for instance, the statement that it was wrong for Bill to lie to Fred is normative, and its normativity is to be explained by reference to the fact that it implies that there was a reason for Bill not to lie to Fred. The relevant reasons are, of course, normative reasons. So I am explaining the notion of a normative statement in terms of another normative concept. This would be a problem if I were trying to reduce the notion of the normative to something else, but that is not my aim. I shall assume that we have some conception of reasons in the normative sense, always bearing in mind the complexities explored in the previous chapter.

As I explained earlier, what is *implied* by statements, in the sense intended here, follows from them *without further ado*. That is to say, it follows from them without the help of additional assumptions, other than ones that merely make explicit features of the content of these statements. Nothing about reasons follows, without further ado, from the statement that the milk in the fridge has curdled. There might, of course, be further ado pertaining, say, to getting hold of fresh milk or getting rid of a smell in the fridge.

Arriving at a precise criterion of normativity is not a routine matter, even once it is settled that normativity is to be explained in terms of normative reasons. A natural proposal is that normative statements are ones that imply some statement to the effect that there is a reason for an agent or agents to do this or that.[55] Here is one problem for such a view. Let P be a non-normative statement and

---

[54] A similar conception of normativity is explicit in Skorupski (1997) and Raz (1999).
[55] Skorupski (1997) relies on such a criterion. I am grateful to Gideon Rosen, who reminded me that criteria of this sort are not straightforward, and to Peter Sullivan, who alerted me to errors in my earlier attempts to deal with the matter.

Q a statement about reasons of the type just specified. P implies P v Q. If P v Q is a normative statement, then a non-normative statement implies a normative statement and the criterion for normativity is, therefore, too liberal. Fortunately, P v Q is not normative, in the sense I am trying to capture, despite its having a normative statement, Q, as a disjunct. Although Q, by stipulation, is a statement of the specified type—a paradigmatic normative statement—P v Q does not count as normative simply in virtue of having a normative disjunct. The consideration that either Washington DC is the capital of the United States or there is reason for me to believe that interest rates will rise is not a statement to the effect that there is a reason for me to do anything, nor does it imply any other statement of the required type. (It can, of course, constitute a reason to believe something, but that is a different matter.)

Another problem arises. I have stipulated that P is not normative. ¬P might also not be normative. Suppose that it is not. Still, ¬P & (P v Q) turns out to be normative by the criterion because it implies Q—a statement of the specified type. But given that P v Q is not normative, as argued above, and that ¬P is not normative, it might look as if we should not count the conjunction, ¬P & (P v Q), as normative. So the criterion might seem to be inadequate. The right response here is to resist the idea that a conjunction of non-normative statements cannot be normative. Paradigmatically, normative statements are to the effect that there is a reason for some agent or agents to do a certain thing. Other statements can be normative in virtue of implying statements of the paradigmatically normative type. The puzzle about taking our conjunction to be normative arises from the thought that a conjunction of non-normative statements cannot be normative. This thought can seem compelling if we think of non-normative statements as necessarily lacking normative subject-matter. The idea would be that if a statement lacks normative subject-matter then it would be inexplicable how it could have any role in accounting for the normativity of a conjunction of which it is a conjunct. But there is good reason to reject the view that non-normative statements always lack normative subject-matter. What we need is a distinction between being normative and having normative subject-matter.

Consider the following two statements:

(i) What Bill did was wrong.
(ii) Had Bill acted wrongly he would have been distressed.

Statement (i) is normative because it implies that there was reason for Bill not to do what he did. The fact that the concept of being wrong is brought into play by (i) contributes to the explanation of why (i) is normative. But the explanation of why (i) is normative is not simply that it brings the concept of being wrong into play. The explanation is that in (i) the concept of being wrong is applied to what Bill did, and on that account (i) implies that there was reason for Bill not to do what he did. The concept of being wrong is normative because it has the power to contribute to the logical powers of statements in this sort of way. But that is not to say that whenever it is brought into play by a statement the statement has a paradigmatically normative implication. (ii) brings the concept of being wrong into play and so has normative subject-matter. But (ii) is not normative by our criterion because it does not imply a paradigmatically normative statement. Though it brings the concept of being wrong into play, the role of that concept in relation to (ii) is not such as to generate an implication of the required sort. With these considerations to hand, we can make sense of the idea that, although P v Q, understood as above, is not normative, it has normative subject-matter introduced by Q. Because it has this subject-matter it is no mystery that, in the case under consideration, the conjunction ¬P & (P v Q) should be normative.[56]

There is a related problem. Consider the principle that for any person x, if x were to receive a gift, that would be a reason for x to thank the giver. The principle does not imply that there is a reason for anyone to do anything. It rather tells us, in effect, that if a fact of a certain sort were to obtain there would a reason for someone to act in a certain way. Principles of this reason-specifying sort are liable to strike us as being normative. But they do not imply a statement of the paradigmatically normative sort. Here too we need the distinction between being normative and having normative subject-matter. The principle is not normative by our criterion, though it has normative subject-matter in virtue of bringing into play the concept of a reason

---

[56] By parity of reasoning, we may think of the assumptions ¬P and P v Q as comprising a normative set because a statement of the paradigmatically normative sort is derivable from them.

to do something. We could think of the principle as being normative in a broad sense in virtue of its subject-matter, while thinking of statements that satisfy our criterion as being normative in a strict and more basic sense.

Concepts are sometimes said to be normative on the grounds that they implicate norms or standards. This is said of the concept of rationality, for example.[57] No doubt rationality, or some particular concept of rationality, is normative, but if so we cannot adequately account for its normativity simply by invoking the notion of norms or standards. The judgement that a person is tall applies a concept whose use is governed by a norm for tallness. But if it is a normative judgement, then we are on a slippery slope leading to the unhelpful conclusion that all judgements applying concepts of magnitudes are normative. And why stop there? All concepts might be thought to implicate norms, since the things falling under them have to satisfy a norm which things have to meet to fall under those concepts. Unless there is some restriction on the sorts of norms that count, explaining normativity in terms of norms gets us nowhere. The norms that count are either standards for judging things in terms of their being or not being commendable, admirable, or desirable, or standards for judging what agents ought or ought not to do, think, or feel. Either way they are reason-linked. The commendable or admirable or desirable is what there is reason to commend, admire, or desire. What an agent ought to do, think, or feel in one central sense of 'ought' is what there is reason for the agent to do, think, or feel. The 'ought' of expectation also yields to this treatment. To judge that someone ought, in this sense, to emerge from a house in two minutes is to judge that there is reason to expect the person to emerge in two minutes.

I shall not attempt to argue that reason-linked normativity is the only normativity. It suffices for my purposes that the normativity that matters for this book is reason-linked. Normativity in this sense is what is at issue in the classic areas of normative philosophical enquiry—ethics, value theory, and epistemology.

Normative statements are sometimes taken to contrast with descriptive statements. Examples of the latter would include statements

---

[57] See e.g. Davidson (1985: 345): 'Irrationality, like rationality, is a normative concept. Someone who acts or reasons irrationally, or whose beliefs or emotions are irrational, has departed from a standard.'

to the effect that a person is tall, that a building is a mansion, or that a room is cold. This way of thinking is misleading because normative statements are descriptive too, by any ordinary standards. The statement that an action is treacherous is surely descriptive of the action, but it is also normative, since it implies that there is reason to condemn the act. A way of trying to accommodate the fact that normative statements can be descriptive is to distinguish between the *merely* descriptive and the descriptive. The statement that an act is treacherous would be descriptive in virtue of its merely descriptive implications, but because it has normative implications it would not be merely descriptive. The trouble with this move is that it assumes that when a normative statement is descriptive this will always be due solely to the fact that it has merely descriptive implications. Such a view is certainly not sanctioned by our ordinary notion of the descriptive. The description of an action as treacherous is richly descriptive because it implies something highly specific about the action—it describes it as a betrayal. Yet the action's being a betrayal is itself a normative matter. It describes the action in terms of an indisputably moral category. A description of a decision as perverse is richly descriptive. It implies that the decision was taken despite there being compelling reasons for not taking it. Those who make the distinction between the normative and descriptive attempt in doing so to capture a distinction that does need to be marked—that between the normative and the non-normative. They run up against the fact that normative statements are as descriptive as any.[58] Even a judgement to the effect that an action or decision is wrong is descriptive in any ordinary sense. Unlike the judgement that an action is treacherous, it is, as one might say, thinly descriptive, because it does not tell us what it was about the action or decision in virtue of which it is judged to be wrong.

The concept of a commitment that has been the focus of this chapter is normative in the reason-linked sense. In what follows I am going to take it for granted that beliefs and intentions, at least as possessed by rational agents, incur commitments in this sense. This

---

[58] Toulmin and Baier (1952) observe that 'descriptions of character demand to be expressed in moral terms'. R. M. Hare defines a descriptive term as one to misuse which is to break the descriptive rule attaching the term to a certain kind of object; see Hare (1963: 8). The problem here is that the definition presupposes what has yet to be explained—a notion of *kinds of object* that is guaranteed to be non-normative.

does not settle whether the concepts of belief and intention are normative. Consider the following statements:

(1) Sally intends to buy a present for her brother.
(2) Sally incurs a commitment to doing what is necessary if she is to buy a present for her brother.

By my account, (2) is normative because it implies a paradigmatically normative statement. If (1) is true then (2) is. At any rate, so as not to beg important questions, assuming that Sally is a rational agent with appropriate reflective capacities, if (1) is true then (2) is true. I shall express this by saying that (1) has *normative import* which is captured by (2). The claim that (1) has this normative import is weaker than the claim that it is normative. (1) is normative, in the strict sense, only if it implies some statement of the pardigmatically normative sort. That (1) has normative import does not establish that it has such implications. In Chapter 4 I consider an attempt to account for the normative import of statements like (1) without invoking the assumption that (1) is normative. Here I introduce the general strategy.

I shall draw upon an example from ethics used already (in Chapter 1, Section 4). My neighbour is at my door, in distress, and calling on me for help. The consideration that this is so—call it C—looks to be non-normative. (I shall not suggest otherwise.) Prompted by it, I may think that I ought to help because I take C to give me a reason to help that is not countervailed by other considerations. Thus, in effect, I treat C as having normative import. There need be nothing mysterious about this. It would be some explanation of why I regard C as having normative import to point out that I accept, at least implicitly, a principle to the effect that the fact that one's neighbour is in distress and calling on one for help is a reason to help. This principle is a reason-specifying principle. It connects a certain type of non-normative consideration with a certain type of normative consideration. If the principle holds, it goes some way to explaining the normative import of the consideration in question. In the light of my acceptance of the principle, it is explicable that I should count the consideration as providing me with a reason to help my neighbour.

A similar line of thought can be applied to the issue of how to explain the fact that (1) above has normative import which is captured by (2). We just need to invoke an appropriate connecting principle.

The following principle, which I shall call the *Means–End Commitment Principle*, would fit the bill:

(3) For any x, φ, if x intends to φ then x incurs a commitment to doing what is necessary if x is to φ.

The explanation for the normative import of (1) which is captured by (2) would be that (2) follows from (1) and (3). Analogous considerations would apply to statements ascribing beliefs. In connection with these, the following *Implication Commitment Principle* might be invoked:

(4) For any x, π, if x believes π, then for any θ, if π implies θ, then x incurs a commitment to believing θ, if x gives any verdict on θ.

I shall argue that this strategy is much more problematic than it seems, and that an adequate account of the normative import of statements ascribing beliefs and intentions to people must treat these ascriptions as being normative. The eventual upshot will be that the concepts of belief and intention are in some respects like the concept of a promise.

CHAPTER 4

Explaining Normative Import

1. The way ahead

Concepts of belief and intention are concepts like *believing that summer is coming to an end* and *intending to learn more about European history*. In this and the following chapter I argue and defend the view that such concepts are normative concepts. The claim that I believe P brings into play the concept of believing P and on that account implies that I have incurred a commitment to believing any implication of P on which I give a verdict. Similarly, the claim that I intend to Φ brings into play the concept of intending, and on that account implies that I have incurred a commitment to doing whatever is necessary for me to Φ. This view is controversial on at least the following two counts. First, it is not widely accepted that the concepts of believing and intending are normative; if my view is to emerge as being plausible and interesting, I need to explain how it can be that they are. That requires me to explain how the psychological dimension to believing and intending relates to the normative dimension and why acknowledging both dimensions is important for personal understanding. I address these matters later in this chapter when I introduce the notion of a psychological commitment, and then further in Chapter 7. Second, some of those who accept that the concepts of belief and intention are normative may deny that believing and intending implicate *commitments* in the sense introduced in Chapter 3. One might think that those concepts are normative simply because rationality is a normative concept and because believing and intending are inextricably linked to rationality. Those who think that the concept of rationality is normative are not bound to suppose that its normativity should be explicated in terms of normative commitments. The central role that I accord to normative commitments should turn out to be plausible and to do some work.

In framing the issues, I shall assume a certain view about the character of concepts of belief and intention. I take these concepts to apply to people. If they apply to things other than people these things will be organized systems, like animals. When we ascribe a belief to a person, we apply a concept of belief to that person and ascribe the corresponding belief-property.[59] Thus, in applying the concept of believing that summer is coming to an end we ascribe the belief-property *believes that summer is coming to an end*. A parallel claim holds for concepts of intention and corresponding intention-properties. Talk of beliefs or intentions as psychological states is shorthand for talk about the state of someone's believing something or of someone's intending something. In other words, it is about belief-properties and intention-properties.[60] It is not about properties possessed by structures in the brain, nor is it about particulars located at some place in the brain.[61]

Given the distinction between concepts and properties, it is clear that distinct concepts can pick out the same property. Thus, to take a minimally controversial example, I can pick out the property of being water as I have just done by deploying the concept of being water. But if I had just written the word 'water' on my whiteboard I could also pick out the property as that which is referred to by the concept expressed by the word I have just written on my whiteboard. A more interesting, and also more controversial, example of distinct concepts picking out the same property is provided by the concepts of being water and of being H_2O. (The example is used in precisely this connection in Gibbard 2002, though the thinking has its routes in Putnam's 1975a theory of natural kind terms.) The idea is that the property of being water is identical with the property of being H_2O, yet the concept of being water and the concept of being H_2O are distinct. Someone might have the concept of water and lack the concept of H_2O, knowing nothing about hydrogen, oxygen, and

---

[59] Some theorists think of properties in a more restricted sense. Here properties are the semantic values of concepts. A thing's possessing the property of being G is what makes it true that the thing is G.

[60] I am going to take this view for granted. With respect to belief, it is defended in considerable detail and in opposition to alternatives by Lynne Rudder Baker (1995).

[61] For a penetrating critical discussion of 'particularism' in the philosophy of mind, see Steward (1997).

their combination to form molecules of H_2O. Irrespective of whether this approach to the concept of being water and its corresponding property is right, it is at least intelligible that it should be thought that specifying the property in terms of the concept of H_2O brings out the nature of water in a way that specifying the property in terms of the concept of being water does not. Pointing at water, we can reasonably ask, 'What is this substance?' When we are told that it is H_2O, we seem to learn about its nature—about what any substance would have to be if it were to be this substance.

Even if this is the right way to think about some concepts and their corresponding properties, it is certainly not the right way to think of all of them. The concept of a teacher is the concept of an individual who occupies a specified role. It is certainly possible to pick out this property without using the concept of a teacher. I can run through the kind of exercise illustrated above in connection with the concept of water—I write the word 'teacher' on the board and pick out the property via reference to the word. But there is no underlying nature to being a teacher—a nature that is not specified by the ordinary role-specifying concept of a teacher. There can be all kinds of wisdom about what it takes to be good teacher—wisdom that a person with a grasp of the concept of a teacher is not bound to have. But if so, that is wisdom about how to fill the role well, given the duties and responsibilities that define it. It is not about an underlying nature common to all teachers.

The stance taken here is that concepts of belief and intention are more like the concept of a teacher than they are like the concept of being water, understood on the model sketched above. There is no more to believing that summer has come to an end or to intending to learn more about European history than is specified by, respectively, the concept of believing that summer is coming to an end and the concept of intending to learn more about European history. So we should not expect there to be true identity statements specifying underlying natures for the beliefs and intentions to which these concepts apply, which are not captured by the concepts.

The discussion in this and the following chapter is an attempt to expand on what is implied by ascriptions of beliefs of the form, 'A believes that p' and ascriptions of intentions of the form, 'A intends that he/she Φs'. These are ascriptions that attribute certain propositional attitudes, specified in terms of their category (belief or intention) and their content. In the next section I discuss a view according to which concepts of propositional attitudes are non-normative psychological concepts. I shall then consider how, in terms of this view, we might attempt to explain the normative import of ascriptions of beliefs and intentions.

2. Dispositionalism

Each of us has a vast range of beliefs, desires, intentions, hopes, fears, and so on, yet only a very few of those are, as we say, before our minds at any given time. While focusing on some task in hand, we need not think of other things we plan to do. At any given time, much that we believe lies dormant, having no immediate effect on what we are thinking or doing. None the less, our various propositional attitudes have the potential to impact on thought, desire, action, or feeling under appropriate circumstances. This suggests that we might think of having a propositional attitude as a matter of having various dispositions, for instance to form beliefs, to perform actions, or to acquire feelings and desires. (Here as elsewhere I shall concentrate on belief and action.) I have a standing belief that there is a farmers' market in town on the second Saturday of each month. To have this belief might involve my having a disposition such that, for instance, were I set on buying the sorts of things I generally buy at this market I would be liable to go there. Of course, that could hardly be the only disposition associated with the belief. My having this belief has the potential to manifest itself in many different ways. For instance, were I to be asked when the farmers' market is held I would be liable to answer by saying something to the effect that it is held on the second Saturday of every month.

According to the theory I consider in this chapter, propositional attitudes, or at least those propositonal attitudes that are standing states, are essentially dispositional. The dispositions are taken to be akin to the paradigm cases of dispositions in philosophical literature. These include dispositions such as solubility in water, flexibility, and fragility. Roughly speaking, a thing has the disposition of flexibility provided that, if it were put under suitable pressure, it would bend.

A widely held view of such dispositions is that they are higher-order properties or states. On this view, a thing has the disposition of flexibility if it has the property of possessing some property that accounts for its bending if put under suitable pressure. That property—the lower-order property—is the *ground* of the disposition.

Suppose it occurs to me at a certain moment that I should be at a meeting. If that is an attitude it seems, even so, to be an occurrence and so, one might think, is not something dispositional. Whether it should be regarded as a distinct attitude, rather than a recollection of something one believes, is a moot point. In any case I shall bypass problems like this. The view I am about to describe may be understood to be a view about propositional attitudes that are standing states, even though they may be short-lived. The attitudes that are my main concern—beliefs and intentions—are naturally understood as being states of this sort. Acquiring a belief and abandoning a belief are events, but that is no reason to think that the belief in question is anything other than a standing state.

What I shall call *dispositionalism* about propositional attitudes is the view that the attitudes (at least those conceived as standing states) are dispositional and that our concepts of the attitudes are dispositional concepts. In addition, the relevant dispositions are conceived as being analogous to the paradigm cases of dispositions, such as flexibility, fragility, and the like.

There are notorious problems about trying to specify dispositions relevant to the characterization of propositional attitudes in terms of conditionals stating what would happen if a certain condition were fulfilled. People who believe conditionals and come to believe their antecedents are not bound to come to believe their consequents. Whether they do so depends on a wide range of factors, such as whether or not they are interested in the truth or falsity of the consequent, and whether the play of thoughts running through their minds is such as to prompt belief in the consequent. It seems a hopeless task to specify the relevant factors except in the vaguest terms. (Some attempts in this direction are made in Millar 1991: chapter 2.) And even when this is done, a realistic formulation of the antecedent of the conditional will almost certainly have to include a hedging clause to the effect that there should be no countervailing conditions. (Problems about laws containing hedged clauses are explored in Schiffer 1991. Fodor 1991 is a response to this.) In what follows I shall cut through these issues by specifying dispositions in terms of what subjects are *liable* to do under a certain condition. A subject is liable to Φ in condition C if, when C obtains, he or she is liable to Φ. The idea is that being in C raises the chance of the subject's being liable to Φ. The cases that interest us are ones in which, for those who believe the relevant conditionals, it would be no surprise if a subject in C were to Φ. This may be so even though it is not the case that in C it is likely that the subject will Φ. In some cases the strongest claim that could justifiably be made is that in C the subject might well Φ. I choose this approach not just because it is conveniently rough-and-ready. I suspect that it is not in general possible to provide realistic specifications of dispositions associated with propositional attitudes in more precise terms and that including hedging clauses gives an illusion of definiteness.

I turn now to a somewhat more precise characterization of dispositionalism. Propositional attitudes are individuated by content and category. Thus, the belief that Stirling has a castle and the belief that Edinburgh has a castle are different attitudes because they have different contents, though they belong to the same category—belief. A belief that it will be cold on Tuesday and a desire that it will be cold on Tuesday are different attitudes because they belong to different categories—belief in one case and desire in the other. I shall say that a set of dispositions is *characteristic* of an attitude, individuated in the way just explained, provided that one would have that attitude if and only if one had those dispositions. With these notions to hand, I can be more precise about what dispositionalism is. I take it to be the conjunction of the following claims:

(A) For any propositional attitude (individuated as above) there is a set of dispositions that are characteristic of that attitude.
(B) For any propositional attitude (individuated as above) to have that attitude is to have the dispositions in the set characteristic of that attitude.
(C) Dispositions are conceived by analogy with the philosopher's paradigm cases, for instance flexibility and fragility.

(A) tells us nothing about either the metaphysics of propositional attitudes or the concepts of propositional attitudes. It merely states that propositional attitudes are paired with sets of characteristic dispositions. (B) gives us a metaphysics. It tells us that possessing, for instance, a belief-property like *believing that Stirling has a castle* consists in having the appropriate dispositions. In keeping with my earlier remarks about propositional attitude concepts and properties, I take it that to possess the property *believing that Stirling has a castle* is nothing other than to fall under the concept *believing that Stirling has a castle*. So (B) reflects a view about concepts of attitudes: the idea is that, when we think of an attitude as the attitude of believing that Stirling has a castle, we do so in dispositional terms. In more general terms, for any propositional attitude Ξ, the concept of Ξing that p is just the concept of possessing such-and-such dispositions—those that are characteristic of Ξing that p. There is an issue as to how a concept of an attitude is supposed to represent the dispositions characteristic of the attitude. I address this in Section 6.

(C) is crucial. The view that I shall eventually defend is compatible with (A) and (B) provided that the notion of a disposition is broadly conceived. It differs from the dispositionalism characterized above in specifying the dispositions characteristic of propositional attitudes in terms that are normatively loaded. (C) highlights the fact that the dispositionalism presently under discussion treats dispositions in the standard non-normative way.

It is important that dispositionalism incorporates a view about concepts of attitudes because, so understood, it yields an account of how ascriptions of attitudes to agents bear upon expectations about, and explanations of, what these agents will think and do in virtue of having these attitudes. The idea is that we are sometimes in a position to *anticipate* what people are liable to think and do if they have certain attitudes because,

(i) in virtue of having a grasp of relevant attitude concepts, we associate these attitudes with their characteristic dispositions, and
(ii) we are in a position to anticipate that circumstances likely to lead to the manifestation of some of these dispositions (triggering circumstances) will obtain.

Further, according to this view, we are sometimes in a position to *explain* why agents form certain beliefs or perform certain actions because

(iii) we are in a position to judge that what the agent has come to believe or do results from the manifestation of dispositions linked to attitudes we ascribe to the agent.

This last condition will be satisfied if we are in a position to judge that the manifestation of relevant dispositions results in the subject's being *liable* to form the belief or perform the action to be explained, *and* that the subject's being so liable led to the formation of the belief or the performance of the action.

In Chapter 1, Section 3, I presented a familiar reason for thinking that rationalizing explanations are causal explanations. One might wonder whether this view is compatible with the dispositionalist view of propositional attitudes. If a fragile cup falls off the shelf and breaks on the stone floor, it manifests its disposition to break on being put under suitable stress. But what caused the manifestation, it might be said, is not possession of the disposition—the higher-order property. Rather, it is possession of the property that is the ground of the disposition. It is this property that figures in the causal process leading from the triggering cause—the cup's being put under suitable stress—to its breaking. The cup's fragility is not a further property with a role in that process. It is simply the property of having some property or other that has such a role. So if one is keen to regard propositional attitudes as states that can figure in causal processes leading to beliefs, actions, or feelings, one might prefer to suppose that to have a propositional attitude is to have the various properties that are the grounds of the relevant dispositions.[62] I do not myself think that we need to go down this path. It would be overly fastidious to take the fact, if it is a fact, that dispositions are not causes to be a reason to deny that rationalizing explanation is causal under dispositionalism. If rationalizing explanation is *dispositional explanation*, then, certainly, it is more like explaining the breaking of the cup in terms of its fragility than it is like explaining the breaking of the cup in terms of its hitting the floor. But the dispositional explanation of the cup's breaking is not a non-causal explanation. It presupposes that there was some triggering cause, even though it need not specify this cause. It also presupposes that there was a causal process associated with the

---

[62] This sort of consideration is appealed to by Jackson and others. See e.g. Jackson (1995) and Braddon-Mitchell and Jackson (1996: 96–103).

disposition, leading from the triggering cause to the breaking of the cup. The dispositional explanation is therefore a way of telling part of the story of the processes leading to the breaking of the cup. It is open to the dispositionalist about propositional attitudes to think of rationalizing explanation in similar terms. Some may wish to withhold the notion of a cause from dispositions. My point is that, even if there is reason to do so, this would be no objection to treating dispositional explanations as causal explanations, albeit explanations that provide limited insight into the causation of what is to be explained (compare McLaughlin 1995: 123–4).

Dispositionalism seems to me to be the most plausible alternative to the view for which I shall be arguing. But it does face some serious problems when it comes to explaining the normative import of ascriptions of propositional attitudes.

3. Dispositionalism and the explanation of normative import

At least part of the normative import of ascriptions of beliefs and intentions is captured by statements about (normative) commitments incurred through having the belief or intention ascribed. These statements are statements that would be true if the corresponding ascriptions were true. One way of accounting for the normative import of an ascription is in terms of the assumption that the ascription is normative. If the ascription were normative, then statements that capture its normative import would follow from it without further ado. Towards the end of the previous chapter I described a strategy for explaining the normative import of ascriptions of beliefs and intentions to rational agents without invoking the assumption that these ascriptions are normative. I envisage the dispositionalist adopting this strategy. In this and the following two sections, I argue that the strategy is unsuccessful.

To recall: the strategy was to explain the normative import of ascriptions of beliefs and intentions to rational agents by invoking principles connecting beliefs and intentions, conceived in non-normative terms, with normative commitments. To this end the following two principles might be invoked, where 'x' ranges over rational agents:

The Means–End Commitment Principle: For any x, ϕ, if x intends to ϕ then x incurs a commitment to doing what is necessary if x is to ϕ.

The Implication Commitment Principle: For any x, π, if x believes π, then for any θ, if π implies θ, then x incurs a commitment to believing θ, if x gives any verdict on θ.

I can best approach the problem I aim to identify by considering an analogous problem in the sphere of ethics. To illustrate this, I draw again on an example used earlier. This was the case in which my neighbour appears at my door in distress and calling on me for help. I regard this as a reason for me to help. Let us suppose that my doing so reflects my acceptance of a principle to the effect that the fact that one's neighbour is in distress and calling on one for help is a reason for one to help. This is a reason-specifying principle connecting the non-normative with the normative. Suppose now that I am pressed to say what it is about my neighbour's being in distress and calling on me for help that gives me a reason to help. Although my acceptance of the principle contributes to the explanation of my reaction to the situation, I cannot address this enquiry simply by alluding to the principle. If there is a puzzle about how the consideration about my neighbour constitutes a reason for me to help, there is as much of a puzzle over what makes the connecting principle acceptable.

The query about what makes the consideration in question a reason for me to help need not be motivated by scepticism about practical or moral reason. It crops up in normative moral philosophy, for instance in discussions about what makes killing wrong when it is wrong (see, e.g. Norman 1995). We do not advance this enquiry simply by citing a plausible principle to the effect that the fact that an action would be a killing is, in the absence of special circumstances, a reason against doing it. In keeping with this, the main types of response to the issue are all concerned with providing a deeper explanation of why such a principle holds. Consequentialists look for an answer in terms of the consequences of individual acts of killing for the general good, or in terms of the consequences of there not being widespread acknowledgement of a strong prescription against killing. Theorists inspired by Kant look for an answer in terms of the view that persons are ends in themselves who, as such, are worthy of respect. If we were to follow Scanlon's distinctive kind of contractualism, we would try to show that some appropriate covering principle could not reasonably be rejected by anyone motivated by a concern to live with others on terms that could be justified to them provided that they shared such a concern (see Scanlon 1998: chapter 3). All of these strategies explain the wrongness of wrong killing in terms of a failure to have due regard to something that is held to be good in itself or worthy of some special kind of concern. For the consequentialist it is the general good. For Kantians it is persons viewed as ends in themselves. For Scanlon it is the ideal of living with others on terms they could not reasonably reject. (Scanlon 1998: 154 explicitly regards this as an ideal.) In each case the normative import of the consideration that an action would be a killing is traced to a basic assumption about what is valuable or worthy of special concern. The same general strategy would apply to the consideration about my neighbour. The connecting principle in this case is not self-explanatory. If it is acceptable, its acceptability will be grounded in considerations about what is of value or worthy of regard.

The question now is, How is the dispositionalist to explain why having a belief or an intention incurs a normative commitment of the sort I have considered? Invoking the Implication Commitment Principle and the Means–End Commitment Principle will not do the trick. We need to know why these principles are acceptable. It can easily seem that there is no real issue here. Dispositionalism about belief and intention *looks* plausible, and the principles in question *seem* acceptable. My brief discussion of principles in ethics connecting the non-normative to the non-normative is intended to dislodge such complacency. It will emerge that there is an issue about whether the principles would be acceptable if the dispositionalist view of belief and intention were correct. To lead into the issue, I first draw attention to a problem for dispositionalism that is often overlooked and which initially might seem to be quite independent of the problem of explaining normative import.

4. How we relate to our current intentions and beliefs

Imagine that I have an intention to take a holiday. According to dispositionalism, this is a matter of having the dispositions that are characteristic of that attitude. If the dispositionalist were right, it would be easily intelligible that I should adopt a purely *contemplative* stance towards this intention. By that I mean a stance in which I simply register that I have the intention, without taking that fact to have any normative import applying to me. For the dispositionalist, my taking this stance would not reflect any deficiency in my understanding of what it is to have the intention in question or in my appreciation of the implications of my having this intention. For the case would be analogous to that of the distressed neighbour. Suppose that I had not taken the consideration that my neighbour is in distress and is calling on me for help to be a reason for me to help. This might reveal a degree of insensitivity on my part. But it would not in itself show that there is some deficiency in my understanding of what it is for my neighbour to be in this state. Viewed from the dispositionalist perspective, the case in which I adopt a purely contemplative stance to my own intention would be exactly parallel. There is the consideration that I intend to take a holiday, which I accept. According to the dispositionalist, this consideration is non-normative and so does not, in and of itself, imply that I incur a commitment to doing what is necessary to carry out the intention. It is possible that I should adopt the purely contemplative stance, just as it is possible that I should have viewed the situation of my neighbour as having no normative import for me. Dispositionalists might well agree that if I did adopt such a stance I would be foolish or irrational. But it is not open to them to suppose that my adopting the stance must reflect a deficient understanding of what it is for me to intend to take a holiday or a deficient appreciation of what is implied by the consideration that I have this intention.

In taking this view of the matter, dispositionalists treat intentions as being analogous to character traits. This is not surprising since character traits *are* dispositional. Suppose that I am prone to irritability. In certain kinds of situations, in which many others remain unruffled, I become irritable. Knowing this, I might adopt a practical stance towards this trait. I could decide that I should do something about it or that it is best left alone. (Maybe I think that trying to deal with it would make me even more prone to irritability.) But I could adopt a purely contemplative stance in which I simply register that I am easily irritated. I could be indifferent or just curious about how I will react in situations I am about to encounter. In any case, the matter would be of merely theoretical interest.[63] While such an attitude might be foolish and imprudent, it is surely possible, and readily intelligible.

In conceiving of intentions as being in this way like character traits, the dispositionalist misrepresents the character of our normal relationship to our current own intentions. The peculiarities of this relationship can be brought out by reflection on self-ascriptions of current intentions. Suppose that I formed my intention to take a holiday by taking a definite decision to do so. I might have thought to myself, and perhaps voiced the thought, 'I intend to take a holiday.' My thought here represents me as intending to take a holiday, but it does more than that. I do not merely report on a state that I am in, as I might report on the state of my health or on some character trait that I have. For there seems to be an intimate connection between thinking the thought and recognizing that it manifestly has normative import for me. To adopt a contemplative stance to my intention would fly in the face of this.

Decisions are not always made by thinking thoughts that explicitly self-ascribe an intention. I might have thought, 'I'm going to take a holiday.' The content of this latter thought would simply be that I shall take a holiday. But in a context in which I am making up my mind, I would in thinking that thought implicitly self-ascribe an intention. In that case too it is hard to make sense of a purely contemplative stance towards my intention. It would fly in the face of the fact that my having the intention manifestly has normative import for me.

Suppose that later, as I pass a travel agent, I recall that I intend to take a holiday. The recollection, like the thought by which I made up my mind, does more than merely represent me to have an intention: it is a renewal—an endorsement—of a previously formed intention. It is not the same as thinking that I intend*ed* to take a holiday. My actual thought is about a current intention—about something I currently intend. Again, it is hard to see how in having the thought I could fail to acknowledge its normative import.

These considerations are problematic from the dispositionalist perspective. If intentions, and indeed beliefs, were dispositional in

---

[63] I was prompted to emphasize the contrast between contemplative/theoretical and practical stances by related work by Richard Moran; see, in particular, Moran (1988; 2001).

the way character traits are, then self-ascriptions of current beliefs and intentions would merely represent one to be in a dispositionally characterized state of mind. In that case, adopting a purely contemplative stance towards our current intentions and beliefs would be readily intelligible. I am suggesting that such a view distorts the phenomenology of belief and intention.

Jane Heal has suggested that the peculiar character of self-ascriptions of some mental states is best explained in terms of the idea that they have a constitutive role in relation to the states they ascribe (Heal 1994a; 2002). Her principal focus, it should be said, is on beliefs, but she thinks it plausible that this general approach works also for intentions (Heal 2002: 18). Applied to the cases I have been considering, the idea would be that my self-ascription of an intention to take a holiday not only represents me as having that intention, but *constitutes* my having the intention. So there is an analogy between the self-ascriptive thoughts in question and performatives. A performative proper is an utterance that in appropriate circumstances makes true what it represents to be so. Saying to my father 'I'll visit this weekend, I promise' both represents me as promising to visit my father and makes it the case that I have so promised.[64] On Heal's approach, the self-ascriptions under consideration would be taken to have a performative-like character on the grounds that they make true what they represent to be so. On this account, the thought that is my making up my mind to take a holiday represents me as intending to take a holiday and makes it true that I do so intend. An attractive feature of the account is that it offers an explanation of the peculiar authority that conscious self-ascriptions of intentions seem to have. In the absence of circumstances rendering the performance, in Austin's words, 'unhappy', like being befuddled by alcohol or deranged, a conscious self-ascription would, according to the account, be authoritative just because it constitutes the obtaining of the very state of affairs it represents to be so. This is a strikingly imaginative way to deal with the peculiarities of self-ascriptions of intentions, but I am not convinced that it works. Two problems arise.

[64] The classic texts are those of J. L. Austin (see Austin 1961: ch. 10; 1962). Austin himself believed that performative utterances are neither true nor false. It is certainly right that if my utterance made a promise, then what I said was not *false*. But since it makes it true that I promised *and* I said that I promised, the most natural way of describing the proceedings is to say that the utterance makes true what it represents me to have done.

The account raises a question to which it is difficult to give a clear and convincing answer: how can merely thinking a thought conjure up the motivational potential characteristic of intentions? This matters because it is plausible that the thinking constitutes an intention only if, when the conditions are 'happy', it guarantees that one has the intention and therefore the motivation that goes with it. How can the self-ascriptive thinking, even in 'happy' conditions, guarantee that? It is true that when I decided to take the holiday I must have already had, or conceived then and there, a desire for a holiday, for otherwise I would not have made the decision. So it might be suggested that my deciding merely channels existing motivation towards taking a holiday and creates some additional motivation, the latter being the added motivation associated with my having settled on a course of action. On this view, the question posed rests on a misunderstanding. The thinking that is the deciding—the making up of one's mind—does not conjure up the motivation: it merely directs it towards action and adds to it. The problem now, I think, is that this response merely shifts the problem. How can the mere thinking of the thought suffice to bring it about that the motivation I already had to take a holiday comes to be channelled towards action and supplemented by additional motivation? We are to suppose that the thinking is like a conduit for existing motivation. So long as the water is high enough prior to the conduit's being opened, it flows through and its force is somehow increased. The model makes it look as if, because the thinking was the making up of one's mind, it explains how the existing motivation is channelled and supplemented. It remains unclear how thinking the thought is supposed to do this.

The second problem—perhaps a more serious one—concerns whether the constitutive account can cope with self-ascriptions that are false. I imagined that when I thought 'I am going to take a holiday', or 'I intend to take a holiday', I was making up my mind to take a holiday. In that case, in thinking the thought I formed the intention. But it could have been that it only seemed to me that I had made up my mind. Perhaps on such matters I am liable to vacillate and shilly-shally. The phenomenology—what it struck me that I was doing—would not settle the matter because it need not differentiate between the case in which I truly made a decision and the case in which I did not.

Against this, it might be suggested that there is no real problem. If I am a vacillator I will be liable to make decisions and then quickly unmake them and then remake them again. Certainly, we should not set the standards for having made a decision so high that we cannot accommodate quick changes of mind. The borderline between having and not having made up one's mind may not be sharp. But nor should we lose track of the fact that making up one's mind about what to do, or for that matter about whether something is so, is *settling* on what to do or think. If I am a vacillator, I may not have made up my mind even though it seems to me that I have. From the inside, so to speak, a case of my not having made up my mind need be no different from one in which I have. That is why a self-ascription can be false. Now, the constitutive account that appeals to the performative-like character of self-ascriptive thoughts can accommodate some cases of false self-ascription—those in which the conditions under which the ascription is made are unhappy. But the edge is taken off this account if the conditions that can render a self-ascriptive thought unhappy are to include cases in which, with a clear mind, a person seems to him- or herself to form an intention, while lacking adequate motivation. On the approach suggested by Heal, unhappiness conditions were to be conditions like being drunk or deranged. But so far as intention is concerned, this is a misleading picture. It is relatively easy, even with a clear head, to suppose that one intends to do something when one does not. People can think to themselves that they intend to give up smoking, or reduce their intake of alcohol or fatty food, and be mistaken. If I really made up my mind to take a holiday, it was not just in virtue of explicitly or implicitly thinking the self-ascriptive thought, but in virtue of thinking the thought in the setting of the wider motivational state I was then in. The self-ascription could not have constituted the intention, since it could not have guaranteed that I had really made up my mind, even in the absence of incapacitating conditions like drunkenness or derangement.

Self-ascriptions of intention *are* peculiar. There *is* more to a self-ascription of a current intention than a mere report of a state of mind. The peculiarity lies in the fact that adopting a purely contemplative stance towards our own current intentions is barely intelligible. I put this down to the fact that having a belief or an intention manifestly has normative import.

Similar considerations apply to belief. When I ascribe a belief to myself I represent myself to be in state that manifestly has normative import for me. But here too it seems best to avoid the constitutive account. One can think one has settled in one's mind that something is so when one has not. A constitutive account can accommodate this fallibility, but at the price of making out that the cases in which the self-ascriptions are false are relatively rare. But mistakes about what we think we believe can easily happen when strong emotions are engaged, as when people are trying to make up their minds whether someone close to them is trustworthy. In such situations the phenomenology is not bound to discriminate between entertaining the thought that something is so and reaching the conclusion that it is so. Whether one really has reached the conclusion will depend on the degree to which one is motivated to use the content of the thought as an assumption in subsequent thinking. That might not be clear to the subject until later.

In the light of these considerations, we need to return to the issue of how the dispositionalist attempts to explain the normative import that ascriptions of beliefs and intentions have. The sense of there being a problem here can easily slip away. If I intend to do something, then, of course, I have made it my *goal* to do that thing. And if I have made it my goal to do that thing, then, surely, I incur a commitment to doing what is required to achieve that goal. That is true, but if the dispositionalist is right, to have made something my goal is just to be disposed to take such steps as I think will bring about that thing. It has yet to be explained why my being so disposed should be thought to have any normative import. My being prone to irritability can contribute to providing a reason for me to do something about this trait, since it is both personally disadvantageous and unpleasant or even harmful to others. So we can explain why there is reason for me to control my proneness to irritability in terms of the desirability of not disadvantaging myself and of avoiding being unpleasant or harmful to others. The dispositionalist thinks that intentions are like character traits and so must explain the normative import of ascriptions of intentions in a similar fashion. The mere having of an intention, or a belief, under dispositionalism does not explain why it is commitment-incurring.

The dispositionalist needs an explanation of

(i) why, if we intend to Φ, we should avoid retaining that intention while never getting around to doing what is necessary if we are to Φ, and
(ii) why, given that we believe P, we should avoid retaining that belief while giving verdicts other than belief on implications of P.

There are two lines of objection to the dispositionalist's enterprise. The first draws attention to its oddness. The second raises problems for attempts to carry it out.

The oddness lies in the very idea that we need to explain the Implication Commitment and the Means–End Commitment Principles in terms of some value that accounts for why it should matter that we do the things that would discharge the commitments incurred by a belief or intention. This is a road that in my view leads to a dead end. If we go along it, and imagine ourselves contemplating our own current intentions or beliefs, it will look as if we need to posit a concern to realize something of value to explain why we take ascriptions of belief and intention to have normative import. (Note once again the analogy with the ethical case.) But it should, I think, strike as odd that such an explanation is needed. It brings too many concerns into the picture to account for a problem that looks unreal.

The other line of objection to the proposed strategy for explaining normative import is that there are problems in attempting to carry it out. To fail to discharge the commitments incurred by a belief or by an intention is to fail to satisfy an ideal of reason (Chapter 3, Section 2). Recall that the Implication Ideal is

For any π, θ, if θ is implied by π, then avoid believing π while giving a verdict on θ other than belief.

And the Means–End Ideal is

For any ϕ, avoid intending to ϕ while never getting around to doing what is necessary if you are to ϕ.

Granted that these are ideals of reason, it might seem that we could explain the normative import we attach to ascriptions of beliefs and intentions in terms of the value we place on conforming to those ideals. Indeed, the dispositionalist might invoke this idea to explain the oddity of adopting a contemplative stance to one's own current beliefs and intentions. The oddity would be taken to lie in representing oneself as intending to do something or as believing something and yet being so irrational as to be indifferent to whether or not one satisfied the relevant ideal. This approach does not address the present problem. Valuing conformity to the ideals of reason certainly makes sense. But given dispositionalism, it becomes an issue whether reason does hold up to us the relevant ideals. If beliefs and intentions are as they are represented under dispositionalism, it becomes problematic that the supposed ideals are indeed ideals of reason. For if intentions and beliefs are dispositional in the way that proneness to irritability is dispositional, why should it be that, in so far as we are rational, we aspire to satisfy the Implication Ideal and the Means–End Ideal?

These considerations have a bearing upon another move that dispositionalists might make. It might be suggested that the Implication Commitment Principle and the Means–End Commitment Principle are necessary truths, even though ascriptions of beliefs and ascriptions of intentions are non-normative. If this is meant to provide the sought-for explanation of why we should think these principles true, it hardly succeeds in this task. Merely stipulating that the principles are necessary truths illuminates nothing. We need an explanation for why they should be thought to be necessary truths. My claim is that there is no reason to suppose that they are necessary truths if ascriptions of beliefs and intentions are non-normative. Once you take seriously the idea that the ascriptions are non-normative, then it becomes a mystery why, if they are true, a claim to the effect that the subject incurs a normative commitment is true as well.

5. Intentions, beliefs, and psychological commitment

A crucial feature of the view I shall defend is that the Implication Commitment Principle and the Means–End Commitment Principle are *constitutive principles*—partial specifications of what it is to believe something or intend something. They are also conceptual principles. Grasping the concept of intention commits one to accepting the Means–End Commitment Principle; grasping the concept of belief commits one to accepting the Implication Commitment Principle. That there should be constitutive normative principles is not puzzling. I shall comment on two such principles that serve as analogues for the Means–End and Implication Commitment Principles. The first is the

> *Promise Commitment Principle*: For any x, ϕ, if x promises to ϕ then x incurs a commitment to ϕing.

The other is the

> *Dean Commitment Principle*: For any x, if x is Dean then x incurs a commitment to carrying out the duties of Dean.

These are not principles connecting the non-normative to the normative in the way the Means–End and Commitment Principles are supposed to do, on the dispositionalist reading to which I have been objecting. They are constitutive principles. The first partially specifies what it is to promise something. The second partially specifies what it is to be Dean. They are also conceptual principles. Grasping the concept of a promise commits one to accepting the Promise Commitment Principle. Grasping the concept of Dean commits one to accepting the Dean Commitment Principle. I take the Means–End Commitment Principle and the Implication Commitment Principle to be analogous to the Promise Commitment Principle and the Dean Commitment Principle, at least in the respect that they are constitutive and conceptual.[65]

Part of the reason for taking seriously the idea that the Means–End Commitment Principle and the Implication Commitment Principle are constitutive and conceptual principles is that if they are then we can avoid the problems posed by the dispositionalist explanation of the normative import of ascriptions of beliefs and intentions. If these principles are constitutive and conceptual, then the normative import of ascriptions of beliefs and intentions is explained by the

---

[65] John Searle (1969: 33–44) made use of the idea of a constitutive rule in his early work on speech acts. His constitutive rules are akin to the rules that govern what I call practices. On Searle's view they commonly take the form of imperatives or state what counts as what, for example what counts as making a promise. In her second Locke Lecture (in draft), Christine Korsgaard talks about constitutive standards. She takes the hypothetical imperative, understood as the principle, 'If you will an end, you must will the means to that end', to be a constitutive standard for action in the sense that it is a 'standard that we must at least be trying to follow if we are to count as acting at all'. The various commitment principles I have picked out are not constitutive standards in this sense. They are not principles one can follow or fail to follow. You can have an intention or belief and fail to discharge the commitment it incurs, but that is not the same as having a belief or intention and not incurring the corresponding commitment. What I called requirements of rationality in Ch. 3, Sect. 2, are, I think, akin to Korsgaard's constitutive standards.

normativity of the ascriptions. Can we shed some light on how this can be so?

Promising in and of itself gives rise to commitments on the part of the one making the promise. Being Dean incurs a commitment to carrying out the duties of the Dean. In both of these cases an explanation of why a normative commitment is incurred is available in terms of the notion of a practice and the commitments incurred by participating in a practice (see Chapter 3, Sections 4–5). Promising is a move in the activity of giving and reacting to promises. Participating in the practice in and of itself incurs a commitment to following its governing rules. Among the rules is that, roughly speaking, one does what one promises. So the commitment to following the rules generates a commitment to doing the thing promised. The Promise Commitment Principle is constitutive because it expresses the constitutive link between making a promise and incurring a commitment to doing the thing promised. It tells us something about the nature of promising and the concept of promising. Parallel claims hold for the concept of a Dean. But where believing and intending are concerned, the style of explanation that invokes practices will not serve the purpose. As I noted in the previous chapter, the commitments incurred by intentions and beliefs are grounded in ideals of reason that are not linked to practices.

We gain some insight into the normativity of intention by comparing intentions with desires. An intention, by my account, in and of itself incurs a normative commitment to doing whatever is necessary to do the thing intended. In this respect intention contrasts with desire. If I want to take a holiday, then I have some motivation to take a holiday, but I need not be *psychologically committed* to doing so. My desire consists in my finding the prospect of taking a holiday attractive—perhaps so attractive that in suitable circumstances I would decide to do so. But it could be that, even though I have this desire, I am not motivated to do what is necessary to satisfy it, because of the time and inconvenience of making suitable arrangements, or because other matters are more pressing. If this is so, and yet my desire to take a holiday persists, I need not be in breach of any ideal of reason. There can be good reasons not to satisfy a desire, which are not reasons to try to get rid of the desire. But if I intend to take a holiday, then I have settled on a course of action—made up my mind to pursue it. It is in this sense that I am psychologically committed to taking a holiday and thus doing whatever is necessary to that end. If, despite being so committed, I fail to do whatever is necessary, then I will not have done what I am psychologically committed to doing—the intention will not be fulfilled. Desires and hopes are often not fulfilled. The prospect of their not being fulfilled does not in and of itself demand anything of the subject. But this is precisely where intention contrasts with desire and hope. *An intention is a state of mind such that the prospect of its not being fulfilled demands a response on the part of the subject—either to give up the intention or to ensure that it will, after all, be carried out. The reason for thinking that intentions are intrinsically commitment-incurring is that their psychological role is shaped by the subject's responsiveness to this demand.*

This, I think, sheds some light on the status of the Means–End Ideal which grounds the normative commitments incurred by intentions. We can understand why this ideal is an ideal of reason in terms of the character of intentions. Though it might initially seem odd, there is reason to think of intention as having a constitutive aim distinct from the aims in which particular intentions consist. Intentions are clearly directed at doing the thing intended, but they are not directed at doing the thing intended *come what may*. There is, as it were, psychological work for an intention to do even if there is no prospect of its being carried out or reason not to carry it out. That work is to ensure that the agent does not let things drift but gives up the intention. An intention that is not going to be fulfilled calls for a change of mind. This can be captured in terms of the idea that the constitutive aim of intention is to ensure either that the intention is carried out or that the agent changes his or her mind. The explanation for why it is an ideal of reason that when we have an intention we either carry it out or give it up is that to do neither of these things is incompatible with intention's constitutive aim.[66]

Conceived as psychological commitments, intentions impact on thought and action in ways that are shaped by the normative commitments they incur. Consider two scenarios. In the first I am exploring a town I have never visited before. I drift along turning

---

[66] It is important to recall that failure to satisfy such an ideal is not necessarily irrational. Care must be taken over the relation between ideals of reason and requirements of rationality, if the latter are conceived in such a way that to fail to satisfy a requirement is *ipso facto* irrational. See Ch. 3, Sect. 2.

this way and that. My exploration of the town is, of course, intentional, and when I turn to go along a particular street my doing so is usually intentional. (It might not be if I'm daydreaming.) But I am not carrying out an intention to follow a particular route. I just go where I feel like going at each point at which there are options. In the second scenario, I am again visiting a strange town, but I intend to visit the castle and my choice of route is directed to this end. In the first scenario there is no way I have to go—which is to say, no way I am committed, in the normative sense, to going. In the second scenario there is. This difference is a normative difference, but it is reflected in a difference in my psychology in the two cases. Whether or not I succeed in doing what I intend, my thoughts and actions in the second scenario are guided by the means–end commitment that the intention incurs. I will have discharged this commitment provided that I do the necessary or give up the intention. If I do the necessary by way of carrying out the intention, I shall have been guided by the means–end commitment. If I give up the intention, because of a change of mind or because I see that I am not going to be able to carry it out, I shall again have been guided by the commitment. For this to be so it is not necessary that I operate with any theory of intention. All that is necessary is that I am aware of what I intend and, as we say, of what I have to do to carry it out. Some might respond at this point by questioning whether intention is inextricably tied to such awareness. I think it is harder to make a case for thinking that intention is not so tied than to make out a corresponding case for desire. Intentions are not simply forces that steer us towards the thing intended. An intention's characteristic work is done via the agent's knowledge that he or she has that intention. This is at least part of the explanation for why it is so natural, when explaining that one did not mean to do something, to say that one did not realize one was doing it. If I have been joking in a manner that has upset a friend, my saying that I did not realize that I was upsetting the friend would generally be taken to indicate that I did not intend to do so. At least typically the things we do intentionally are the things we do knowing what we mean to do. I explore the matter further in the next chapter.

It will come as no surprise that I regard belief too as a psychological commitment by analogy with intention. My believing P is a psychological commitment to using P as an assumption in my thinking, should the need to do so arise. If I believe P then the prospect of giving a verdict other than belief on an implication of P is not something I am in a position to view with indifference. It calls for a reaction.

It is in the nature of the psychological commitment in which believing P consists that the way it impacts on my thought and action is shaped by the implication commitment that it incurs—the normative commitment to believing any implication of P on which I give a verdict.[67] The normative commitment can have this shaping role only if the subject has appropriate reflective capacities—including a capacity to reflect on the implications of things believed. It might be doubted that beliefs essentially involve such capacities. My point is that, since beliefs in the realm of personal understanding—the beliefs we ascribe to one another—implicate reflective capacities through the exercise of which the impact of those beliefs is shaped, we should acknowledge a distinction in psychological kind between those beliefs and any belief-like states the impact of which is not so shaped.

Just as means–end commitments are grounded in the Means–End Ideal, so implication commitments are grounded in the Implication Ideal. But how should we explain the status of the Implication Ideal? Consider first a weaker ideal of reason—the ideal of avoiding inconsistency in one's beliefs. We can account for this ideal in terms of the idea that belief constitutively aims at truth—an idea discussed at some length in Chapter 2, Section 2. Suppose now that I believe P and that P implies Q. I might avoid believing P and believing ¬Q, and so avoid inconsistency, yet still fail to satisfy the Implication Ideal. For I might believe P and withhold both belief and disbelief from Q. (In that case I give a verdict other than belief to Q, despite believing P.) The view that belief constitutively aims at truth does not explain what has gone wrong in the situation envisaged. It looks as if we cannot account for what is wrong here in terms of the idea that belief aims at truth. The situation is one in which I have a picture of how things are on which both P and Q are true, and yet I give a verdict on Q that is out of kilter with its being part of that picture—the very picture that I use to steer my thoughts, actions, desires, and feelings. What is wrong here is that, although I believe P, I do not exploit P in

---

[67] Isaac Levi (2002) stresses the commitment character of beliefs and contrasts this conception with the idea that beliefs are dispositional.

a way that is relevant to the issue as to whether or not Q is true. With that in mind, I suggest that the Implication Ideal has to do with our need to exploit correctly what we already believe when this is called for. If one fails to satisfy the Implication Ideal, then something that one believes is not playing the role that believing it accords it. Belief not only aims at truth; it aims at the correct exploitation of what is believed when the need arises. This is reflected in our actual psychology, since the realization that one is giving a verdict other than belief to an implication of what one believes is liable to prompt a readjustment. Of course, the right adjustment need not be to believe the implication. It might be to give up belief in what implies it.

The notion of a psychological commitment helps to account for the difference between self-ascriptions of current beliefs and intentions on the one hand, and self-ascriptions of current character traits on the other. (Recall that the failure adequately to account for this is a problem for dispositionalism.) In self-ascribing a character trait, for instance proneness to irritability or aggressiveness, I merely represent myself to have the trait and thus the dispositions in which the trait consists. Even if the self-ascription is true, it does not settle whether I should do anything, or whether I am committed to doing anything, about the matter.[68] It does not in and of itself give rise to any normative commitments, and the psychological impact of having the trait is not necessarily shaped by any such commitments. By contrast, when I represent myself as having a current belief or intention, I thereby represent myself to have incurred a normative commitment. That is why it is not possible for me to adopt a contemplative stance towards my own current beliefs or intentions. Barring barely intelligible befuddlement, I cannot but acknowledge that the belief or intention has normative import for me.

It should be stressed that the problem for dispositionalism of accommodating the peculiarity of our relationship to our own current intentions and beliefs does not *depend* on the assumption that ascriptions of beliefs and intentions are normative. The problem arises because it is not readily intelligible that we should think of ourselves

---

[68] There might be an issue arising from writings of Frankfurt (1998) about whether we can in some sense identify with a character trait. I do not think, however, that identifying with a trait could plausibly be regarded as treating the having of the trait as a normative matter. Interesting discussions of identification may be found in Buss and Overton (2002).

as currently intending to do something, or as believing something, and yet adopt a contemplative stance towards our having this belief or intention. The trouble is that, on the dispositionalist account of the nature of beliefs and intentions, this would be readily intelligible.

The general stance I have adopted sheds some light on Moore's paradox as applied to thought. (See Moore 1942; 1944. For suggestive discussions from which I have benefited, see Heal 1994a and Moran 2001.) There is something odd about thinking, 'I believe that p, and it is not the case that p', even though the thought is not self-contradictory. The thought represents me as believing that p and therefore as being normatively committed to believing whatever is implied by the proposition that p. It therefore represents me as being normatively committed to believing that p. But the second conjunct of the thought is the proposition that it is not the case that p. The oddity lies in the fact that my accepting the second conjunct is at odds with what the first conjunct represents me to be committed to. The analogue for intention of the paradox for belief just discussed is, 'I intend to Φ, but I shall not do what is necessary if I am to Φ.' This yields to an analogous treatment. Accepting the second conjunct is setting oneself not to do what the first conjunct represents one to be committed to doing.

To sum up, part of the case for thinking that ascriptions of beliefs and intentions are normative is that this conclusion accounts for the peculiarity of our relationship with our own current intentions and beliefs. The other part of the case concerns the inadequacy of the dispositionalist account of the normative import of ascriptions of beliefs and intentions. Here the argument was that under dispositionalism the Implication Commitment Principle and the Means–End Commitment Principle become problematic. Though they are in fact acceptable, the dispositionalist lacks a satisfying account of why they are so. Further support for my own view is provided by the light shed on Moore-type paradoxes.

6. The problem of representing the dispositions characteristic of beliefs and intentions

In this concluding section of the chapter I aim to provide further support for the view that ascription of beliefs and intentions are normative by discussing another problem for dispositionalism. We have seen that, according to dispositionalism, to believe something or intend something is to have certain non-normatively specifiable dispositions. There is a problem for this view that has received inadequate attention. This is the problem of *representing the dispositions*. How is an ascription of a belief or intention supposed to represent the dispositions that are characteristic of the attitude ascribed?

When illustrating dispositionalism about the attitudes, we tend to use examples that turn on logical concepts expressible by, for instance, 'everything...', 'something...', 'if...then...', 'either... or...', '...and...', and 'it is not the case that...'. That is because the case for dispositionalism about propositional attitudes looks strongest when the focus is on candidates for plausible dispositions that mirror the logical properties of these logical concepts. Grasp of the disjunction-concept, for instance, might be taken to implicate a disposition such that, roughly speaking, if one believes a disjunction and comes to believe the negation of one of its disjuncts, one is liable to come to believe the other disjunct. Departing from such examples, we might try dealing with concepts, like those of a bachelor or of an uncle, that have a tolerably, though not indisputably, clear inferential role. Then we might try to say something plausible about colour concepts like *being red*. To have that concept might be thought to implicate a disposition to come to believe that something before one is red when one has a visual experience such that there seems to be something before one that is red.[69] Beyond such examples it becomes quite unclear what to say.

The problem that concerns me now arises even if we bypass worries about hedging clauses (see Section 2) and settle for rough specifications of dispositions in terms of what the subject is liable to do under certain conditions. Suppose that we learn that Tom, a keen gardener, thinks that his flower beds lack adequate nutrients. How does that inform us about Tom's dispositions to thought or action? The picture suggested by the dispositionalist theory is something like this. We are given an ascription to Tom of a belief **B**. In virtue of our grasp of what it is to have that belief, we take Tom to have a number

---

[69] A systematic attempt to carry out this sort of exercise is Loar (1981).

of dispositions. That puts us in a position to anticipate how Tom is liable to think and act and not to be surprised when he thinks and acts in particular ways. Notice that this view requires not just that in having **B** it is determined, in the sense of fixed, that one has certain dispositions. It requires that we should be able to read off specifications of the dispositions from the ascription of **B**. There is a question, though, as to how we are supposed to be able to do this.

How Tom will think or act as a result of having **B** will obviously depend on what else he thinks, what he wants, what circumstances he encounters, how he is feeling at the time, and many other factors. How are we supposed to have a grip on the potential of **B** to hook up with all of this? Examples turning on logical concepts are easier to handle, because in these cases the potential that a belief has to hook up with others seems to have a definite shape. It looks plausible that, if I believe that either Mary is arriving by plane or she is arriving by train, then I am disposed in such a way that, roughly speaking, were I to come to believe she is not coming by plane I would be liable to believe that she is coming by train. In this sort of case there is *some* plausibility to the idea that we can read off the disposition from the category and content of the attitude in question. But how is the potential for Tom's belief **B** to combine with other beliefs and attitudes to produce thought or action supposed to be written into the category and content of **B**? Again, the fact that the category of attitude is belief tells us a lot. It tells us that **B** has the potential to link up with other beliefs to produce further beliefs, and that it has the potential to link up with intentions to produce actions. But it is not so clear in this case how the content is supposed to tell us which sorts of beliefs and what sorts of intentions it can combine with. There can easily seem to be no problem, because it is not difficult to think of scenarios in which we might well form certain expectations about what Tom will think or do in view of what he takes to be the state of his flower beds. Knowing him to be a keen gardener who likes to keep his flower beds in tip-top condition, we might expect him to apply fertilizer. The question though is how we are able to do this. I see no prospect of spelling this out in non-normative terms that are psychologically realistic. It is clearly crucial that **B** concerns flower beds and the property of lacking nutrients, considered as applying to flower beds. So **B** is apt to combine with beliefs that Tom has about flower beds, and about what it is for flower beds to lack nutrients, to produce some further belief. It would be nice from a theoretical point of view if we could demarcate this potential with the help of rules for drawing implications from the content of **B** that turn on the concepts of flower beds and of lacking nutrients. But there is no reason to expect such a project to be feasible. I do not appeal here to a general scepticism about conceptual truths. The point is simply that there is no reason to suppose that all of the concepts brought into play by **B** have a non-normatively specifiable conceptual role which makes it possible to spell out, in non-normative terms, its potential to contribute to the basis of other beliefs.

How should we then characterize the dispositions to thought and action characteristic of believing **P**? The answer, I think, is implicit in the previous discussion:

> In virtue of believing P subjects are so disposed that, should the need arise, and given suitable prompts, they are liable to use P as an assumption in reasoning, constrained by the basic implication commitment incurred by the belief, and by the derivative commitments incurred when it combines with other attitudes, including other beliefs.

For my purposes, what needs to be stressed is that, while on this approach beliefs are dispositional in nature, the dispositions characteristic of them are normatively specified. For theoretical purposes we could delve further into the nature of the disposition just specified—conceiving of it as implicating dispositions linked with particular concepts brought into play by the belief and other attitudes with which it combines. (I shall turn to this matter in Chapter 6.) But these dispositions will themselves be normatively specified. The moral is that we represent the dispositions characteristic of a belief via our grasp of the commitments incurred by the belief. They are, roughly, speaking, dispositions to discharge the commitments. That is why it is no surprise that, when trying to think up examples of the dispositions characteristic of beliefs, by way of illustrating dispositionalism, we first think of the normative commitments of the belief we have selected and try to gerrymander a non-normatively specified disposition to fit. We might hit on a specification of a disposition that looks just about plausible. If it *is* plausible, that will be because behaving as one would if the disposition were manifested would be a way of discharging a commitment incurred by the belief. What gets overlooked in these exercises is that, absent our grasp of normative commitments incurred by a belief, and we have no way of representing the potential of the belief to affect thought and action.

There is, of course, no suggestion, that the use of the assumption P by someone who believes P will always be properly constrained by the relevant commitments. The person who has the belief may fail to realize that some proposition is an implication of the content of the belief and on that account may fail to discharge the implication commitment with respect to that implication. It is also possible for people to be mistaken about what is implied by something they believe. What it takes to discharge a belief-relative commitment may not discharge a commitment that is not belief-relative (Chapter 3, Section 2).

It might seem a simple matter to specify the dispositions characteristic of intentions in non-normative terms. For surely those who have an intention are so disposed that, roughly speaking, given convenient opportunities and assuming they do not lose track of their intention, they will be liable to do what they believe to be necessary to carry it out. That is right so far as it goes, but it does not suffice to account for the explanatory and predictive use we can make of ascriptions of intentions. What we are trying to do is characterize the potential of an intention with a specified content to combine with beliefs and other intentions to produce action. In a case in which content of the intention is a disjunction, say, to travel to London by plane or by train, it is clear that the disjunctive form of the content serves as an index of the potential relevance of certain beliefs to carrying out the intention. But, as in the case of belief, once we move away from the logical form of contents, the matter is much less clear. The content of an intention does not have parameters for all of the possible variable factors that might affect the intention's potential to combine with beliefs to produce action. About all we can say, in advance of consideration of actual or possible scenarios in which the intention comes into play, is that the intention will impact on thought or action in ways that make some kind of sense. What makes some kind of sense will reflect the commitments the intention and the subject's beliefs incur.

It might be suggested that the points about which I have been making a fuss simply reflect a familiar and widely accepted thesis in the current philosophy of mind—the thesis that the mental, at least so far as it concerns propositional attitudes, has a holistic character. It has long been recognized that the way in which any given attitude impacts on thought and action depends on what other attitudes the agent holds, and therefore that there is no hope of specifying the psychological (functional) roles of the attitudes one by one. A familiar response to this is to suppose that the role of any given attitude can be specified only with the help of a total theory of the formation, maintenance, and adjustment of attitudes (Lewis 1972; Loar 1981; see Schiffer 1987 for trenchant criticism). The problems I have been throwing up, it may be said, arise from trying to say something in general terms about the roles of particular attitudes taken individually. This fails to come to grips with the issues I have been raising, but it helps to clarify those issues. I have not been trying to specify the role of attitudes one by one, but rather to say something about the potential of attitudes to articulate with other attitudes and thereby to impact on thought or action. There are two problems for the contrasting approach now under consideration. The first is that, even assuming that there is some theory that, when applied, generates non-normative specifications of the roles of particular propositional attitudes, it seems implausible that we actually draw upon the assumptions of such a theory in our commonsense thinking. Recall that we are trying to become clearer about how attitude-ascriptions can provide a basis for our expectations about, and explanations of, people's thought and action. The assumptions of the imagined theory must be available to us, and it must be plausible that we rely upon them. As things stand we have very little idea of what the theory is, which is why we lack any full-blown attempt to spell it out, beyond illustrations of how the logical concepts and some observational or sensation concepts might serve to characterize psychological roles.[70] The second problem puts in question whether there really is a theory that generates non-normative specifications of the roles of

---

[70] It does not help to treat the theory as being tacit, as do Stich and Nichols (1992), since the issue is to explain how we are able to treat certain considerations as reasons for expecting agents to think and act in certain ways, and not simply to explain how behaviour is moulded in sub-personal ways by sub-personal data-structures.

particular propositional attitudes. There is little reason to be confident that a non-normative specification of the potential of an attitude to impact on thought and action is obtainable from its content and category. The trouble is that, when considering how the belief or intention is likely to affect thought and action if these scenarios obtain, or were to obtain, we have no recourse but to think of what it would make sense for the subject to do in the circumstances. In other words, we are constrained to think about what will or would happen by thinking about normative matters. The normative commitments that have been so central to the preceding discussion are crucial for such thinking.

7. Back to explanatory irrelevance

Earlier (Chapter 1, Section 5) I described a line of thought deriving from Harman according to which moral judgements and principles are explanatorily irrelevant. The idea is that, if we want to understand why a person makes a moral judgement about some situation, we need never invoke the truth of the judgement or the truth of any principles that underpin it. We need only advert to non-normatively specifiable features of the situation and psychological facts about the person making the judgement. Those who take this view about moral judgements might well be tempted to extend it to cover normative judgements generally. Why, they may ask, should we think of thought and action as being shaped by *the commitments* incurred by beliefs and intentions, rather than by *beliefs* of subjects to the effect that they have incurred those commitments? On this approach there is no need to suppose that normative commitments come into the picture other than as believed.

I do not, of course, deny that the commitments incurred by our beliefs and intentions do their work via our appreciation that we have incurred those commitments. But it is important for the overall picture I am presenting that 'appreciate' here is a success verb. What we appreciate to be so is so. Suppose that you want to hail a taxi. You wait at the kerb of the pavement until you see one coming. When one appears you raise your hand in the usual way. You do so because you believe that a cab is approaching. In this case we do not hesitate to suppose that you have this belief because a cab is approaching. Indeed, this explanation for your belief is highly relevant to understanding what you are doing. Why should you be raising your hand in these circumstances, if not to hail an approaching cab? Now suppose that we know that you believe that if the stock market falls further then interest rates will be lowered. It turns out that the stock market falls further but interest rates are not lowered. When you affect not to be surprised by this, we take pleasure in reminding you that you are, or have been, committed to thinking that interest rates would be lowered. We can say this confidently not because you have told us of what your beliefs commit you to, or because you have voiced any beliefs as to what you are committed to—you had no need to tell us. We know what you thought and thus what you were committed to, and in this case we expect that, because you were so committed, you will appreciate that you were and will agree that you were wrong in thinking as you did. Just as in the taxi case the fact that the cab is approaching is independent of, and explains, your believing that it is, so in this case the fact that you are committed to believing a certain implication of things you believe is independent of, and explains, your believing that you are so committed. That you incur the commitment is as much a fact you encounter as is the fact that the cab is approaching. The commitment only makes a difference to what you think if you are aware of having incurred it. But it would be just as wrong to ignore the explanatory role of the commitment as it would be to ignore the explanatory role of the fact that the cab is approaching. I discuss the explanatory role of normative considerations more fully in Chapter 7.

CHAPTER 5

The Reflexivity of Intention and Belief

1. The high conception of beliefs and intentions

I have argued that beliefs and intentions influence thought and action in ways that are shaped by the commitments they incur. They are so shaped because subjects who have beliefs and intentions understand what these beliefs and intentions commit them to, and respond in the light of this understanding. On this view our beliefs and intentions involve reflective capacities—capacities to think about what we think and what we intend, and to see what our beliefs and intentions commit us to. These capacities are capacities we know that we have. When we believe something we have the capacity to think about what we believe, considering whether it is true or false, whether it is something others believe or are doubtful about, and so on. Similarly, when we intend something we have the capacity to think about what we intend—whether there is any point to it, whether it might give rise to practical problems, or objections from others, and so on. An inchoate notion of commitment, along the lines I have made explicit, pervades our thinking. When we think of what we have to do in view of intending to do certain things, we are thinking of means–end commitments. When we appreciate the practical significance for our thinking of the fact that this would have to be true if that were true, we are thinking of implication commitments.

Some may think that the position I am taking is open to objection because it implies that only creatures with the capacity to think about their beliefs and intentions, and the commitments they incur, can have beliefs and intentions. There is a strong tendency in current philosophy of mind to suppose that concepts of beliefs, desires, intentions, and so on apply alike to human beings and to at least some non-human animals. Those who make this supposition do not of course deny that human believers are able to think about their own propositional attitudes and about considerations in the abstract. Nor do they deny that this enables human believers to engage in *deliberative thinking*—thinking about what to do or think in the light of this or that consideration. What they deny is that the explanatorily central elements among our attitudes—beliefs, desires, and perhaps intentions—necessarily involve the reflective capacities required for deliberative thinking. The attraction of such a view is obvious. It is entirely natural to think of a pet dog, say, as wanting its food and believing that it is about to get it. Or consider the squirrel in my garden, which is clearly trying to get at the nuts suspended in a mesh basket from the bird-table. First it tries to reach the nuts from the pole that supports the table. When this does not succeed it climbs on to the table and tries to reach down for the nuts. Feeling it is losing balance it comes back up and then, with its tail curled around part of the structure on the table, it stretches upside down to its full length and reaches the basket. It seems natural to describe the squirrel as wanting to get at the nuts, even as intending to do so. It adopts various means to this end until something works. If nothing had worked it would eventually have given up. Assuming that dogs and squirrels lack the capacity for deliberative thinking, it might seem that we are faced with the option of either denying an intentional psychology to such creatures or denying that beliefs and intentions implicate a capacity for deliberative thinking. But these options are not exhaustive. There is also a view that accommodates *both* the claim that believing and intending, as they figure in our ascriptions of beliefs and intentions to one another, implicate the capacity for deliberative thinking, *and* the claim that non-human animals lacking the capacity for deliberative thinking have an intentional psychology. We can, without inconsistency, credit dogs and squirrels with, for instance, belief-like states, or with beliefs in some thin sense that covers different psychological kinds, while holding that *our* beliefs are inextricably tied to a capacity for deliberative thinking. So the desirability of making sense of animal intentionality is not a decisive objection against the high conception of belief and intention that I am defending. But is it yet clear that we should adopt such a conception?

The issue facing us at this point concerns two distinct ways of thinking of the difference between human intentionality and the intentionality of non-human animals lacking the capacity for deliberative thinking. On one way of thinking, widely represented in current philosophy of mind, the difference is that between first-order intentional states and higher-order intentional states. Creatures with only first-order states lack the capacity to have intentional states that are about intentional states. Creatures with second-order intentionality can think about individuals as, for instance, believing this and desiring that, where the beliefs and desires in question are first-order. Creatures with third-order intentionality can think about second-order intentional states, and so on. On the picture now under consideration, the difference between the intentionality of creatures lacking the capacity for deliberative thinking and human intentionality is that between creatures with only first-order intentionality and creatures with higher orders of intentionality. This approach does not require us to think of the believing and intending of dogs and squirrels as differing, *qua* believing and intending, from our believing and intending. The difference between their believing and intending and ours lies in the range of subject-matter that can figure in the relevant contents, not in the intrinsic psychological character of the believing and intending. On the other approach, which I favour, believing and intending, conceived as psychological commitments with a normative dimension are at the centre of human intentionality. What is the fundamental reason for adopting this approach? The answer is implicit in the discussion of Chapter 4. It is that any theory that represents believing and intending as lacking an intrinsic normative dimension fails to provide an adequate account of the psychological role of beliefs and intentions. Among other things, it is powerless to explain the peculiarity of our relationship to our own current beliefs and intentions (recall Section 4 of Chapter 4). If intending to Φ is simply a matter of being so set that under suitable conditions, and in the absence of a change of mind, distractions, and so forth, one will Φ, then it would be readily intelligible that I should adopt a purely contemplative stance towards my current intention to Φ. It would be just as intelligible as my adopting a purely contemplative stance towards a character trait that I know I have. If this were right there would be no difference, other than of content, between my predicting that I will become irritated in the presence of someone I dislike, and my predicting that I shall be taking certain steps in order to carry out an intention. In both cases the prediction would be based on the assumption that dispositions I take myself to have will, under suitable conditions, be manifested. This presents a distorted picture of our relationship to our intentions and our expectations about how we shall carry them out.[71] In regarding myself as currently intending to Φ I regard Φing as an end I have set myself. In doing that I think of my Φing not simply as something that, under suitable conditions, will come about. Rather, I view my Φing as something that, in and of itself, enjoins me either to do what is necessary or to give up the intention. If I anticipate doing the necessary, I do so on the ground that I am (psychologically) committed to Φing and, therefore, to doing what that takes. In this way I think of myself as the agent of my Φing, and of what has to be done to that end. I do not view myself simply as one who, because I have certain dispositions and tendencies, is likely to do certain things.

All this is implicit in the previous chapter. It helps to address a problem that some might think affects the dialectic presented there. I discussed a strategy on which it is conceded that ascriptions of beliefs and intentions have normative import for those to whom the beliefs and intentions are ascribed, and an attempt is made to explain that normative import without using the assumption that the ascriptions are normative. The idea was that, when an ascription of a belief or intention to someone is true, then some statement to the effect that the subject incurs a certain commitment is also true, but we are not to suppose that this statement is *implied* by the ascription. I criticized this strategy. Some may feel that the criticized strategy is too concessive to my position. If normative import is to be understood in terms of the notion of normative commitment, and normative commitments can be incurred only by creatures with suitable capacities, then it should not be assumed that all ascriptions of beliefs and intentions have normative import. They will have normative import for those to whom the beliefs or intentions are ascribed only if

---

[71] Closely related themes may be found in Hampshire (1959; 1965).

these subjects have appropriate reflective capacities. For this reason theorists who take it for granted that creatures lacking such capacities have beliefs or intentions might think that things have been unfairly stacked up against their position.

In fact, I did not presuppose that all ascriptions of beliefs and intentions have normative import. The claim was that ascriptions *to rational agents*, conceived as having appropriate reflective capacities, have normative import. Those who think that non-human animals have beliefs and intentions, in just the same sense in which we have beliefs and intentions, still need to explain why, for those who have the requisite capacities, beliefs and intentions incur normative commitments. Any attempt to provide an explanation will run into the problem already identified. If believing and intending lack an intrinsic normative dimension, then it is hard to see why our beliefs and intentions, in the presence of appropriate reflective capacities, should give rise to the commitments. As I observed earlier, there is a question of whether the Means–End Ideal and the Implication Ideal would be ideals of reason if intending and believing lacked a normative dimension. These ideals become problematic on the assumption that there is no intrinsic normative dimension to believing or intending. If we are to think of belief and intention as being on a par with proneness to being irritable, so far as its dispositional character is concerned, then it is obscure why reason enjoins, for instance, that we avoid persisting with an intention while never getting around to carrying it out. We would need to posit some value or concern to explain why we have reason to abandon the intention or take the steps necessary to carry it out. Suppose it is said that, if we have an intention *and* it is desirable, or it matters to us, that the intention be carried out, then there is reason to avoid persisting with it while never getting around to carrying it out. The trouble then is that it is bizarre to imagine that it is open to us to discriminate between intentions that we care about fulfilling and others that we do not care about fulfilling. Our intentions set our ends and our ends are what we care about achieving. Some no doubt matter to us more than others, but nothing is truly an end unless we have some concern that it should be achieved. There is no need to posit an additional value or concern to explain why we should do the necessary or abandon the intention; it is enough that we have the intention.

The lesson I think we should draw from these reflections is that some of our knowledge of ourselves is not about mere habits or dispositions, non-normatively conceived. It is knowledge of ourselves as being subject to, and set to shape our thought and action by, commitments incurred by our beliefs and intentions.

2. Reflexivity

It is an implication of the view I have been defending that believing and intending involve a certain *reflexivity* since their impact on thought and action is shaped by the subject's knowledge of those very beliefs and intentions. One can appreciate what a belief or intention commits one to only if one knows one has that belief or intention. In what follows I provide further support for the overall picture by focusing on considerations that make reflexivity plausible but are independent of the view that belief and intention are inextricably normative.[72] The following two sets of claims are crucial.

(a) A characteristic role of intentions is to get us to do things by way of carrying out those intentions. When we carry out an intention, or attempt to do so, we know what we are doing. That involves knowing that we have the intention and that doing the thing in question is by way of carrying it out.
(b) A characteristic role of beliefs is to supply assumptions that form or contribute to our reasons for belief or action. When our beliefs do this we know that the assumptions are ones we believe and that we are relying on them.

These claims do not imply that the *only* psychological effects of beliefs and intentions are ones that depend on the subjects' knowledge of what they believe or intend. When it seems right to assent to some suggestion, we need not know what motivates our assent. The explanation for its feeling right to assent might lie in other beliefs we have. But the very fact that we are unclear about the basis of our

---

[72] It is not unusual to think of intentions as sophisticated states implicating reflective capacities. It has been claimed that intentions implicate belief or knowledge that one has the intention (Hampshire 1959: 101–3; Harman 1976: sect. II) and that intentions have contents that are self-referential (Harman 1976; Searle 1983; Velleman 1989). I touch on the latter view below.

assent casts doubt on whether this is a case of assenting *for a reason*. There will be a reason why, but that does not suffice to make the case one of believing for a reason. It is also important to stress that the view does not imply that subjects always know what they believe or what they intend. The point is that when beliefs and intentions function in the characteristic ways specified, respectively, by (a) and (b), subjects know that they have the beliefs and intentions in question. This is compatible with its being possible that subjects should have beliefs and intentions of which they are unaware.

3. Intention and reflexivity

On any plausible view of the matter, having an intention involves being in a state that has motivational power. Agents who have such intentions must be motivated to do what they intend and must have some propensity to take the steps they believe to be necessary to this end. With regard to many of our intentions, there is a significant period of time between their formation and their fulfilment. For much of that period the agent is not preoccupied with, or in any way engaged by, activities relevant to carrying out the intention. So it is of some interest to consider how intentions like these get us to do the things we intend. I argue that we can make sense of how such intentions lead to actions that consist in, or are steps towards, carrying them out only on the assumption that the agent views these actions as done by way of carrying out the intention. I shall consider two aspects to this issue. The first concerns plans for carrying out intentions to act some time later. The second, which I discuss in the next section, concerns what I call the *precariousness* of some of these intentions.

If we intend to do something some time hence, then we need to have some idea of how to go about it. In this connection it is common to speak of intentions as implicating a plan for carrying them out (see e.g. Bratman 1987; Mele 1992). That is fine so far as future-directed intentions are concerned, but it needs to be borne in mind that the plan may be very rough and ready. It may involve little more than an idea of the steps that would be needed to go about finding out what needs to be done and some idea of the time-constraints on carrying out the intention. How will my intention to have a holiday abroad within the next couple of months lead to action, assuming that it does? It may not do so immediately. What is likely to happen is that I find myself from time to time saying or thinking things like, 'I'd better settle on where to go' and 'I'll need to book flights'. Once I have settled on where to go, I shall probably have further thoughts—'I still have not booked a hotel for my trip', 'I must make arrangements for the cat to be looked after'. In one way or another, I am prompted to do things necessary to carry out my intention and to deal with what I shall not be able to do if I am on holiday. Whatever the details, any action towards carrying out the intention is not done blindly. I take action *with a view to* carrying out the intention and thus in the knowledge of what I intend.

The importance of knowledge of one's own intentions in these cases can be further brought out by consideration of how plans are implemented. I take a plan to be a more or less detailed specification of a course of action leading to a certain goal.[73] A plan in this sense is not necessarily a plan for carrying out an intention. (Contingency plans are still plans.) To have a plan for carrying out an intention is to have an intention to carry out the intention by implementing the plan. Does that mean that there must be a further plan—to carry out the intention to carry out the original intention by implementing the original plan, and so on indefinitely? No, because not all intentions need plans. At some point in implementing a plan one simply acts without the need of a plan. For instance, having walked to the local travel agent, I turn into the office at the right point. This is intentional but the relevant intention does not require a plan. I need no plan for getting myself to turn into the travel agent when the appropriate point comes. I just do it. (Yet I do not do it blindly. In so far as I do it by way of carrying out my intention to call at the travel agent, I know what I am doing.)

It is not a sufficient condition of a plan's being implemented that I merely do the things specified in it. Though it would be strange, it is certainly possible that I should do the things specified by my plan for taking a holiday even though my motivation for doing these things has nothing to do with the intention. Suffering from amnesia, I could forget all about the intention and then, by remarkable coincidence,

---

[73] In this respect I follow Mele (1992: 109).

do the various things required by the plan. To implement the plan for carrying out my intention, I must be *guided* by the plan. Notice that it is not even enough that when doing the things specified by the plan, like booking flights, I should think of these things as things that enable me to take a holiday. Though it would be strange, I could think of them in this way while it is still an open question for me whether I am going to take a holiday. To be implementing the plan I must be doing things it specifies *by way of*, that is *with a view to*, taking the intended holiday.

Opponents of reflexivity might resist these claims by suggesting that subjects can be guided by a plan without representing the plan to themselves. This way of thinking might be encouraged by discussions of rule-following. There are various activities that seem to be rule-governed although those who engage in these activities need not explicitly represent the relevant rules to themselves. When we use language meaningfully in speech and writing we do not do so haphazardly. We conform by and large to various regularities. We tend to apply the term 'dog' to dogs and not to elephants, and those who hear us use the term 'dog' will generally take us to be talking about dogs. Rules are said to come into the picture because uses of words can be correct or incorrect and thus, one might think, in accord with or in breach of some rule. If I apply 'dog' to a fox whose foxy nature is manifest—it's standing right in front of me—it looks as if I have not only falsely applied the term but have made some kind of linguistic mistake. My use of 'dog' does not seem to be governed by the right rule.[74] The problem in this area is to make sense of what it is to be guided by a rule. On the one hand, it is clear that to be guided by a rule it is not enough that one's behaviour should be in accord with the rule. On the other hand, it is no good supposing that being guided by rules is like being guided by the instructions in a recipe book.[75] The problem arises precisely because there are activities that it is tempting to regard as being rule-governed *despite* the fact that explicit representations of the rules are not available. There is, in addition, the consideration that a regress threatens on the assumption that the rules

---

[74] Discussions of rule-following do not routinely distinguish between mere false application and failure to observe a rule. A fuller discussion of related matters may be found in Ch. 6.
[75] This dialectic has it origins in Wittgenstein (1958). It is explicitly set out in Sellars (1963a), Millikan (1990), and Pettit (1993).

function as explicit instructions: there would have to be rules governing the interpretation of the rules, rules governing the interpretation of *those* rules, and so on. (This line of thought is fairly explicit in Wittgenstein 1958.) The problem then is to make sense of being guided by rules of which one does not have explicit representations. Though it is fair to say that there is no generally accepted way of spelling this out, the upshot has been a willingness to believe that there must be some sense in which people are guided by rules that they do not explicitly represent to themselves. Against this background, it might seem that I have not done justice to the idea that those who intend to do something may in some sense be guided by a plan associated with the intention that they do not think of as the plan for carrying out the intention.

Whatever is the right approach on the problem of rule-following, there are obvious differences between being guided by plans of action and being guided, if we are, by rules governing the use of language. In the language case there is pressure, arising from the phenomenon itself, to take seriously the idea of being guided in the absence of explicit representations of what guides us. There is not the same kind of pressure arising from the phenomenon itself to take seriously the idea of being guided by plans that we do not explicitly represent to ourselves. Plans are the sorts of things that people do represent to themselves. And, as I stressed above, not all intentional action requires the implementation of plans. Some pressure to consider modes of guidance by plans that do not implicate explicit representations of plans linked to intentions comes from the supposed desideratum that a theory of intention should confine itself to first-order intentionality. The motivation for taking this to be a desideratum is supplied by the familiar thought that there are non-human animals that have an intentional psychology, yet lack the resources to represent plans or intentions to themselves. As I have been at pains to stress already, even if that thought is true, it does not dictate that such creatures have *intentions* or, if they have intentions, that they carry them out by implementing plans. It is hard not to believe that non-human animals pursue goals guided by information they receive about their environments. The squirrel in my garden is regularly bent on getting at the nuts that are meant to be for birds. Though this makes it fairly natural in everyday talk to describe the squirrel as intending to get at the nuts, we are not compelled to ascribe full-blown intentions to it, even on the assumption that it has an intentional psychology. Not all goal-directed activity is intentional action (see Chapter 2, Section 2). We ourselves engage in sub-intentional goal-directed activity in the course of doing things intentionally. When intentionally walking through doors, we adjust our movements in ways that usually ensure that we do not bump into door frames or into people coming in the opposite direction. Usually such adjustments are sub-intentional. They are directly controlled by perceptual cues without any need on our part to form intentions to execute particular movements. It is not just that there is no need for the *conscious* formation of intentions. The point is that we as agents are not involved in making the adjustments in the way that we are involved in doing what we intend.[76] Sub-intentional activity, so long as it remains sub-intentional, is always sensitive to perceptual cues the practical significance of which need not surface at the level of propositional attitudes. Let it be granted that the squirrel displays sub-intentional goal-directed activity. In attributing to it an intention we go beyond the attribution of sub-intentional activity, using a description that over-determines the state it is in.

There is good reason not to assimilate acting on an intention to the kind of goal-directed activity that may account for the sub-intentional activity I have been talking about. The point I am making can be made vivid with the help of a fictional example. One of the classic films of Cold War paranoia is John Frankenheimer's *The Manchurian Candidate*. In the film some American soldiers are captured by the enemy and 'brainwashed'. One in particular has been put into a state such that he will obey any instruction he is given once he has been primed by a procedure that involves turning over playing cards. (Sometimes the procedure is initiated by others. Sometimes the agent is prompted to go through it himself by a formulaic phone call, to which he is also primed to respond.) The enemy's aim is to use him as an assassin, and eventually to make him kill a presidential candidate back in the United States. When the agent receives the instructions he intentionally carries them out. He intends to kill a specified target, and when he does what this requires it seems that he

---

[76] Velleman (2000b: 19) calls the kind of activity I am talking about *sub-agential*.

knows that it is with a view to killing that person. What he lacks is any idea of what is causing him to act as instructed. He has intentions to kill particular people and intentions to take appropriate means, but he does not intend *to do whatever he is instructed to do following the procedure with the cards* and does not know why he is set on killing the target when he is. (This interpretation is at least consistent with the action. Presumably in these phases we must suppose that he lacks the normal means of monitoring the significance of what one is doing, for otherwise he would be stopped from killing by his realization that he does not know why he is set on doing so). There is a plan to which this man is conforming. The plan is that he act as instructed following the card-turning procedure. Moreover, it is no accident that he is conforming to this plan because, we are to suppose, he has been 'programmed' to do so. Some may wish to describe him as being guided by the plan. But even if he is guided by it, in the sense of being programmed to do as the plan specifies, it is not a plan for carrying out an intention to do whatever he is instructed to do following the procedure, for he has no such intention. I am not suggesting that there are theorists who would ascribe to this character such an intention. The point is this: suppose that an agent is conceived as implementing a plan for carrying out an intention, without knowing that he is doing so, or even knowing that he has the intention. Then his relation to the supposed intention would be like this character's relation to whatever it is that disposes him to do whatever he is instructed to do following the procedure. But the strangeness of his behaviour lies precisely in the fact that he is programmed to follow the instructions issued after the procedure. In thinking of him as being programmed, we are contrasting his state with that of someone who intends to do whatever he is so instructed to do. He does behave in a goal-directed manner, but the goal governs his behaviour at the sub-intentional level.

At this point it might be suggested that, although agents who implement plans linked to those intentions must represent *the plans* to themselves, they need not represent themselves as having those intentions. In pursuing the means to carrying out my intention, it might be said, I need to think of what I am doing as something I need to do *in order to take a holiday*; the representations I need are about relations between possible actions, not about my intention. But everything depends on the nature of the relationships. I may know that ordering flight tickets will contribute towards my taking a holiday and yet it might not be the case that the point of my ordering the flight tickets is that it will enable me to take a holiday. Of course, it is part of the scenario that I do what is in the plan in order to take a holiday, but what we are considering now is whether we can make sense of this without invoking thinking on my part about my intention. I do not myself see how we can.

The claim that future-directed intentions are reflexive is in harmony with the view that the contents of intentions are self-referential (Harman 1976; Searle 1983: chapter 3; Velleman 1989: 96; contrast Mele 1992). The idea is that if I intend to Φ then the content of my intention is *that I Φ by way of carrying out that very intention*. The simplest way to see why it might be thought that intention is self-referential is through examples in which a person, who intends to Φ, Φs because of the intention, yet not by way of carrying out of the intention. In a variant of a famous example of Davidson (1973/1980: 79), a climber forms an intention to rid himself of the weight at the end of his rope, knowing that the climber attached to the rope will fall to his death. He becomes so nervous at the very thought that the other climber will fall to his death that this causes him to let go of the rope. The intention led to his letting go of the rope, but he did not let go of the rope by way of carrying out the intention. To carry out an intention to Φ it is not enough that one Φ, or even that one's intention should have led to one's Φing. One must have Φed *by way of* carrying out the intention. But now, if an intention is carried out only if the action intended is done by way of carrying out the intention, this should be reflected in the content of the intention: the content should specify a condition necessary and sufficient for the intention to be carried out. As we have seen, it is not sufficient for carrying out my intention to Φ that I should Φ. By the assumption about content, it follows that the content of my intention is not given by the proposition that I Φ; it must be given by a clause to the effect that I Φ *by way of carrying out this intention to do so* (Searle 1983: 83–6). The content of my intention, therefore, must make reference to that very intention. It seems plausible that this view presupposes that intention is reflexive in my sense. It is hard to see what doing something by way of carrying out an intention would be if the agent need not know that he or she is carrying out, or at least trying to carry out, the intention.

4. Precarious intentions

If we are to carry out intentions to do things some time hence, our intentions have to connect psychologically with the steps we take to carry them out. I have been arguing that the connection involves our knowledge of what we intend and of the fact that we take the steps with a view to carrying out the intention. Cases of precariousness serve to reinforce the point. These are cases in which the intention might easily not be carried out because it does not come to mind. If it is carried out, this is thanks to a bit of luck. The luck consists in the occurrence of something that brings the intention to mind but which might easily not have done so.

Intending to do something is settling on doing that thing. For it to be true that one is settled on doing something, the psychological commitment to doing that thing must be fairly stable. One will tend to change one's mind only if there seems to be a reason to do so. This stability should not be conflated with what I shall call *inertia*.[77] An intention has inertia—is something like an inertial force—if it will lead to action aimed at fulfilling it so long as there is no change of mind and there are no obstacles or distractions. By 'obstacles' I mean factors that block attempts to carry out the intention. By 'distractions' I mean factors, like having one's attention diverted, that cause one to lose track of an intention that would otherwise have been acted upon. My intention to take a holiday has inertia. It takes a lot to arrange the holiday and because of this I shall be prone to think about it from time to time. Some intentions may not loom so large in one's thinking. Working at home, I form an intention to return a book to a colleague from whom I have borrowed it. I mean to take the book with me when the time comes to set out for the campus. I do not expect to do anything in the interim, trusting that I shall remember to take the book. But suppose that I forget all about the book. Intentions can easily end up in this way. The phenomenon raises an issue about how

---

[77] Thus my use of the term 'inertia' is somewhat different from that of Bratman (1987).

we should conceive of the motivational power of an intention. On the one hand, we are inclined to suspect that avowals of intention are insincere if nothing happens towards carrying out the avowed intentions, even though there are no distractions, or obstacles, or a change of mind. This is where the model of intention as inertial force comes into play. On the other hand, it seems that we can have intentions and yet do nothing to carry them out, even though we are not distracted, there are no obstacles, and we do not change our minds. It is these cases that I am describing as precarious.

Imagine two scenarios in which I intend to return the book. In one scenario, nothing else pertaining to taking the book occurs to me until I spot it as I am preparing to leave home. I duly take it. In the other scenario everything is exactly the same except that I do not spot the book and so do not take it. It would be entirely in accord with our everyday notion of intention to suppose that in the first scenario I carried out an intention I formed earlier. Not only did I do what I intended to do; I did it, not blindly, but by way of carrying out my intention. Had I been asked why I was taking the book I would unhesitatingly have replied by saying something to the effect that I had to return it to my colleague. If in this scenario there was an intention formed and carried out, then it is hard to see why the second scenario should not be a case of genuine intention. Note that in this scenario there is no change of mind—the intention is retained. Nor is it a case of being prevented from carrying out the intention—nothing interfered with carrying it out. Nor was there any distraction in the sense in which I have been using that term—I was not distracted from doing something I would have done but for the distraction. I just forgot about the intention. Some intentions—the precarious ones—need a bit of luck. One who has an intention to do something some time hence had better have that intention come to mind, but whether the intention does come to mind can easily depend on co-operation from the surrounding world or from the haphazard comings and goings of our mental life. Intentions are retained in memory, at least for a time, or recorded in lists or diaries. But whether an intention stored in this way is recollected—the memory or record accessed—depends on the contingencies of the agent's circumstances and mental life. It requires a fair wind. In a case of intending to return the book, the element of fair wind might have been supplied by my happening to glance at the book as I packed my bag before leaving. Had the book been covered by a sheet of paper or been on a shelf I might well have gone without it. My glancing at the book was to a degree a matter of luck, but it is not so lucky that my not having taken steps in advance to eliminate that element of luck counts against my having genuinely intended to take the book. Well-organized people take special steps to increase the chance that they will carry out their intentions. They make lists, keep diaries, and solicit the help of others to remind them of things. But intentions are not the prerogative of the well organized. Of course, if I know I am absent-minded and liable to forget things, then one might wonder how serious my intention is if I don't take steps to make it more likely that I will remember it. An agent who leaves too much to chance lacks serious intent. But we set the requirements for intention too high if we overlook the fact that carrying out intentions can depend on chance factors. All intentions have some degree of stability in that they are resistant to changes of mind without reason, but not all intentions have inertia. Precariousness contrasts with inertia but is compatible with stability.

I have discussed examples of future-directed intentions that lack inertia to reinforce the point that the psychological thread connecting our intentions with future action that consists in, or is a step towards, carrying it out depends on our knowledge of our own intentions. In the case of precarious intentions, it is especially clear that the knowledge has to come to mind in (conscious) recollection, for it is only such recollection that prompts action.

5. Unreflective intention

One might wonder though whether it is plausible that intentions in general are reflexive. What are we to say about unreflective intentions—the ones that have not been consciously formed and may not give rise to conscious thoughts about carrying them out?

When I am at the university I usually intend to return home in the evening. I do not decide in advance each day that I shall do so. And because I do not need to remind myself that I intend to return home, and hardly ever need to tell anyone that I am on my way home, the intention rarely comes to mind in any very definite form and so is rarely consciously endorsed. I just go home as part of a regular routine. It might seem less natural than it is in the cases I have been considering to think of this sort of intention as being reflexive. What is true is that carrying out my routine intention to return home does not require me to recollect that I so intend. But in carrying it out I know what I am doing, and if things do not go smoothly then, barring some odd psychological condition, this knowledge will come into play. If my car were to break down I would be liable to wonder how I was going to get home. If for some unforeseen reason I had to go somewhere other than home, I would be liable to take into account my family's expectations and let them know what was happening.

In some cases in which things do not go smoothly, the effect of the absence of knowledge of what we are doing is striking. While working in my university office, I realize that I need some envelopes. I set off for the departmental store to get some, but I am distracted by thinking about other things. By the time I get to the store, I have forgotten why I needed to go there. My arrival at the store is certainly caused by my having formed an intention to get some envelopes and setting off to do so. I intentionally headed towards the store, knowing what I was doing; but by the time I arrived at the store I did not know what I was doing. At that point I was not carrying out my intention. As I ceased to know what I was doing, it ceased to be true that I was carrying out an intention to pick up some envelopes and that I was there for that reason.

6. The reflexivity of belief

In Section 2, I summed up the reflexivity of belief in these terms:

A characteristic role of beliefs is to supply assumptions that form or contribute to our reasons for belief or action. When our beliefs do this we know that the assumptions are ones we believe and that we are relying on them.

Irrespective of whether one accepts these claims, it is hard to deny that our beliefs very often figure in our psychology in ways that bring into play reflective capacities. At least typically, if we believe P we are able to (i) acknowledge that we believe P if the issue arises, (ii) engage in reflection as to whether P is true, plausible, or compatible with other things we believe or know, and (iii) engage in reflection as to why we believe P. These points can hardly be denied. The serious question is whether, if believing is stripped of these reflective abilities, we are left with anything recognizable as believing. Theorists have, I think, been too ready to give an affirmative answer to that question. One motive, which I have touched upon more than once, derives from a concern to make sense of animal intentionality. Another derives from the assumption that the thought-and-action-guiding role of belief simply does not require subjects to have those reflective capacities. When we drive along a road with busy traffic we are constantly adjusting our speed and more or less radically adjusting our direction of travel. If it is our perceptually gained beliefs that are guiding us then, it might be thought, they must surely do so in ways that do not involve our knowingly, far less consciously, relying upon the truth of their contents. What is surely right about this line of thought is that, as a result of perception, we have information-bearing states that control our behaviour in a fairly direct manner. If, as mooted earlier, we engage in sub-intentional goal-directed activity, then it seems plausible that such activity is guided by cues that do not figure at the level of beliefs. When we register such cues it is by means of sub-doxastic informational states that stand to beliefs as sub-intentional aims stand to intentions. It can hardly be doubted that we take in information in the way that I am calling sub-doxastic. We do so when catching a ball that has been thrown high in the air, or returning a shot at table tennis. In either of these cases, we track the trajectory of the ball and adjust our position and hand movements accordingly. The cues to which we are responding are not all registered at the level of belief. (Try spelling out what the beliefs are in ways that are specific enough to account for the all the adjustments we make in response to perceived cues.)

It is doubtful that we need to posit beliefs shorn of the reflective capacities that are at least typically linked to our beliefs in order to make sense of the intentionality of creatures that lack such reflective capacities as are implicated in our own mental life. To argue that there is such a need, it would have to be shown that the functions that seem to call for the ascription of beliefs and intentions could not be fulfilled by sub-doxastic states. I suspect that the cases in which we can confidently ascribe beliefs and intentions with specified contents coincide with the cases in which subjects have the kind of reflective capacities that I have been considering.

I shall leave the matter there for the present but I discuss closely related matters in later chapters. In Chapter 7, I shall argue that we can make clear sense of what it is to believe or act for a reason only when subjects know what their reasons are. In Chapter 6, I make a case for thinking that the employment of the concepts that our propositional attitudes bring into play implicates reflective capacities.

7. Self-deception

I have claimed (Chapter 4) that beliefs and intentions are psychological commitments that, as such, have a normative dimension. When we consciously attribute to ourselves a current belief, for instance, we endorse the normative commitments that having such a belief incurs. It might be thought that this view is falsified by examples showing that we are perfectly capable of taking a more detached attitude to our own current beliefs.

Michael Martin discusses the case of a mildly self-deceiving father who believes that his son is a fine painter on no very good evidence. (The example originates from Dennett 1978: chapter 3, and is discussed by Peacocke 1998, to whom Martin is responding.) If the father were to reflect on the facts of the matter carefully, he would probably reach the judgement that his son is not a fine painter at all. Yet, reflecting on his own beliefs, he might realize that he does really think that his son is a fine painter. Martin suggests that it is possible that the father 'should be led to a sense of a lack of inner integrity, feeling forced to distance himself from what he recognizes is one of his own strongly held convictions' (Martin 1998: 115). He cites other cases, which avoid the complications of self-deception but, he thinks, illustrate this kind of distancing. For instance, in pursuing a philosophical issue one might find that one has a strong conviction that something is so, though one lacks firm arguments in its support. Martin suggests that in such a case one's conviction might guide action, for instance by taking one's research in a particular direction, even if one distances oneself from its commitments. The distancing might be manifested by hesitancy in discussion with others. The tendency of these considerations is against the view that in self-ascribing a current belief one thereby endorses the normative commitments that such a belief incurs.

I think the best response to Martin's cases is to draw upon some observations made in Chapter 2 Section 2. There are attitudes other than belief that are directed at truth. Some of these we mark with special terms, like 'conjecture' or 'guess'. Reflection on cases may suggest that there are other truth-directed attitudes for which we have no names readily to hand. In ordinary usage the term 'belief' ranges widely, covering attitudes that really should be distinguished. Nothing, I think, compels us to describe the father as both consciously recognizing and yet distancing himself from a belief to the effect that his son is a fine painter. There is an attitude that could be described as *not quite believing but being prepared to think and act as if –*. My own inclination is to think that, in so far as the father does truly distance himself from an attitude he has about his son's painting skills, this attitude is better described in these terms rather than as belief. The attitude has a role that is in some respects like belief. The father will be liable to encourage his son, praise him when speaking with others, hold back from criticizing his son's work, and so on. There is a genuine phenomenon here. Martin thinks of it in terms of the father's distancing himself from one of his own beliefs. I find it more plausible to think of him as having an attitude that falls short of, but in some respects resembles, belief. The difference might emerge only in a situation in which the issue as to the son's abilities is forced, as it would be if an expert were to provide cogent reasons for doubting the quality of the work.

This approach also works in relation to the other cases Martin alludes to. We already have names for belief-like attitudes that might be in play in these situations. They are hunches or conjectures. If the degree of conviction informing hunches or conjectures sometimes seems stronger than is suggested by so calling them, this may be because the subject invests a great deal of effort in trying to show that the propositions in question are true.

More complex cases of self-deception may raise doubts about the conception of intention that I have been defending. A common view of what is happening in self-deception is that the agent intentionally acts to suppress or sustain certain beliefs in order to bring about desired ends. According to this view, it is in the nature of such cases that the self-deceiving agents are unaware of, or not fully aware of, what they are doing. So, although they are supposed to be carrying out intentions, they do not think of themselves as having those intentions or as carrying them out. Indeed, if they did think of themselves in this way the intention would be abandoned. I have acknowledged that intentions (and beliefs) can have psychological effects of which the subject is unaware, and I have not ruled out of court the possibility that there might be beliefs and intentions of which the subject is unaware, but I have defended the following claim about intention that I set out at the beginning of Section 2:

(a) A characteristic role of intentions is to get us to do things by way of carrying out those intentions. When we carry out an intention, or attempt to do so, we know what we are doing. That involves knowing that we have the intention and that doing the thing in question is by way of carrying it out.

If we can carry out intentions that we do not realize we have, then (a) is false. If the phenomenon we call self-deception requires us to posit such intentions, then we should reject (a). I do not think we need posit the kind of intentions that present the problem. In what follows I discuss a subtle and imaginative defence of a view about self-deception that on the most plausible reading implies that there are such intentions.

Sebastian Gardner (1993) has argued that 'all self-deception involves what can be called a *structure of motivated self-misrepresentation*'. This is defined as:

A structure in which a psychological state S prevents the formation of another state S′, where (i) S involves a misrepresentation of the subject, (ii) this feature is necessary for S to prevent the formation of S′, and (iii) this structure answers to the subject's motivation. (Gardner 1993: 18)

Gardner thinks there is a special kind of self-deception—*strong self-deception*. This is 'a structure of motivated misrepresentation in which S and S′ are *beliefs* and the process occurs through an *intention* of the subject's' (1993: 19). Gardner argues for strong self-deception drawing upon an analysis of, among other things, the self-deception

154 THE REFLEXIVITY OF INTENTION AND BELIEF

ascribed by Tolstoy to his character Anna Karenina. It is useful to have before us the passage Gardner discusses:

At first Anna had avoided the Princess Tverskoy's set as much as she could, because it meant living beyond her means and also because she really preferred the other [intellectual set]; but since her visit to Moscow all this was reversed. She avoided her serious-minded friends and went into high society. There she saw Vronsky and experienced a tremulous joy every time she met him. She met Vronsky most frequently at Betsy's, who had been born a Vronsky herself and was his cousin. Vronsky went wherever there was a chance of meeting Anna and whenever he could spoke to her of his love. She gave him no encouragement, but every time they met her heart quickened with the same feeling of animation that had seized her in the train the day she first saw him. She knew that at the sight of him joy lit up her eyes and drew her lips into a smile, and she could not quench the expression of that joy.

At first Anna sincerely believed that she was displeased with him for daring to pursue her; but soon after her return from Moscow, having gone to a party where she expected to meet him but to which he did not come, she distinctly realized, by the disappointment that overcame her, that she had been deceiving herself and that his pursuit was not only not distasteful to her, but was the whole interest of her life. (Tolstoy 1954: 143)

On Gardner's analysis, Anna's self-deception is a case of motivated misrepresentation. The states involved (corresponding, respectively, to S and S′ in the schema above) are a *promoted belief* that she is displeased with Vronsky's pursuit of her, and a *buried belief* that she ought to renounce Vronsky. There are two chains of causation: (a) Anna's desire for Vronsky causes her to desire to bury the belief (not to believe) that she ought to renounce him; (b) her desire to bury this belief causes her to desire to believe that she is displeased with Vronsky.

There are two main steps in the argument to show that there is intentional self-misrepresentation here. The first is the claim that in both the causal sequences identified there is a relation of instrumentality (Gardner 1993: 21). Anna's burying the belief that she ought to renounce Vronsky is instrumental to satisfying her desire for Vronsky. Her promoting the belief that she is displeased with Vronsky is instrumental to satisfying her desire to bury the belief that she ought to renounce him. (If she were to believe that she is displeased with Vronsky, then no danger would be attached to being in his company and there would be no need to believe that she ought to renounce him.) The second main step in the argument is in support of the claim that there is no way of explicating the relations of instrumentality other than on the assumption that Anna intends certain means towards ends that she desires (1993: 21). The idea is that Anna intended to bury the belief that she ought to renounce Vronsky *in order to* satisfy her desire for Vronsky, and that she intended to come to believe that she was displeased with Vronsky *in order to* satisfy her desire to bury the belief that she ought to renounce him. Gardner argues:

> Any sparser story, that seeks to dispense with an intention in favour of wishful thinking and non-rational dispositions, will entail a conception of mental processing in which a desire can avail itself of the services of the right means miraculously—i.e., without the need of reasoning to determine which are the right instruments for a desire to make use of. It follows that self-deceptive intent is required by the nature of practical reason. (Gardner 1993: 22)

The suggestion is that it would be a miracle if Anna were to be caused by her desire for Vronsky to bury her belief that she ought to renounce him if she had not intended to satisfy her desire by burying the belief. Similarly, it would be a miracle if Anna were to be caused to believe that she was displeased with Vronsky by her desire to bury the belief that she ought to renounce him if she had not intended to satisfy the desire by coming to believe that she was displeased.

If this account is right, then either Anna is carrying out intentions without realizing that she is doing so, or a part of her represents herself to herself as carrying out those intentions. The latter option is unappealing. Apart from the doubtfulness of positing parts of the self, functioning in effect as distinct centres of agency (on which, see Gardner 1993: chapter 3), it seems implausible that the intentions should be ones about which Anna would know at any level. The problem is to see how the intentions could survive the realization by Anna *at any level* that she has them. But if we avoid positing parts of the self, functioning as distinct centres of agency, then we seem driven to conclude that Anna does not know she has these intentions and so does not know that she is carrying them out. This conclusion is at odds with the account of the role of intention that I have been defending. On that account, we know what we are doing when we carry out intentions, even if we do not consciously think of ourselves as carrying them out. We are not compelled, however, to believe that cases like that of Anna exhibit intentional self-deception.

The central belief is that she is displeased with Vronsky. There are three important points about this belief. The first is that it has a certain effect that from Anna's point of view is advantageous. So long she believes herself to be displeased with Vronsky, she can think of being in his company as holding no danger for her. The second point is that there is some reason for Anna to be displeased with Vronsky. She is a respectable married woman with a child whom she adores, a high social standing among the intellectuals of St Petersburg, and a husband who has an influential role in government. Her position would be threatened were she to pursue a liaison with Vronsky. Further, as Anna is aware, Vronsky had only recently been paying much attention to young Kitty Shcherbatsky, the sister of Anna's sister-in-law. At the stage of the narrative to which the quoted passage relates, Vronsky had behaved badly towards Kitty by ignoring her and being openly preoccupied with Anna. Given these considerations, Anna has reason to be displeased with Vronsky. So by thinking that she is displeased her gaze is deflected from the moral turmoil of not really being displeased when there are clear reasons to be so. The third point is that Anna was in an agitated state in which her own emotions were not wholly clear to her but in which she would certainly have experienced twinges of apprehension about her feelings towards Vronsky. The hypothesis that she *is* displeased with Vronsky would provide a way of making sense of at least some aspects of her agitation, quite apart from the advantageous effect of believing it true. There is, of course, a fact about Anna's state that is at odds with the idea that she is really displeased. She lights up in Vronsky's presence, and she knows that she does. But the danger attached to desiring him makes it unthinkable that she should indulge any such desire. So she does not think about the evidence of her desire and latches on to the less plausible hypothesis that she is displeased with him. She is sustained in believing this hypothesis by its psychological benefits—its enabling her to feel safe in Vronsky's company and to ignore the moral turmoil of being in his company—and by the fact that it provides a way of making sense of her emotional state. If Anna is deceived, it is only in the sense that her emotions have led to poor reasoning, and thereby to a false conclusion, about the state of her desires and feelings.

Under this interpretation, Anna does not act intentionally to bring it about that she believes herself to be displeased. Yet it is no miracle that she should come to have this belief. Here again, the notion of goal-directed sub-intentional activity can do some work. The goal is being comfortable both about being with Vronsky and about her acknowledged pleasure in his company. The activity that is directed towards this goal is a combination of evidence-avoidance and belief-sustenance. The evidence of her desire and of the dangers of attempting to satisfy that desire is ignored. She believes she is displeased because this makes some sense of her feelings. She avoids the evidence to the contrary because the belief does psychological work. She feels comfortable in Vronsky's presence.[78]

What then should we think about the idea that Anna intentionally buries the belief that she ought to renounce Vronsky? Certainly, we need an explanation of why she does not so believe, given that there clearly are reasons for her to renounce Vronsky. But an explanation is provided by the goal-directed activity already posited. Anna's avoidance of thinking about reasons for renunciation is of a piece with her avoidance of the evidence of her desire and the dangers of satisfying it. All this avoidance is directed at the goal of feeling comfortable about her relationship with him. The goal is achieved and the avoidance-activity reinforced.

This view of Anna's case treats her deceived state as a case of motivationally biased reasoning (Mele 1997; Lazar 1999). It is a case of blindness brought on by her desires, fears, and other feelings, rather than intentional self-deception. Anna is in a sense deceived, but if she is self-deceived, it is only in the sense that it is she herself who is misled by the workings of her own psychology.

José Bermúdez, defending intentional self-deception against the account of the phenomenon in terms of motivational bias, suggests that self-deception is selective in that '[a]ny explanation of a given instance of self-deception will need to explain why motivational bias

---

[78] Johnston (1988) is a perceptive account of the role of sub-intentional processes in self-deception.

occurred in *that* particular situation' (Bermúdez 2000: 317). This generates a *selectivity problem*: to explain why in some cases but not in others the desire that something be true should lead to the belief in it. The objection to this approach is that we are not bound to think of the phenomenon as one in which the subject wants something to be true and on that account comes to believe it. There *is* a selectivity problem: to explain why people do not always form beliefs when doing so would be psychologically advantageous to them. But to deal with this problem it is not necessary to posit desires to believe and self-deceptive intentions to satisfy these desires. In Anna's case there is a belief that she is displeased with Vronsky. The thought that she is displeased, as I have already suggested, is among those that might easily strike Anna as being true. In addition, her holding this belief enables her to think that being in Vronsky's company is not dangerous. That in turn enables her to feel comfortable in his presence. There is no need to assume that she starts out from a desire to believe that she is displeased which causes her to form the belief that she is. Rather, to sum up, there is a hypothesis about her condition with some initial plausibility, an alternative that is unthinkable, and subintentional—but goal-directed—avoidance of the evidence of the true state of her desires and feelings.

I have dwelt on a fictional example, yet it seems plausible that the phenomenon usually described as self-deception can in general be accounted for along the lines of my interpretation of Anna. If this is right, then it provides no objection to the view that intentions, when carried out, are knowingly carried out. I should repeat that it is not an implication of this view that the only psychological effects of our intentions are effects that we know stem from those intentions. For all that I have said, an intention to do something particularly unpleasant, or something that one feels guilty about, or which is otherwise troubling, might wreak psychological havoc that the agent does not realize is induced by the intention. A parallel claim holds for the effects of beliefs.

CHAPTER 6

Meaning and Intentional Content

1. The topic

So far I have been concerned with the normative dimension of believing and intending conceived as psychological commitments. My arguments have focused on characteristics of the attitudes of believing and intending. In this chapter I explore the normativity of meaning and of conceptual intentional content. The overarching aim is to make plausible the idea that *all* propositional attitudes, conceived as having conceptual content, have a normative dimension.

The issue about meaning arises from Saul Kripke's (1982) discussion of Wittgenstein on rule-following.[79] Kripke asks us to consider the relation that holds between meaning *plus* by '+' and answering questions like, 'What is the sum of 68 + 57?' A dispositional theory has it that if you mean *plus* by '+' then you will probably answer '125'. That is because, according to such a theory, to mean *plus* by '+' *is*, roughly speaking, to be disposed, by and large, and among other things, to answer such questions with the correct sum. Kripke wants to emphasize, by contrast, that if you mean *plus* by '+' then, faced with the question 'What is 68 + 57?' you *should* answer '125' (Kripke 1982: 37; cf. 11 and 23 f.). One could sum up the assumption about meaning that appears to underpin this criticism of dispositional theories in terms of the slogan that meaning is normative. Allan Gibbard gives us a way of reading that slogan which is suggested by Kripke's brief remarks:

The crux of the slogan that meaning is normative... might be another slogan: that *means* implies *ought*. To use roughly Kripke's example, from

---

[79] Much of the discussion of Kripke has, quite naturally, focused on meaning scepticism. I do not address that matter here. The articles in A. Miller (2002) address this topic, as does Tennant (1997).

statements saying what I mean by the plus sign and other arithmetic terms and constructions, it will follow that I *ought* to answer '7' when asked 'What's 5 + 2?' (Gibbard 1994: 100)

This way of interpreting the issue is in keeping with a central feature of the position on normativity adopted in this book. It assumes that there are certain statements that are paradigmatically normative—in this case, statements about what a subject ought to do—and it explains the normativity of other statements by reference to how they relate to the paradigmatic statements. (For some complications attached to this approach, see Chapter 3, Section 7.) Gibbard's paradigmatically normative statements—certain ought-statements—can be plausibly interpreted as implying statements that I regard as being paradigmatically normative—certain statements about reasons. However, for me the intuitive slogan about the normativity of meaning should be not 'Means implies ought', but 'Means implies (normatively) committed'. Recall at this point that it may well be that what a subject is committed to doing is not something the subject ought to do. A person may be committed to writing a letter of resignation by his intention to resign from his job, but it may be that he ought not to write the letter. Perhaps he ought to give up his intention to resign.

2. Normativity, correctness, and use

The claim that meaning is normative is sometimes formulated in terms of the idea that the meanings of words are associated with conditions of correct use. In this section I highlight a crucial ambiguity in the notion of correct use.

In his state-of-the-art article addressing issues raised by Kripke, Paul Boghossian writes:

> The normativity of meaning turns out to be . . . simply a new name for the familiar fact that, regardless of whether one thinks of meaning in truth-theoretic or assertion-theoretic terms, meaningful expressions possess conditions of *correct* use. (On the one construal, correctness consists in *true* use, on the other, in *warranted* use.) (Boghossian 1989: 513)

What interests me in this statement is the fact that 'use' is clearly being understood to mean something like *application* and correct use is understood to be true or warranted application.[80] To apply the term 'oak' is to predicate it of some object and thus say of that object that it is, depending on the context, oak (the type of wood) or an oak. With use understood to be application, correct use, naturally, is taken to be true or warranted application. But this is not the only way to characterize correct use. A number of discussions of rule-following (for example Wright 1980; McDowell 1984; McGinn 1984: 60) formulate the notion of correctness differently. They have it that a use of an expression is correct if and only if it is in accordance with (in keeping with, faithful to) the meaning of the expression.[81] Sometimes the two ways of thinking about correctness seem to be run together. Simon Blackburn, also addressing Kripke's discussion, writes:

> The topic is that there is such a thing as the correct and incorrect application of a term, and to say that there is such a thing is no more than to say that there is truth and falsity. I shall talk indifferently of there being correctness and incorrectness, of words being rule-governed, and of their obeying principles of application. (Blackburn 1984/Miller 2002: 28–9)

The chief point here, I think, is that where there is correctness and incorrectness in application there will be rules governing use, and there will be principles of application. That is fine, but the passage raises the question of whether correctness/incorrectness of application is the same as obeying/disobeying rules of use or being/not being faithful to the rules. Similar issues are raised by the following more recent explanation of the idea of the normativity of meaning:

> It is a central ingredient in understanding an expression to grasp that there are associated with it conditions for its correct application. Put another way, it is essential to any expression's possessing whatever meaning it does, that there are rules for its correct use. In this sense, meaning is normative. (from the glossary to Hale and Wright 1997: 674)

The passage invokes the notion of correct application, but also seems to allude to the idea that correct use is use in keeping with an expression's meaning—the meaning being fixed by rules for correct

---

[80] Even where correctness of use is not identified with truth or warrantedness of application, uses that are applications are commonly used to illustrate correctness of use. See e.g. McCulloch (1995: 100); Loewer (1997); and Horwich (1998: 92 ff.).

[81] The notion also seems to figure in Boghossian's discussion at the point at which he emphasizes that normativity has to do with a relation between meaning something by an expression at some time and the use of that expression at that time (Boghossian 1989: 513).

use. Furthermore, the explanation could be taken to suggest that these notions amount to the same thing. In any case, as with Blackburn's statement, the passage invites consideration of (a) the relation between application and use, (b) the relation between the two characterizations of correctness, and (c) the relation between what I shall call conditions of correct application and rules of correct use.

Use and application

Evidently use is wider than application. I use the term 'oak' when I ask, 'Is that an oak?' or when I say, 'Had that been an oak we would not have cut it down.' In neither of these cases do I apply the term to an object in the sense explained above, for my use of it does not consist in anything that amounts to saying of something that it is an oak. Further, it is convenient to think of uses of a word as encompassing not only utterances of that word but also dealings with the word when understanding, or trying to understand, utterances of it. I use the term 'oak' if I infer from someone's saying 'The oak is in splendid condition' that he is referring to a tree. We can think of these as *interpretative*, as opposed to *expressive*, uses of the word. Interpretative uses are not applications.

The two characterizations of correctness

Using a term in keeping with a meaning contrasts with misusing it, on a very natural conception of misuse. If, though I aspire to use a word in keeping with its received meaning, I am wrong about its received meaning, then I may misuse it. If I thought 'arcane' meant *ancient* then I would be liable to use the word as if that is what it meant. In so doing I would fail to respect the conditions of true application of the term; that is, I would be using the term as if its conditions of true application were other than they are. The term is truly, and in that sense correctly, applied to something if and only if that thing is known only to the initiated, but I would have used it as if it truly applied to something if and only if it was ancient. In that respect my use would be a misuse. None the less, I might on occasion apply it to some ritual, say, to which it does truly apply. On those occasions I would apply it correctly, in the sense of *truly*, but I would misuse the word none the less. I use it meaning to say something to the effect that the ritual is ancient, but the word I use is not suitable for the purpose.

Suppose that there is systematic mismatch between what I say when I apply the term, and what I mean to say when applying it, and yet it just so happens that I always apply it truly. Are these applications misuses? I would say that they are. When we make statements we give it to be understood that what we say is true and that we said what we meant to say. This dictates that the words we use when we state something to be so should be apt to say what we mean to say. Even if, as it happens, my applications of 'arcane' are always correct in the sense of *true*, they are not apt to convey what I meant to say. They are misuses because in so using the term I treat it as having conditions of true application that are not fixed by *its* meaning. In that sense I fail to respect its conditions of true application.

In the case just described, there is misuse explained by my being wrong about what a term means. There are also misuses in cases in which the user knows what the term means. Slips of the tongue are misuses of this type. I might say 'That tree is an oak', but my use of the word 'oak' is a slip of the tongue—I meant to say 'beech'. Here I apply the term 'oak' to a certain tree picked out demonstratively. My application of 'oak' to the tree may well be incorrect in the sense of being false. But however that may be, it is certainly incorrect in that it is a misuse—a use that is not in keeping with the relevant meaning of the term. This meaning dictates that, when applied to something, the word ascribes the property of being an oak. It is not in question that I said of the tree that it is an oak, for what I said is fixed in part by the relevant meaning of the term 'oak'. So I have ascribed to the tree the property of being an oak. But what I said is not what I meant to say. The word is not a suitable word for ascribing the property I meant to ascribe—that of being a beech. I might have applied the term correctly, in the sense of truly, since the tree I meant to call a beech might actually have been an oak. Still, in that case I would have used it as if it meant something else and thus failed to respect the condition of its true application.

The cases of misuse considered so far are ones in which people say something that they do not mean to say. The situation is more complicated in relation to the next example, adapted from a well-known example considered by Tyler Burge (1979). Fred says to his doctor, 'I have arthritis'. He says so without realizing that you only have arthritis if you have inflamed joints. Fred has no idea whether or not he has inflamed joints and would consider the matter irrelevant anyway. When his doctor points out to him that arthritis is a painful condition due to inflammation of the joints, and that the pains in his arms are due to rheumatism, Fred stops thinking that he has arthritis and resolves to bring his use of the term into line with received medical usage. It is not at all unnatural to think of Fred's use of the term, in his statement to his doctor, as a misuse. He uses the term as if it meant something other than it does. To use a term in this way is to fail to respect its conditions of true application. After what his doctor says Fred aims to use the term correctly in future, that is, in keeping with its meaning. But, unlike my imagined misuses of 'oak' and 'arcane', Fred's case is not a case of saying something he does not mean to say. For Fred really thinks he has arthritis and means to say so. He intends to, and does, pick out the property of having arthritis and ascribes it to himself. It is just that he has a wrong idea of what arthritis is and that leads him to use the term as if it meant *any persistently painful condition of the limbs or joints*.

This way of thinking about Fred's case sometimes provokes the suggestion that, at the point at which he says to his doctor 'I have arthritis', what he meant by 'arthritis' was something like *any persistently painful condition of the limbs or joints*. Correspondingly, on this view, the concept he applies to himself was not his doctor's concept of arthritis, and the condition he picks out was not that which the doctor's concept picks out. The problem here is that, even if on some ways of filling out the scenario this would be a correct description of the situation, there are other ways of filling it out that are in keeping with the view that Fred meant to pick out the condition arthritis all along. (Of course, on any way of filling out the scenario Fred meant to pick out a condition he thinks is called arthritis, but that is not the same as meaning to pick out arthritis.) Fred could quite naturally explain his adjustment of use by saying that, whereas he thought that arthritis was any persistently painful condition of the limbs or joints, he now realizes that this is incorrect. The change is a change in thinking about arthritis, which is accompanied by a change in the use of the word 'arthritis'. It is not a change from using the word to stand for a condition other than arthritis to using it to stand for arthritis.

Note too that, if Fred's doctor mistakenly applies 'arthritis' to a patient, he would have applied the term incorrectly, in the sense of falsely, but would not on that account have used the term incorrectly, in the sense of *not in keeping with its meaning*. A false application may respect the conditions of true application of the term. We may suppose the doctor to know what these are and to have used the right term for what he meant to say.

The upshot is that a use is correct in the sense of being in keeping with the relevant meaning provided that it is not a misuse. It is a misuse when it fails to respect the conditions of correct (= true) application of the term, that is, when it involves using the term as if those conditions of application, which are fixed by its meaning, were other than they are. An application that is correct, in the sense of being true, may or not be correct, in the sense of being in keeping with the relevant meaning. An application that is correct, in the sense of being in keeping with the relevant meaning, may or may not be correct, in the sense of being true. Thus correctness of use, conceived as true application, is not the same notion as correctness of use, conceived as use in keeping with meaning.

It is open to those who take correct application to be warranted, rather than true, application to adopt a modified version of the position just reached. Use in keeping with meaning would, on the modified theory, be use that respects the relevant conditions for warranted application. I shall not explore further in that direction but will work with the idea that use in keeping with meaning is use that respects the relevant conditions for true application. The theory of meaning can hardly avoid making conditions of true application central. I assume that any further refinements required by consideration of conditions of warranted application would still leave in place a conception of use in keeping with meaning as use respecting conditions for true application.

Conditions for correct application and rules for correct use

Conditions for the correct (= true) application of a term are not the same as rules for correct use. Rules may be followed or flouted; conditions may or may not be satisfied. Conditions of correct application, I am now assuming, are just conditions that are either necessary or sufficient for an application to be true. Still, conditions for the true application of a term surely bear upon all uses of the term, since any use of a term, whether an application or not, can be assessed in terms of whether it respects or fails to respect the conditions of true application. Suppose you say to me 'Cut down the oak', referring to the one and only oak tree in the garden. I understand what you are saying and thus know to which tree you are referring. Though I use the term 'oak' in this context I do not apply it. Even so, my use respects the conditions for true application of the term. It has a meaning on which it applies to oak trees. That is the sense that is relevant in this context and that is how I take it. But if I take you to be referring to a tree, that is in fact a lime, then that may be because I fail to respect the relevant conditions of true application, thinking falsely that the term 'oak' applies to trees that, unknown to me, are limes. With these considerations in mind, it is not hard to see why it is plausible that conditions for true application give rise to rules, even though they should not be identified with rules. There is a sense of the term 'oak' in which it is given true application to an object if and only if that object is an oak tree (as opposed to oak, the type of wood). So it is plausible that those who use the term in that sense are subject to the rule: when that sense is in play, use 'oak' only in ways that respect those conditions of true application, that is, only in ways that are in keeping with its meaning *oak tree*. I shall take it that the use of terms is subject to rules of this sort.

3. Normativity and truth

I have been distinguishing between two notions of correctness. Notwithstanding that there is this distinction, it might be thought that we can make sense of the idea that meaning is normative in terms of the notion of correctness as true application. When we answer '125' in response to the question 'What is 68 + 57?' we give the correct, in the sense of 'true', answer. Kripke also says it is the answer we *should* give. Perhaps, then the normativity of meaning has something to do with a requirement to give true answers to questions and, when we assert things, to assert truly.

Certainly the meaning of '+' contributes to fixing the correct answer to the question posed. But why is the correct answer something we *should* give? Perhaps we should answer '125' because we *intend* to give the correct answer. In that case normativity arises from an intention that we might or might not have and provides no reason to think that meaning is intrinsically normative. Perhaps one ought from a moral point of view to give the correct answer. Even if that is so, it has nothing to do specifically with meaning, but depends on a conception of the moral proprieties of communication.[82] A different approach would be to claim that it is in the nature of correctness that it imposes an obligation on us to answer questions correctly and in general to assert truthfully. If that were so, the obligation to speak truthfully would arise out of what it is for a statement to be correct, in the sense of 'true'. The trouble is that there is no reason to believe that there is any such obligation, that is, no reason to think that correctness itself gives rise to a demand to speak truthfully (compare Heal 1987/8: 98-102). The scepticism to which I am giving voice here is compatible with supposing that the speech act of assertion is governed by a rule of truthfulness dictating that one assert P only if P is true.[83] If there is such a rule, it depends on the character of assertion and thus on the practice of making and responding to assertions, *whatever their content*. There being such a rule would not establish that the meaning of expressions has any intrinsic normativity.[84] At this point one might be tempted to conclude that meaning is not intrinsically normative. I shall try to make it plausible that there is room for a different approach.

4. How meaning can be normative

If meaning is normative, then certain statements about meaning imply some paradigmatically normative statements. Two issues need to be resolved simply in order to formulate clearly what is at stake. The first concerns which statements about meaning we should be

---

[82] The points about intention and about morality are both made in Wikforss (2001: 205).
[83] Such a rule is discussed in Williamson (2000: ch. 11). Williamson argues persuasively that there is a stronger rule governing assertion dictating that one assert P only if one knows P.
[84] The point is noted by Wikforss (2001: 206).

considering. Kripke's discussion focuses on what a person means or meant by a word or symbol. In particular, he engages in first-personal reflections on what *he* means or meant by '+'. Some discussions deal with the meaning of expressions. Horwich, for example, though responding to Kripke's discussion, homes in on statements of the form 'x means DOG', where 'x' stands in place of a designation of a word—say, " 'dog' ". The second issue concerns which paradigmatically normative statements best bring out the normativity of the statements about meaning. Kripke's formulations are in terms of how a person *should* use a term, given what that person means by it. Like Gibbard, I take this to amount to the same as how a person *ought* to use the term, given what he or she means by it. Horwich, in keeping with his focus on the meanings of words, considers how a term ought to be used given what *it* means. An alternative approach would take the normative notion of *commitment* to be the key normative concept. On this approach we consider how one is committed to using '+' in virtue of what one means by it or, in the spirit of Horwich's discussion, given what it means. This is the approach I favour.

I shall address both of these issues by expanding on what I take to be a familiar conception of the use of language. Though this conception is by no means uncontroversial, the discussion will at least help us to make sense of claims about normativity in relation to meaning. I think it makes these claims plausible as well.

The term 'oak' has a sense in which it means *oak tree*. On the conception I have in mind, what makes this true is that there is a practice of using 'oak' to refer to a certain kind of tree—the oak. The notion of a practice is that discussed in Chapter 3 and subsequently. A practice is an essentially rule-governed activity. In this case the practice is governed by a rule to the effect that one respect the following conditions for true application of 'oak': 'oak' is given true application to an object if and only if it is an oak tree. The effect of conforming to this rule is that when the relevant sense is in play one respects the conditions specified. Participating in the practice makes one subject to that rule although, as with other practices, like playing a game of soccer, one may participate in the practice and also flout the rules. A significant result of the discussion of commitment in Chapter 3 was that participating in a practice incurs a commitment to following its governing rules and therefore to doing what the rules prescribe. It does not follow that one ought to follow the rules because it might be that one ought instead to withdraw from the practice. It is not difficult to think of practices with respect to which withdrawing would the right way to discharge the commitment incurred by participating. Imagine a group of people who engage in a role-playing game involving stealing cars, ramming them into shop-windows, and stealing the goods. One role is car-stealer, another is car-driver, another is goods-stealer, and so on. Each role, let us suppose, is associated with stylized ways of performing the activity that is definitive of the role. The activity is a practice in which playing a role is governed by a rule requiring that the stylized actions associated with the role be performed. Yet it is not true that if one participates in the practice then one ought to carry out the performances associated with one's role. I am assuming here that 'ought' modifies 'carry out the performance associated with one's role' rather than the whole conditional, 'If one participates in the practice then one carries out the performance associated with one's role.' What is true, and what people mean, or ought to mean, when they say that if one participates in the practice then one ought to carry out the performances associated with one's role, is that if one participates in the practice then one is committed to carrying out the performance associated with one's role. In the role-playing scenario this amounts to saying that one ought to avoid participating in the practice and not carrying out the right performance.

There can be reasons to withdraw from practices of word-use. Arguably, certain words descriptive of insulting and offensive racial or gender stereotypes ought not to be used expressively at all and therefore ought not to be so used in keeping with their meanings. We can still make sense of what is required of us if we are to use these words expressively. For if we participate in a practice of so using them we incur a commitment to using them in conformity with the rules for their use. We can discharge that commitment either by conforming to the rules or by stopping using them. A different kind of example is supplied by words expressing concepts that we no longer have reason to apply. Most of us have no expressive use for the term 'witch'. There is reason not to use it expressively, not simply because there are no witches but because we have no need to go about denying that people are witches. Even so, if we want to keep in touch with the past we had better use words like this interpretatively.

These cases illustrating reasons for withdrawing from a practice are rather rare. One might be wary of motivating a shift from claims about what one ought to do to claims about commitment simply by invoking such examples. But the fundamental reason for the shift derives from general considerations about practices and reasons. The crucial question is not whether there are cases in which people ought to withdraw from the practice, but whether from the mere fact that there is a certain practice we can derive conclusions to the effect that certain individuals ought to conform to its governing rules. According to the account of practices I have defended, in which commitments are central, the answer is, 'No'. There would be a problem with extending the account to practices of using words if there were reason to think that those who participate in such practices ought, just on that account, to follow their governing rules. So far as I can see there is no such reason. It is in our interests to participate in (most of) the word-using practices that prevail in one's community, and therefore to follow their rules. That is a reason that is explained not by the mere existence of these practices, but by facts about the importance to us of communication with others and about what is necessary for such communication.

So far as expression-meaning is concerned, we now have a resolution of the issue, identified above, concerning the key normative concept. We can illustrate the normativity of expression-meaning as follows:

(1) 'Oak' has a sense in which it means *oak tree* (i.e., it stands for a kind of tree—the oak)

implies

(2) When that sense is in play those who use 'oak' are committed to following the rule: use 'oak' in ways which respect the conditions specifying that it is given true application to a thing if and only if it is an oak tree.

Earlier (Chapter 3, Section 7) I distinguished between claims to the effect that a statement has normative import and claims to the effect that a statement is normative. For (1) to have normative import—specifically, normative import captured by (2)—all that is required is that if (1) were true then (2) would be true. The present claim is that

(1) not only has normative import but is normative in virtue of implying (2). This is to be understood as the claim that (2) follows from (1) without further ado. Why should it be supposed that we have a genuine implication here? The reason lies in what makes (1) true. The proposal is that (1) is true in virtue of there being a practice of using 'oak' to stand for a kind of tree. By using 'oak' in this sense one becomes a participant in this practice and thereby incurs a commitment to following the rule specified by (2).

The next step is to relate what has just been said to the notion of a *person's* meaning *oak tree* by 'oak'. What makes it true that on some occasions of use I mean *oak tree* by 'oak'? Here too, practices come into the picture. There is a practice of using 'oak' to refer to a kind of tree—the oak—and I am a participant in that practice. The occasions on which I mean *oak tree* by 'oak' are those in which I am engaging in this practice, that is, using 'oak' to refer to a kind of tree—the oak. The upshot is that, if it is true that on some occasions of use *I* mean *oak tree* by 'oak', then there has to be a practice of so using the term in which I participate. If there is such a practice then it follows that those, including me, who participate in it incur a commitment to following its rule prescribing respect for the relevant conditions of application. So we have another type of implication illustrated by the following:

(3) Sometimes I use 'oak' and mean *oak tree* by it (i.e., I use 'oak' to stand for a kind of tree—the oak)

implies

(4) When I use 'oak' that way I incur a commitment to following the rule: use it in ways that respect the conditions specifying that 'oak' is given true application to a thing if and only if it is an oak tree.

When it comes to formulating a plausible normativity thesis about meaning we do not need to choose between *person-meaning* and *expression-meaning*. The two notions are correlative. What I mean by 'oak' on some occasion is what 'oak', as used by me, means on that occasion.[85] The latter, and therefore also the former, is determined by

---

[85] Though I mean *oak tree* by 'oak', if I apply 'oak' in a slip of the tongue to a lime, I might mean to say that the tree to which I refer is a lime. What I say is determined by what I mean by 'oak'; what I mean to say is not.

whatever contextual factors bring the appropriate expression-meaning, and thus the appropriate practice, into play. In this case they will be factors that determine that *kind of tree*, rather than *type of wood*, is what matters. The concept of expression-meaning is responsible for the normativity of claims of the sort illustrated by (1). The concept of person-meaning is responsible for the normativity of claims illustrated by (3). In each type of case the relevant implication is explained by the theory of practices.

Some discussions of person-meaning in relation to Kripke's discussion of rule-following explain person-meaning in terms of intentions. (Kripke 1982: e.g. 9, 12; Wright 1984). There is no denying that it is very natural to do so. In giving a talk I might say, 'By "convention" I shall mean *convention* in Lewis's sense.' To make such a declaration is undoubtedly to give it to be understood that one intends to use the word in certain ways, in particular, in ways that are in keeping with its meaning *convention* in Lewis's sense. So one might think that meaning something by a word is just intending to use it in keeping with a certain meaning. There is some support for such a view from the fact that saying what we meant to do is just a way of saying what we intended to do. With this notion to hand, we seem to have a distinct explanation of why it is that meaning something by a word incurs a commitment. This explanation simply draws on general considerations about intentions. If intentions incur commitments and meaning something by a word is intending to use it in a certain way, then meaning something by that word incurs a commitment to using it in those ways. And if, as argued in Chapter 4, intentions are *intrinsically* commitment-incurring, then so is meaning something by a word.

It will help us to address this matter if we first consider the relation between participating in the practice of using 'oak' to refer to a kind of tree—the oak—and intending to use 'oak' in keeping with its meaning *oak tree*. It is not at all clear that those who participate in the practice are bound to have the corresponding intention. Indeed, one might wonder whether they are bound to have any intentions at all regarding 'oak'. Might not young children participate in the practice without having reached the stage of having intentions concerning their use of the word 'oak'? And might not even mature participants in the practice lack specific intentions concerning their use of the word? Let it be granted that when people say that p they usually intend to say that p. Still, it is a further step to suppose that they must have had intentions concerning the words they use—intentions expressible as claims about what they mean by the words they use. When I intentionally tell someone something to the effect that it is cool outside, and do so by saying that it's chilly outside, it is not at all obvious that I must have intended to use the word 'chilly' rather than 'cool'. That being so, it hardly seems right to suppose that I intended to use 'chilly' in keeping with its meaning *chilly*. Yet it is true none the less that by 'chilly' I meant *chilly*. A weaker view would be that mature participants must have a more general intention—a standing intention to use words with their received meanings. Even that might be too strong a condition. At any rate, it is a condition that very young speakers are unlikely to meet. What is true, I think, is that part of what it is to be a mature participant in a practice of using a word is that one is so disposed that, were one to discover that one's use is not in keeping with the relevant meaning of the word, one would be prepared to adjust one's use accordingly. The manifestation of this disposition is an intentional adjustment of one's use. This is what Fred does when he learns that he has been misusing 'arthritis'. Had he not been disposed to adjust his use in the light of the information from his doctor, there would no basis for regarding him as having all along meant by 'arthritis' what his doctor means by it. It does not follow that he must have had an intention regarding the word all along, or a general intention to use words with their received meaning, even though when he does adjust his use he does so intentionally and with a view to keeping faith with its received meaning.

There is some reason, then, to resist a position that requires that participating in a practice of using 'oak' in keeping with its meaning oak tree must involve a standing intention to use 'oak' in keeping with its meaning oak tree, when that practice is in play. Still, the existence of the practice depends on there being participants capable of intentionally adjusting their uses of the word in response to the discovery that their existing usage is not in keeping with the relevant meaning. Indeed, a 'participant' who lacked such a capacity—a very young child, for instance—might best be regarded as a participant only in a loose sense. Much use in keeping with meaning is both unstudied and non-accidental. It is non-accidental, since the use will have been honed by encounter with the practice. It is unstudied because falling in with the practice will not have sprung from reflection on the practice or its requirements. But if, as on the present hypothesis, there really are rule-governed practices of using words with certain meanings, rather than mere regularities more or less widely conformed to, then there must be individuals who appreciate, or could be brought to appreciate, what the practice demands. I take that to be a conceptual truth about practices and one that highlights an important difference between the existence of a practice and the existence of by-and-large conformity with some regularity in behaviour. Note however that a person's appreciation of the requirements might just be a matter of being able to recognize that certain uses of a word are wrong and to give some account of why. That does not require having an ability to formulate the rules of the practice.[86]

In the light of the stance on practices and intentions just sketched, let us go back to the idea, introduced three paragraphs ago, that meaning *oak tree* by 'oak' is intending to use it in keeping with its meaning *oak tree*. This was of interest to us because it seemed to provide an account that is different from that which states that your meaning *oak tree* by 'oak' is a matter of your participating in a practice of using 'oak' to refer to oak trees. If this latter idea is filled out as I have suggested, and participation in a practice of using a word does not require having intentions regarding the use of the word, then we have two competing accounts of meaning oak tree by 'oak'.

There are two directions in which we could go at this point. One would be to hold that 'meaning *oak tree* by "oak"' is ambiguous; in one sense it is a matter of having an intention concerning the word and in the other sense it is not. Even if that is right, it cannot be that using a word in keeping with a meaning depends solely on the intentions of individuals. When individuals resolve, and therefore intend, to use a word in a particular way, there needs to be a background of practice and action that makes sense of that resolution and enables uses that carry out the resolution to be understood. The other direction would be to deny that there is a sense in which 'meaning *oak tree* by "oak"' is a matter of having an intention regarding this word. It is not obvious that such a view is wrong.

---

[86] As well as being plausible, this view avoids the regress to which Wittgenstein drew attention deriving from thinking that all conformity to a rule is a matter of following an instruction in the way that one follows a recipe.

Recall my saying that by 'convention' I mean *convention* in Lewis's sense. It is true that by saying this I am, in effect, announcing an intention. But it does not follow that what makes what I say true is that I have this intention. It could be that, although what makes what I say true is that I participate in a practice of using 'convention' for conventions in Lewis's sense, my *saying* what I do indicates that I intend so to use it. It would indicate that I intend so to use it because in saying what I mean by the word I would convey that I recognize that I am committed to using it in keeping with its meaning *convention* in Lewis's sense and would thereby give it to be understood that I shall be using it in that way.

Both of the suggested responses are compatible with taking it that the theory of rule-governed practices can explain and accommodate both the transition from (1) to (2) and the transition from (3) to (4). It is just that defenders of the first response, which invokes an ambiguity in 'meaning something by a word' would need to make it clear that the reading of (1) to which the theory applies is that on which meaning is not a matter of having an intention.

5. Deflationist tendencies

The position I have described captures the idea that, *just in virtue of* there being a sense of 'oak' on which it means *oak tree*, those who use 'oak' in that sense incur a certain commitment. This is the force of the claim that (1) implies (2), for that amounts to the claim that (2) may be inferred from (1) *without further ado*. Deflationists about normativity deny that (1) implies (2) in this sense. They may concede that when (1) is true (2) is true. They think, however, that if (2) is true that is not just in virtue of (1)'s being true but because something else is true as well.[87] The strategy might be applied to the claimed implication between (3) and (4) or to the versions of the normativity theory that make the normative notion that of how one ought to use a word.

Paul Horwich is a deflationist in the sense just explained. At any rate I infer that he is, given what he says about the transition from

(5) 'dog' means *dog*

---

[87] Their strategy is thus analogous to that which, in Ch. 4, I imagined being deployed by dispositionalists to explain the normative import of ascriptions of beliefs and intentions.

to

(6) 'dog' ought to be applied only to dogs. (Horwich 1998: 92 f.)[88]

Horwich accepts that (6) is a normative statement and that if (5) were true then (6) would be. In my terms, he concedes that (5) has normative import captured by (6). He denies that (5) implies (6) (in my sense) and seeks to explain why it is that if (5) were true (6) would be. So in my terms he denies that (5) is a normative statement. His explanation is in three stages (Horwich 1998: chapter 8). First, he invokes the idea that truth in belief is something at which we ought to aim—we ought to believe only what is true. Second, he gives a pragmatic account of why we ought to aim at truth: roughly speaking, action based on true beliefs is more likely to be successful than action based on false beliefs. Third, he argues that since we ought, for the reasons spelled out by the pragmatic account, to apply the concept of a dog only to dogs, and since applying the word 'dog' is applying the concept, we ought to apply the word 'dog' only to dogs. The point of the strategy is to show that, since the normative claim (6) is grounded not just on (5), but on (5) in conjunction with the pragmatic considerations about aiming at truth in belief, there is nothing *intrinsically* normative about meaning.

Horwich's strategy is interesting in that it accounts for the normative import of statements like (5) in terms of a principle to the effect that we ought to aim at true beliefs. The problem with this approach harks back to the ground-clearing operation conducted in Section 2 above, which drew attention to an equivocation in the notion of correctness. As we saw, sometimes when people talk of correct uses they have in mind primarily, if not exclusively, true applications. Sometimes, though, correct use is conceived as use in keeping with meaning. It seems to me clear that when we are exploring the normativity of meaning it is the latter notion on which we need to focus. If, contrary to what I have argued, but in line with Kripke and Gibbard, the normative claims on which we need to focus are claims about how one ought to use words, then the particular ought-claims that need explaining are claims to the effect that one ought to use words in ways that are in keeping with the relevant meaning and in

---

[88] Horwich appears to conceive of normativity as Boghossian does, but with the proviso that the central explanatory consideration is about correct, in the sense of true, application.

that sense are correct. If that is the issue then the considerations that Horwich adduces are irrelevant and could only seem relevant because of an equivocation over the notion of correctness.

Lying to conceal a mistake, I say to you 'The tree I cut down was an oak', though in fact I cut down a beech. I said just what I meant to say. Here I apply the term 'oak' incorrectly (falsely) but I do not misuse it. My use respects the conditions for correct (= true) application of the term—it is a use that is entirely consistent with respecting those conditions. What makes my use faithful to the meaning of the term? Nothing that has to do with what is required for me to achieve the aim of believing only what is true. What makes my use correct, in the sense that matters, is simply that it respects the conditions for true application of the term. Given that I wanted to say to you that I had cut down the oak, I needed to use a term to refer to the oak, and I did so. My use was in keeping with the meaning of the term I used and thus correct in that sense. Aiming at truth is irrelevant to explaining why the use of the term is correct. It is respecting the conditions of true application that matters, not aiming at true applications. Similar considerations apply to slips of the tongue, which I have already discussed in Section 2. If, in circumstances in which I cut down the beech, I meant to tell you that I had cut down the oak but said by mistake, 'I cut down the beech', I would have spoken truly. None the less, I would have used the wrong word to say what I meant to say. I misused that word because I used it as if its conditions of application were other than they are. But, again, this has nothing to do with what is required to achieve the goal of believing only what is true.

A different deflationary strategy would be to concede that the oughts or commitments in which we should be interested are those linked to correct use, in the sense of use in keeping with meaning, but to argue that these oughts/commitments can still be explained away without invoking the idea that meaning is intrinsically normative. Suppose it is conceded that if 'oak' means *oak tree* then those who use 'oak' incur a commitment to using 'oak' in those ways that are in keeping with its meaning *oak tree*, that is, in those ways that are specified by the rule of the relevant practice. Still, it might be said that the reason why these people are so committed is that they are aiming to communicate using 'oak', and so had better use 'oak' in keeping with its meaning oak tree. Again, the idea is to invoke a goal that is extrinsic to their meaning what they do by it. This strategy strikes me as being significantly more plausible than the one just considered. None the less, it fails to identify the issue. It is true that, if you intend to communicate with the folks around here, and propose to use the word 'oak', then, unless you make it explicit that you are going to use it in some peculiar way, you are committed to using it in keeping with its meaning *oak tree* or *oak (the type of wood)* as the case may be. It is also true that this commitment is incurred just in virtue of having the intention in question. If you carry out the commitment, you will fall in with the prevailing practices of using 'oak'. But the issue is not about what you are committed to in virtue of intending to communicate. There are other commitments on the scene, in particular, those you incur once you are a participant in the prevailing practices. An analogy with rule-governed games helps here. You may be committed to playing a game of soccer. The commitment might have been incurred by your having said that you would play, or by your having a standing commitment to play, or some such thing. What explains these commitments is not what explains your commitment to obey the offside rule once playing in the match. The latter commitment is explained by the fact that as a participant in the game you incur a commitment to playing by the rules of the game. The moral is: don't conflate a commitment to participating in a practice with commitments incurred as a participant in a practice. The deflationary strategy under consideration does just that.

6. Words and concepts

In the remainder of this chapter I present a view on which normativity attaches to *conceptual intentional content* and thus to the contents of all of our propositional attitudes. To lead into this, I need to consider whether there are analogues at the level of thought of the considerations about meaning that I have been discussing.

Philosophical interest in concepts focuses on the link between possessing concepts and forming propositional attitudes. We possess the concept of a dog, for example, if and only if we are able to form propositional attitudes with contents that are about dogs, thought of as dogs. (It is, of course, possible to think about a dog not as dog, but just as some kind of animal, or as the thing I am looking at now. For that, there is no need to possess the concept of a dog.) It might seem odd to introduce the notion of a concept in terms of what it is to possess a concept rather than by directly spelling out what concepts are. I do so because I take it that the concept of, say, a dog, is whatever it is the possession of which enables me to *manage* attitudes that are about dogs thought of as dogs.[89] Managing attitudes covers forming them, retaining or abandoning them in the face of this or that consideration, and also exploiting them, as when a belief contributes to the basis of other beliefs.[90] Concepts themselves are abstract entities. They can be applied and withheld from application. They can be grasped more or less adequately.

The concept of meaning something by a word is normative because of the link between meaning and commitments. Meaning is therefore normative in the reason-linked sense. The parallel claim for concepts is that the concept of possessing a concept is normative in the same reason-linked sense. It will turn out that this latter claim emerges quite naturally from a development of the previous considerations about meaning. Before addressing the issue head-on, some analogies and disanalogies between words and concepts need to be taken into account.

Words have meanings, and concepts have contents. The meaning of a word is what it means. The content of a concept is what it is a concept of. Whereas words can change their meanings without changing their identity, concepts are individuated by their content. The content of a concept is just whatever it is that makes it the concept that it is. So although a word can have different meanings, a concept cannot have different contents. In view of this, it is somewhat less natural to speak of using concepts than it is to speak of using words. Words, like tools, can be used in one way and then used in some other way. And there can be differences in uses of a word that reflect differences in meaning. If concepts are individuated

---

[89] This is in the spirit of Christopher Peacocke's (1992: 5) Principle of Dependence.
[90] 'Manage' is not an entirely happy term. It could be taken to imply that when managing is going on the subject is necessarily engaged in intentional action. I use it simply as an abbreviation for forming attitudes and the rest.

by their contents, then for concepts there is no analogue of differences in use that reflect differences in meaning.

There is, however, a sense in which concepts can be used. We can be said to use concepts when we exercise the capacities in which their possession consists. Thus we use them in managing the propositional attitudes we have. I distinguished in Section 2 between expressive and interpretative uses of words. A word is used expressively when it is used in making an utterance. We use a word interpretatively when we understand an expressive use of it in a certain way, thereby taking the word, as used on the occasion in question, to have a certain meaning. The analogue for concepts of the expressive use of a word is the use of a concept in managing propositional attitudes. We could be said to use concepts interpretatively when we form, abandon, or exploit attitudes that are about other attitudes, or about considerations, claims, and the like. For when we do these things we need to exploit our grasp of the concepts brought into play by the attitudes, considerations, claims, and the like about which we are thinking. Note, however, that *all* uses of concepts occur in the management of propositional attitudes. There is nothing else for uses of concepts to be. So the interpretative use of concepts is a special case of expressive use.

Another key notion in the discussion of meaning was *application*. We apply the term 'dog' to something when and only when we predicate it of something, thereby saying of that thing that it is a dog. There is a fairly straightforward analogue for concepts. You apply the concept of a dog to something if and only if you judge it to be a dog. The restriction to judgement, rather than belief, is deliberate. Judgement, unlike belief, is an act rather than a standing state, so we can think of the person judging as truly using concepts when doing so. You do not use concepts simply in virtue of having stored beliefs, intentions, hopes, and so forth. It is when these stored attitudes are adjusted or exploited in some way that the concepts they implicate are truly used. It is worth noting that, while there can be insincere utterances, there cannot be insincere judgements. Saying that p is compatible with not believing that p. Judging that p implicates believing that p.

At the heart of the discussion of semantic meaning was a distinction between two kinds of correctness in the use of terms. A use of a term can be correct in virtue of being a true application, or it can be correct in the sense of being a use in keeping with the term's meaning. If we are to find analogues for the normativity theses advanced earlier in this chapter, there will have to be conceptual analogues of these two notions of correctness. There is no problem about correctness in the sense of true application. Obviously concepts can be truly or falsely applied. But since concepts are individuated via their contents, it might seem that there is no scope for using a concept in a way that is not in keeping with its content. In other words, there is no scope for misusing a concept in a sense of 'misuse' parallel to that in play in the discussion of semantic meaning.[91]

There seems to be no analogue for concepts of slips of the tongue. In the case of a slip of the tongue we mean to say one thing but use a word that is inappropriate for what we mean to say. The slip consists in the use of inappropriate means to carry out an intention. Judging, unlike saying something, is not an intentional action. So one cannot intend to judge something but by a slip judge something else. But it is possible to employ a concept yet not do so in keeping with its content. Suppose Bill hears that Tom is Sally's uncle and infers from this that Tom is the brother of one or other of Sally's parents. He might have overlooked the fact that an uncle can be the husband of an aunt. Here Bill employs a concept in the course of exploiting information he receives. The situation is entirely compatible with his employing the concept of an uncle. He just fails to employ the concept correctly—in keeping with its content—because he takes the information he receives to have an implication it does not have. In this case he misuses the concept in that he fails to respect the conditions of its true application. He treats the concept as if it were other than it is.

There is no doubt, then, that there can be misuses of concepts. Less obviously, there can be *systematic* misuses of concepts. Even if Bill is ignorant of the fact that uncles can be husbands of aunts, he could still be using the regular concept of an uncle. Burge's patient (Fred) not only systematically misuses the term 'arthritis', he systematically misuses the concept of arthritis. These claims are liable to be met with some resistance. There is a tendency to suppose that one's concept of

---

[91] Colin McGinn (1984: 147) has taken the idea of misusing concepts to be problematic on somewhat similar grounds.

an uncle is just the way one thinks about uncles—one's conception of what it is for someone to be one's uncle. But examples such as that of Burge's patient suggest that we should distinguish between concepts and conceptions. Fred has an inadequate conception of arthritis that guides his use of the concept of arthritis. His conception is his idea of what it is for a condition to be arthritis. The trouble is that Fred's conception is mistaken even though he possesses the corresponding concept. Differences in conception of X are compatible with sharing a concept of X. Like a chemist, a child may have the concept of sugar, but the child's conception of sugar will be much thinner than that of the chemist.[92]

What makes it the case that a particular concept is the one a person is employing? In the case in which Bill has an inadequate conception of an uncle and fails to realize that uncles can be husbands of aunts, what makes it the case that, despite this misconception, it is the concept *of an uncle* that he is employing, rather than his own deviant 'uncle'-concept? (One's 'X'-concept is whatever concept one would bring into play using the term 'X'. One's 'X'-beliefs/thoughts/judgements, etc., are those beliefs/thoughts/judgements, etc., that bring into play one's 'X'-concept. One's 'X'-conception is the conception one has of what is picked out by one's 'X'-concept.) I suggest that Bill's 'uncle'-concept is the good old concept of an uncle only if his 'uncle'-conception, and thus his use of the concept, is appropriately responsive to information about the property of being an uncle. When Bill learns that the husband of one's aunt is one's uncle, he adjusts his 'uncle'-conception accordingly. If he had not been prepared to adjust his 'uncle'-conception in this way, it would be doubtful that his 'uncle'-concept was the concept of an uncle.

Suppose that, although I systematically use the word 'arcane' to mean *ancient*, I am prepared to adjust my use on learning that it does not mean *ancient* but rather *understood only by the initiated*. What are we to say of my 'arcane'-concept prior to the adjustment? It seems that my 'arcane'-conception is appropriately responsive to information about the property of being arcane—I am prepared to adjust my conception on learning what it is to be arcane. Is my 'arcane'-

---

[92] The sugar example is from Millikan (2000) in the content of a discussion in which concepts are distinguished from conceptions. I take it that something like this distinction is implicit in various works by Putnam, including Putnam (1962/1975b).

concept, prior to the adjustment, the concept of being arcane? It is arguable that it is not, on the grounds that I have an insufficient grasp of what it is to be arcane to count as having the concept of being arcane. I think it should be conceded that my 'arcane'-concept is the concept of being ancient. Even though I adjusted by 'arcane'-conception in response to information about what it is to be arcane, it does not follow that my 'arcane'-concept is the concept of being arcane. Contrast this case with that of Bill in the scenario in which he does not realize that uncles can be husbands of aunts. Not only is he prepared to adjust his conception in the light of information about what it is to be an uncle, the conception includes a partial specification of the property of being an uncle. The same can be said for Fred's 'arthritis'-concept. But my 'arcane'-concept, prior to the adjustment of my 'arcane'-conception, is not the concept of being arcane because, even though the conception is appropriately responsive to information about what it is to be arcane, it is not even a partial specification of the property of being arcane.

This view is consistent with what I have already said about words and practices. In the scenario envisaged I do not have enough of a grasp of the meaning of 'arcane' to count as engaging in the practice of using it to mean *arcane*. To make sense of my being prepared to adjust my use of the word when I learn what it means, it is not necessary to assume that I was engaging in the practice, and thus using the concept of arcane, yet failing adequately to respect the word's meaning (the concept's content). The explanation for my being prepared to adjust my use of the word and, correspondingly, make my 'arcane'-concept the concept of being arcane is that I took myself to be using the word as others do. In effect, I took myself to be participating in the prevailing practice of using the word to stand for *being arcane*, but I was wrong about that.

There is a significant point of contrast between words and concepts pertaining to issues about normativity. On the view I have taken, there are practices of using words in particular ways. The rules governing these practices determine what words mean. This is no reason to think that there are practices of using concepts in particular ways. One and the same word could have been, or could come to be, subject to a rule that is different from that which actually governs it. That is a condition of its making sense to think of the use of words as being governed by the rules of practices, and to think of words as shifting their meanings as the practices evolve. There are, in a sense, rules governing the use of concepts, but they are not rules that govern *practices*. The rules governing the use of concepts are requirements of correct use.

It is the fact that a concept is the concept *of arthritis* that dictates that we use the concept of arthritis in ways that respect the conditions of application, according to which it is given true application to something if and only if it is arthritis. The concept of arthritis is that concept the use of which is subject to the requirement: use it in ways that respect the fact that it truly applies to something if and only if it is arthritis. By contrast, what dictates that we use the word 'arthritis' in ways that respect the conditions of its true application is that using the word is engaging in a practice governed by a rule prescribing respect for those conditions. This difference is closely related to another, deeper, difference. The normative status of the rules governing any practice depends on these rules being implicitly or explicitly acknowledged by some people. (Recall the discussion of undertaking in Chapter 3, Section 4.) On this topic phenomenalism looks right: rules are rules in virtue of being treated as rules. Not so for requirements governing the use of concepts. That certain concepts are in use is determined by there being certain words in use, and therefore by there being certain practices.[93] But, given that certain concepts are in use, it follows from that alone that the corresponding requirements govern their use.[94]

With all of the foregoing preliminary points on the table, I turn now to consider analogues for the normativity claims advanced in Section 4. We are looking first for an analogue of, for instance, the following claim:

(6) 'Uncle' has a sense in which it means uncle (in the strict kinship sense)

implies

---

[93] The point here is that for some concepts it is true there would not be such concepts unless there were words used in certain ways. The point does not turn on whether or not all concepts depend on the use of words.

[94] In this respect I differ from Brandom (1994), where phenomenalism about rules extends, not just to rules for words, but to rules governing intentional content generally. For critical discussion of Brandom on related matters, see Rosen (1997).

(7) When that sense is in play those who use 'uncle' are committed to following the rule: use 'uncle' in ways that respect the conditions specifying that it is given true application to a thing if and only if it is an uncle.

The analogue of (6) for concepts is the truism that the concept of an uncle (in the strict kinship sense) is what it is. None the less, that the concept of an uncle (in the strict kinship sense) is what it is implies that those who use it incur a commitment to satisfying the requirement: to use it in ways that respect its conditions of true application.

Given the normativity of person-meaning,

(8) Sometimes Bill uses 'uncle' and means *uncle*, in the strict kinship sense, by it

implies

(9) When Bill uses 'uncle' in that way he incurs a commitment to following the rule: use it in ways that respect the conditions specifying that 'uncle' is given true application to something if and only if it is an uncle (in the strict kinship sense).

The parallel claim for concept-possession is:

(10) Bill possesses the concept of an uncle (in the strict kinship sense)

implies

(11) Bill incurs a commitment to using that concept in keeping with the rule: respect the conditions specifying that it is given true application to something if and only if it is an uncle (in that sense).

We have already seen how it is possible that someone should misuse the concept of an uncle in the sense of failing to use it in keeping with its content. If this were not possible, it would make no sense to talk of incurring commitments in virtue of possessing a concept. Where commitments are incurred, it must be possible to fail to discharge those commitments. There can be no such failures unless there are misuses of concepts. Indeed, the phenomenon of misuse is the main reason for accepting that possessing concepts is intrinsically commitment-incurring.

7. Content and psychological explanation

Suppose that

(a) what Bill means by 'uncle', in discourse in which he says of someone that that person is so-and-so's uncle, is *uncle* (in the strict kinship sense, even if he misuses the word).

So

(b) when Bill utters 'John is Richard's uncle', what he says is that John is Richard's uncle.

But since

(c) the concepts one uses in saying something are those corresponding to what one then means by one's words

it follows that

(d) the 'uncle'-concept Bill uses in saying what he does is the concept of an uncle (this being the concept attached to 'uncle', given what he means by 'uncle').

Some might dispute whether (c) is true. It might be thought that, in the case in which Bill systematically misuses 'uncle', as when he exploits the meaning of the term mistakenly, the misuse lies purely in his use of words and not in his use of concepts. The thought here is that, although Bill systematically misuses the word, the misuse reflects the fact that he has a distinctive and deviant 'uncle'-concept. On this way of thinking, when he corrects his use, he brings it about that his 'uncle'-concept is the concept of an uncle. The picture competes with that which I am putting forward. The difference between Bill's dispositions and that of someone who has an adequate conception of an uncle are taken to make it the case that Bill has a deviant 'uncle'-concept. If this is right, the problem in Bill's case is that the word he uses to express his 'uncle'-attitudes is misleading as to the contents of those attitudes and what he says is misleading as to what he believes. Since what he believes is fixed in part by his 'uncle'-concept, his belief is one in which John is represented as falling under *his* 'uncle'-concept. On the contrasting picture that I am presenting, there is no mismatch between what Bill means by 'uncle' and the 'uncle'-concept he deploys in saying what he does. The concept he brings into play in his remark about John is not a deviant 'uncle'-concept but the good old concept of an uncle. The belief he expresses is fixed by what he says. This view of the matter fits naturally with the view that concept-possession is commitment-incurring. People who possess a concept may diverge significantly in their use of it and thus in their dispositions to manage propositional attitudes that bring the concept into play. All of them are disposed to use the concept correctly in the sense of being disposed to manage the relevant attitudes in whichever ways are required by its being the concept that it is. But as we have seen, they may be mistaken as to what is required by its being the concept that it is.

Even the defender of the picture I am rejecting should want to accommodate occasional misuses of a concept, as in the case in which Bill knows full well that uncles can be husbands of aunts, but overlooks this possibility in drawing a conclusion from the statement that John is Richard's uncle. It is quite implausible in this case that Bill has a deviant 'uncle'-concept which is momentarily brought into play on the occasion in question. Accordingly, it is implausible to suppose that in accepting what he says in saying 'John is Richard's uncle', he represents John as falling under a deviant 'uncle'-concept. What Bill accepts is simply that John is Richard's uncle. He just overlooks the fact that John could be the husband of one of Richard's aunts. If this is conceded, it significantly weakens any suggestion that there must be a deviant concept in play in cases of *systematic* misuse.

As I said, on the view I have sketched there can be significant variations among those who possess a concept with respect to how they think in virtue of possessing that concept. The way Bill thinks about uncles, if he does not realize that husbands of aunts can be uncles, differs from the way someone with an adequate grasp of the concept thinks about uncles. The way Fred thinks about arthritis differs from the way his doctor thinks about it. This account may seem to present a problem concerning psychological explanation. To illustrate the problem I shall focus on belief. Beliefs are individuated via their contents: beliefs are the same if and only if their contents are. Given that we cite beliefs in giving explanations of why people think what they do and why they act as they do, it is natural to suppose that the content of a belief must reflect the potential of the belief to explain changes in the subject's thought or behaviour. If this is right, then beliefs will have the same (or different) contents if and only if they have the same (or different) explanatory potential. When Fred's doctor believes that someone has arthritis, he is disposed to infer that the person has inflamed joints. Fred is not similarly disposed when he believes that someone has arthritis. On the line of thought I am considering, this is taken to show that the explanatory potential of Fred's 'arthritis'-beliefs is different from the explanatory potential of his doctor's 'arthritis'-beliefs. So, as the argument goes, the concept introduced by the doctor's uses of 'arthritis' must be different from that introduced by Fred's uses of the same word.[95] Suppose we concede that beliefs that share a content must have the same explanatory potential. Does it follow that the 'arthritis'-beliefs of Fred and his doctor have different contents? This would follow if the 'arthritis'-concepts of Fred and his doctor were individuated by their differing conceptions of arthritis. However, the assumption that they are thus individuated is part of what is in dispute in this territory, as we saw above. No doubt Fred's doctor will think of someone who has arthritis as having inflamed joints. That can be explained by the fact that his conception of arthritis is of a painful condition due to inflammation of the joints. But if his having this conception is not necessary for believing of someone that he or she has arthritis, then so believing will not, without further ado, account for transitions in thought to the belief that the person in question has inflamed joints. The less we pack into the content of a belief, the less can be explained by it. But that is precisely what enables us to make sense of the idea that the doctor's 'arthritis'-beliefs and Fred's 'arthritis'-beliefs can be alike in content, bringing into play the same 'arthritis'-concept. It is only if we pack too much into the content of the doctor's beliefs that we are misled into thinking that their explanatory potential must be different from corresponding beliefs held by Fred.

8. Normativity and truth again

It is sometimes argued that there is no need to take intentional content to be intrinsically normative. David Papineau (1999) deploys

---

[95] This line of thought is in the spirit of Loar (1988).

an argument to this effect akin to the deflationary argument deployed by Horwich (1998) and discussed in Section 5. Papineau claims that 'the most significant norms of judgement can be viewed as prescriptions to the effect that, in order to achieve the truth, you ought to judge in such-and-such ways' (Papineau 1999: 18). I shall take it that the relevant ought-claim is best read as a claim about what we are committed to in virtue of pursuing truth in judgement as an end. (Papineau's 1999: 18, footnote 3, suggests that he would be sympathetic to this reading.)

Papineau assumes that if intentional content were intrinsically normative then it would be because truth is intrinsically normative. With a view to defending his view that intentional content is not intrinsically normative, he argues, (a) that truth is not intrinsically normative, and (b) that we can make sense of the norms guiding judgement in terms of the idea that truth in judgement has instrumental or moral value. (A somewhat similar line is taken in Dretske 2000a, and there is an obvious kinship with the approach taken by Horwich on semantic meaning that I discussed earlier.) The point is that normativity does not attach to truth in judgement as such, but depends on ends that we set ourselves, like thriving in our environment, or on moral values that we adopt.

I have been arguing that the use of predicative concepts is governed by a requirement prescribing that they be used in ways that respect the conditions of their true application. In relation to the concept of an uncle, what determines that there is this requirement? Simply that the concept of an uncle is the concept that it is—that concept the use of which is governed by the requirement to respect those conditions of application. There is no need to invoke the goal of truth in judgement to explain why, if we use the concept, we are subject to the requirement. More interestingly, invoking that goal does not explain all uses of the concept. In particular, it does not explain uses of the concept that are not applications. (Note the unsurprising similarity to the strategy I adopted in Section 5 in response to Horwich on normativity and meaning.) If I want to deceive you into thinking that I have a rich uncle, then if I say as much I am using the concept of an uncle, though not applying it. My use is subject to the requirement prescribing that I respect the relevant conditions of application, and I respect those conditions. (I do not proceed as if the conditions of application were other than they are.) What requires me to respect the conditions on this occasion has nothing to do with my aiming at truth in judgement.

9. Reflexivity in relation to concept-use

I have presented a view according to which concept-possession has an intrinsic normative dimension. If this view is correct, then ascriptions of content to propositional attitudes imply that those to whom the ascriptions are made incur commitments in virtue of their possession of the concepts that these attitudes bring into play. These commitments are distinct from the commitments identified in connection with the attitudes of believing and intending. The latter are commitments specifically tied to those attitudes. They are bound up with the character of believing and intending. The commitments of which I am speaking now are commitments linked to concepts and thus to the contents of any attitude. The discussion in this chapter has been concerned with presenting and clarifying the view rather than with arguing that this is how we should think of concepts. There are many other ways of thinking about concepts in the field. I have not attempted to undermine all of these ways of thinking. I hope that I have made my own view plausible. It is important to bear in mind that it is intended to provide an account of concepts that figure in what I have been calling personal understanding. These are concepts brought into play by our propositional attitudes and which figure in the content clauses of our ascriptions of propositional attitudes. The case for thinking that it is the right account of those concepts will turn on whether it can account for the psychological role of the attitudes better than alternatives.

The normative dimension of believing and intending explains both the commitments we generally recognize to be incurred by beliefs and intentions, and the peculiarity of our relationship to our own beliefs and intentions—a relationship for which, I argued, dispositionalism, as described in Chapter 4, could not account. The normative dimension of believing and intending also accounts for how we represent the dispositions that are characteristic of beliefs and intentions. The dispositions are dispositions to discharge the commitments that these beliefs and intentions incur. They are not just dispositions to do the things that will discharge the commitments, but dispositions to take account of the commitments and act accordingly. The principle reason for adopting a corresponding view about concept-possession is that the view best accounts for the psychology of concept-use. I do not claim to have established that this view is the best account of concepts. I do think that it fits the kinds of concepts we possess and ascribe to each other. If that is right, it gives us a reason to distinguish concepts in this sense from analogues of concepts that might be invoked in discussions of the intentionality of non-human animals. Earlier I suggested that we should distinguish between intentions and sub-intentional aims, and between beliefs and sub-doxastic informational states. It seems entirely plausible that the sub-intentional aims and the sub-doxastic informational states should be conceived as non-conceptual intentional states, in contrast with conceptual states like beliefs, intentions, desires, and the rest.[96] If so, we should be looking for something that stands to the non-conceptual states as concepts stand to the conceptual states.

---

[96] The idea that there are non-conceptual intentional states has wide currency. Major influences are Evans (1982) and Peacocke (1992). For doubts about the utility of non-conceptual content in thinking about perceptual experience, see McDowell (1994b).

CHAPTER 7

The Problem of Explanatory Relevance

1. The character of the problem

In Chapter 1, Section 3, I alluded to what I called *the problem of explanatory relevance*. The problem arises in connection with rationalizing explanations—explanations of, for instance, the formation of a belief or the performance of an action in terms of the subject's reason for forming that belief or performing that action. If rationalizing explanations are distinctive *qua* explanations, then one might suppose that the explanatory insight that they yield has something to do with the fact that the relevant propositional attitudes rationalize the belief or action to be explained in the way they do. But if, as I argued in Chapter 1, the explanatory insight provided by rationalizing explanations is causal, and tied to appropriate generalizations, then it is not clear what the provision of the rationalization adds. If the explanation is causal, the insight it yields is provided by the information that the attitudes cited in the explanation figured in the aetiology of the formation of the belief or the performance of the action. That information provides explanatory insight of a limited sort. It implies that the attitudes cited in the explanation are such that, given suitable prompting circumstances, someone with attitudes of that sort would be liable to form a belief or perform an action of the sort being explained. One reaction to the problem would be to deny that rationalizing explanations are causal and that the insight they provide implicates generalizions. I am interested in a solution to the problem on which rationalizing explanations are causal, the insight that they yield implicates generalizations, and the provision of the rationalization in question is, even so, explanatorily relevant to what is being explained. I shall attempt to clarify the issue in terms of an example concerning the formation of a belief.

Suppose that I form a belief on the basis of other beliefs that I have. Let us call the belief formed the conclusion-belief and the beliefs on which it is based the basis-beliefs. The basis-beliefs may supply a rationalizing explanation of my forming the conclusion-belief. When they do, the problem is to explain how the fact that the basis-beliefs rationalize the conclusion-belief in the way they do can be explanatorily relevant to the formation of the conclusion-belief. Suppose that, already believing that Lizzie will go to the party only if Tom is going, I then learn that Lizzie will go and conclude that Tom is going. My reaching this conclusion is a case of forming a belief for a reason. My reason is constituted by the considerations that Lizzie will go to the party only if Tom is going (C^1), and that Lizzie will go to the party (C^2). Of course, there will have been some event that prompted me to draw the conclusion. It might just have been learning that Lizzie was going to the party. Or perhaps I did not link that information with Tom's going until later when the question arose as to whether Tom would be going. An explanation of my forming the conclusion-belief in terms of my reasons for thinking that Tom is going need not refer to any such prompting event. This is not a major defect, given that we are interested in the agent's motivating *reasons*, rather than the details of the causation of the formation of the belief. In explaining beliefs we are often content to home in on considerations constituting the agent's reasons. We may have no interest in why appropriate background beliefs came into play or why one piece of information came to be put together with another.

Thus far the story is compatible with the dispositionalism I criticized in Chapter 4, which treats explanations in terms of propositional attitudes as a species of dispositional explanation, akin to an explanation of why a copper bar comes to be bent in terms of its flexibility. Given dispositionalism, the problem of explanatory relevance arises for rationalizing explanations of belief because, in so far as the explanation is dispositional, the fact that the basis-beliefs *rationalize* the formation of the conclusion-belief in the way they do seems to be irrelevant to why the belief is formed. The burden of explaining why the conclusion-belief is formed is borne entirely by the fact that certain dispositions are manifested, and so must have been triggered. In that story the fact that the beliefs rationalize as they do has no *explanatory* role. Explanations of this kind implicate a generalization that picks out the features of the basis-beliefs which, according to the explanation, lead to the formation of the conclusion-belief. For all that has been said so far, the implicated generalization might be something like:

G For any x, if x believes that Lizzie will go to the party only if Tom is going and comes to believe that Lizzie will go, then, given appropriate prompting circumstances, x is liable to believe that Tom is going.

Although **G** adverts to the contents of the relevant beliefs, it does not advert to any relational property of the basis-beliefs in virtue of which they provide the particular kind of rationalization of the formation of the conclusion-belief that they do. That is why it becomes an issue whether any such property can be explanatorily relevant to why the conclusion-belief is formed.

I shall say that the considerations C^1 and C^2, which form the contents of the relevant basis-beliefs, stand in a *reason-giving relation* to the conclusion that Tom is going to the party. A sufficient condition for this to be so is that were they true they would provide an adequate normative reason for believing the conclusion. The basis-beliefs rationalize the formation of the conclusion-belief in virtue of the fact that C^1 and C^2 stand in a reason-giving relation to the conclusion that Tom is going to the party. The immediate task, then, must be to explain how this fact about the reason-giving relation can be explanatorily relevant to the formation of the conclusion-belief. It should be noted, however, that the provision of such an explanation would not yield a general solution to the problem of explanatory relevance for cases in which conclusions are drawn from assumptions. This is because, when beliefs rationalize the acceptance of some conclusion, the considerations that form the contents of the basis beliefs do not always stand in a reason-giving relation to the conclusion. In some cases the relevant assumptions, even if true, will not provide an adequate normative reason for accepting the conclusion. I return to the problems posed by such cases later.

The problem of explanatory relevance is likely to strike one as being a genuine problem only if one thinks that modes of rationalizing do have an explanatory role. Such a view might be challenged. It might be said that the distinctive feature of *rationalizing* explanations of the formation of beliefs on the basis of others is simply that the implied transition from the basis-beliefs to the conclusion-belief conforms to a certain pattern such that the basis-beliefs rationalize the formation of the conclusion-belief in a certain way. On this approach to the matter, it is neither here nor there whether the kind of rationalization provided has an *explanatory* role. Why in that case would rationalizations be of any philosophical interest? They could still be of some epistemological interest. It might be supposed that we have belief-forming dispositions which when manifested result in inferences that match appropriate reason-giving relations. If this is right, and we know which dispositions people are likely to have, given that they have such-and-such beliefs, then we would be in a position not to be surprised when they go on to form certain other beliefs on the basis of those beliefs. This response to the idea that there is a genuine problem about explanatory relevance is unsatisfactory, if only because sometimes the fact that the belief formed is rationalized in the way it is seems to be explanatorily relevant to why the belief was formed. The example under consideration is a case in point. It is hard to believe that the fact that C^1 and C^2 stand in a reason-giving relation to the conclusion that Tom is going, and on that account rationalize my reaching this conclusion, is explanatorily irrelevant to why I reached this conclusion. The problem is how to shed light on this.

Consider how a dispositionalist might attempt to provide a solution to the problem of explanatory relevance, without invoking knowledge or beliefs that subjects have about their own reasons. (If one is suspicious about my earlier treatment of the role of agents' beliefs about their commitments and reasons in their psychology, then one might well be attracted by this attempt.) The key idea is that the reason-giving relation between C^1 and C^2 and the conclusion that Tom is going to the party is explained by a logical property of these considerations. In particular, it is explained by the fact that the conclusion follows from the considerations in accordance with the pattern of valid inference *modus ponens*. With this in mind, a defender of pure dispositionalism might argue as follows. When I form my belief about Tom, the dispositions manifested are partially constitutive of my having a grasp of the relevant logical property of C^1 and C^2. When these dispositions are manifested I demonstrate an implicit grasp of this logical property—the very property in virtue of which C^1 and C^2 stand in a reason-giving relation to the claim that Tom is going. That is tantamount to my being sensitive to the reason-giving relation between, on the one hand, C^1 and C^2, on the other hand, the conclusion. If C^1 and C^2 had not stood in this relation, and nothing else I believed stood in this relation to the conclusion, then I probably would not have come to believe that Tom is going. This, according to the view, is because, by-and-large, my belief-forming dispositions are such that, when manifested in drawing conclusions from assumptions, the inferences made are valid or in some other manner legitimate.

The fact that my conclusion about Tom results from dispositions that are partially constitutive of my grasp of the relevant logical property of C^1 and C^2 is supposed to show that the way my beliefs in C^1 and C^2 rationalize my coming to accept the conclusion is explanatorily relevant to my coming to accept the conclusion. How does it do so? We have already seen that the relevant reason-giving relations could be thought to be of epistemological significance. But the present question is about the *explanatory* relevance of such relations.

No doubt it will not be accidental that I routinely make inferences in accordance with *modus ponens*. Perhaps I have been 'designed' to do so via a process that selects out the dispositions that ensure that, by and large, I do. In that case, an explanation is available of why I have these dispositions—an explanation that adverts to the patterns in question.[97] But again, it is not clear why this should be supposed to address the problem of explanatory relevance. How the dispositions were acquired is one thing; why a subject forms a particular belief in given circumstances is another. The problem of explanatory relevance concerns the latter. When I form my belief about Tom it is certainly relevant to the explanation of my doing so that the dispositions in question are manifested. Let it be granted that they are

---

[97] Sellars (1963a) is an early, though widely ignored, discussion in which this line is pursued.

partially constitutive of my grasp of the relevant logical property of C^1 and C^2, and that it is no accident that I have those dispositions. The fact remains that, on the present account of the matter, I form the belief simply because (i) I have those dispositions, and (ii) something caused them to be manifested. As yet nothing has been done to show that the relevant reason-giving relation has any explanatory role in the causal–explanatory story of why the conclusion is reached.

Why then might this approach to the problem of explanatory relevance seem attractive? We gain some insight into this from reflection on the problem of deviant causal chains. Kathleen Lennon (1990: 38) has a nice example of a deviant causal chain leading to the formation of a belief. Imagine that through hypnosis I have been put in a state such that whatever belief I next form will lead me to believe that there are six apples on the table. The next belief I form is that there is a group of two apples and a distinct group of four apples on the table. (I am told this or see it to be so.) I duly come to believe that there are six apples on the table. The belief that is the basis of my believing that there are six apples on the table supplies a rationale for my so believing. Yet this basis-belief does not provide a rationalizing explanation for my forming the conclusion-belief. The conclusion-belief is not formed in the right kind of way. The dispositionalist approach I have been describing has the resources to explain why this is a case of deviance. It is a case of deviance because the formation of the conclusion-belief does not come about via the manifestation of *the right kind of dispositions*. The right kind of dispositions comprises those that are constitutive of my having a grasp of relevant reason-giving features of the consideration that forms the content of the basis-belief. In the hypnosis scenario, the content of the basis-belief is wholly irrelevant to the explanation of why I reach the conclusion. In my hypnotized state, I would have come to believe that there were six apples on the table *whatever* I came to believe immediately following hypnosis. This might suggest that in a situation in which I come to the same conclusion on the same basis, but through the manifestation of the right sorts of dispositions, the requirements of explanatory relevance would be met. Granted that the content of the basis-belief is explanatorily relevant to the formation of the conclusion-belief, and its relevance is mediated by the right sorts of disposition, it might seem that we have all we need to secure the explanatory relevance of the reason-giving power of the consideration that forms the content of the basis-belief. But this still does not come to grips with the problem. It is true that the dispositions that the theory counts as being of the right kind are not manifested in cases of deviance. It does not follow that when those dispositions *are* manifested the fact that the basis-beliefs stand in a reason-giving relation to the conclusion-belief is explanatorily relevant to the formation of that belief. It remains unclear why the resources considered so far are supposed to solve the problem. In other words, it is unclear that the proposed approach does justice to the idea that the conclusion-belief was formed at least in part *because* the considerations constituting the contents of the basis-beliefs stand in a reason-giving relation to the conclusion.

At this point is might be suggested that I am working with an overly narrow conception of explanatory relevance. Given that

(i) I already believe C^1, and come to believe C^2,
(ii) C^1 and C^2 stand in a reason-giving relation to the conclusion that Tom is going to the party, and
(iii) I have the right kind of belief-forming dispositions,

it is to be expected that I will arrive at the conclusion, in response to suitable prompting events. If to explain something is just to show that it is to be expected, then the reason-giving relation would be explanatorily relevant to my drawing the conclusion. But leaving aside whether this is a legitimate, if weak, notion of explanation, it is not clear that it helps in the present context. We are considering how a belief comes to be formed on the basis of others, when the contents of the latter stand in a reason-giving relation to the content of the former. The explanatory relevance that is of interest, therefore, is relevance to the explanation of why a belief comes to be formed. Merely showing that, given the reason-giving relation in question, and the other relevant circumstances, it is to be expected that the conclusion-belief should be formed does not show that the reason-giving relation made a difference to the formation of the belief. We need to take a different tack.

In Chapter 1, Section 5, in the context of a discussion of what I called the deflationary strategy for dealing with the connection between propositional attitudes and rationality, I distinguished between two conceptions of rationality. On one conception rationality is a kind of order among one's attitudes and actions. On the other it is associated with *rational agency*. Here is how I characterized rational agents:

[R]ational agents not only think and act in conformity with the sorts of patterns that might be thought to make up the rational order. They sometimes think things and do things because they see, or assume, that there is reason to think these things and do these things. (p. 33)

    The problems we have been running up against in this discussion of explanatory relevance are, I believe, due to the fact that the approach under consideration does not go beyond the first of these conceptions. It attempts to solve the problem of explanatory relevance without reference to the stance that agents have on their own reasons. If we take this stance into account, then we can make sense of how reason-giving relations can have an explanatory role.

    When I formed the conclusion that Tom is going to the party, I did so *in view of* the considerations C^1 and C^2. That is to say, I would have taken it that C^1 and C^2 were my reasons for believing that Tom is going. Though I need not have thought to myself that these considerations constituted a (normative) reason for me so to believe, I would have formed my belief understanding them to constitute such reasons. Knowing that they are *my* reasons for believing that Tom is going, I would presume that they are (adequate normative) reasons for me so to believe. That I do so regard them might easily have become manifest. For instance, if the issue had arisen as to why I believe that Tom is going, or as to whether he will be going, I would have been able to give reasons for thinking it true that he is going. In this situation it *is* explanatorily relevant to my coming to my conclusion about Tom that there is a reason-giving relation between C^1 and C^2 and that conclusion. If C^1 and C^2 had not stood in such a relation to the conclusion, I might well not have believed that they did. That is because my belief that there is such a relation is grounded in the fact that there is. Given that C^1 and C^2 do stand in a reason-giving relation to the conclusion, I am liable to be aware of this in a situation, like that envisaged, in which the consideration and the conclusion are all in play. And had I not believed that there is, I might well not have reached my conclusion about Tom. That is because when we reach conclusions, as opposed to forming beliefs blindly, we take ourselves to be drawing conclusions from assumptions supplying adequate normative reasons for doing so. If we are not confident that we have such a reason, we might well hesitate to draw the conclusion.[98]

This narrative provides a useful model for thinking about the problem of explanatory relevance. It provides us with a case in which it is tolerably clear why the obtaining of a reason-giving relation is explanatorily relevant to the formation of a belief. Moreover, it does so in keeping with the assumption that rationalizing explanations of beliefs implicate true generalizations linking the basis-beliefs with the conclusion-belief. The generalization labelled **G** above was to the effect that anybody with such-and-such beliefs would, in appropriate prompting circumstances, be liable to reach such-and-such a conclusion. All that I have added to the story is an illustration of what explains why **G** holds. I am liable to arrive at the conclusion in question because I recognize that C^1 and C^2 constitute a reason for believing that conclusion. The further removed a case is from the sorts of conditions that obtain in this story, the less clear it is that in that case rationalizing plays an explanatory role.

A number of objections might be raised at this point. Here I consider a few.

An infinite regress threatens if we assume that when people believe something on the basis of other beliefs they must take it that the considerations forming the contents of the basis-beliefs stand in a reason-giving relation to the believed conclusion.

This worry might have its origins in Lewis Carroll's (1895/1995) story of Achilles and the Tortoise. On at least one plausible way of taking the story, the Tortoise's thought leads to two conclusions:

(a) We can never be compelled to accept a conclusion on the basis of premises from which it logically follows because we can always

---

[98] Bill Brewer (1995) writes: 'Epistemologically productive reasoning is not merely a mechanical manipulation of belief, but a compulsion in thought *by reason*, and as such involves some conscious understanding of why one is right in one's conclusions' (p. 242). I am not sure that the understanding must be conscious—it depends what one means by that—but I endorse the thought that, in cases in which one is right, understanding why one is right is crucial. It needs to be borne in mind, however, that in some cases of rationalizing explanation the subject is not right. See the discussion of messy cases in the next section.

raise the question whether we are entitled to think that the conclusion does follow from the premises.

(b) Adding to the premises a further premiss to the effect that the conclusion follows from the original premises will not help, because one can always raise the question whether the conclusion follows from the expanded set of premises; and so on *ad infinitum*.

One lesson of the story might be that (a) is correct. The fact that a conclusion follows from premises that we accept never *compels* us to accept that conclusion, if by 'compel' is meant *makes it psychologically impossible to do otherwise*. That presents no problem for logic, because logic is not about what would in fact compel acceptance. Logic and psychology are not so close. But perhaps the lesson that is more germane to our immediate concerns is that it is a mistake to suppose that, in order to be justified in drawing a conclusion from premises, we need to assume a further premiss to the effect that the conclusion follows from the original premises. That way would lead to an infinite regress. With this in mind, my account of what explains my belief about Tom might initially seem to be suspect. It might be thought to suggest that, to be rationally moved to believe that Tom is going, I need *as assumptions* not just C^1 and C^2, but also the further assumption that C^1 and C^2 stand in a reason-giving relation to the conclusion that Tom is going. Any such suggestion would clearly be wrong.

The objection rests on a misunderstanding of the role that the account assigns to my belief that C^1 and C^2 stand in a reason-giving relation to my conclusion. There is no suggestion that C^1 and C^2 do not by themselves stand in a reason-giving relation to the conclusion. The point is that my belief about the reason-giving force of C^1 and C^2 has a role in explaining why I believe the conclusion on the basis of my beliefs in C^1 and C^2. The content of my belief about the reason-giving force of C^1 and C^2 should not be conceived as a further assumption needed to provide me with an adequate reason to believe the conclusion.

It distorts the phenomenology to suppose that beliefs about reason-giving relations routinely have the kind of role that the story assigns to such a belief.

It has to be conceded that the account thus far might suggest certain misleading pictures of what happens when we base beliefs on others. One picture might be this: I have it in mind that Lizzie will go to the party only if Tom is going (C^1) and that Lizzie is going (C^2), but nothing happens. It has to come before my mind that these considerations stand in a reason-giving relation to the conclusion that Tom is going. Then I believe that Tom is going. There are echoes here of the Tortoise's deliberations. For it is as if I need a further premiss, beyond C^1 and C^2, to be persuaded.

The picture is certainly misleading in this respect. But it is not how we should think of the phenomenology. The story is that when I believe that Tom is going to the party, I do so in view of C^1 and C^2, on the understanding that they provide me with a reason for me so to believe. It is compatible with this that I should have reached my conclusion *unreflectively* in the sense that I did not think to myself that C^1 and C^2 stand in a reason-giving relation to the conclusion. But the fact, if it is a fact, that I formed the belief in this way does not show that I formed it *without regard to* whether there is such a reason-giving relation between C^1 and C^2 and my conclusion. If I had not been confident that C^1 and C^2 stand in a reason-giving relation to the conclusion, I might well not have formed the conclusion.

If I am right about the role of beliefs about one's own reasons, then believing for a reason is far less common than philosophers think.

This objection might be motivated by reflections on intentionality in non-human animals along the lines that I have touched upon more than once. Why does the pet dog dash to the front door and bark excitedly? Perhaps because it believes that there has been a certain sort of sound outside, and on that basis expects its owner to enter the house. Here we have an intentional description and explanation. The objector might suggest that it is just the sort of explanation for which it is useful to have the notion of rationalizing explanation. Yet the dog presumably is not capable of forming thoughts about reason-giving relations. What the dog is responding to is the sound from outside, which it associates with the entrance of its owner.

In this connection it is important, once again, not to become bogged down with terminological matters. The substantive issue is about when the obtaining of reason-giving relations has an explanatory role in relation to the formation of a belief. The point of the story about how I formed my belief about Tom was to provide a reasonably clear case in which the obtaining of such a relation had an explanatory role. In this example the role of the relevant reason-giving relation was mediated by my taking it, in effect, that my reasons were (normative) reasons to believe that Tom was going to the party. The dog is presumably not equipped to have such beliefs. We are not on that account debarred from applying *a* notion of rationalizing explanation to the dog, but it will be a thinner notion than that which applies to us. With the thinner notion in play, the fact that the dog's 'belief' rationalizes its expectation in some way is not explanatorily relevant to why its belief was formed. Explanations will be rationalizing in this thinner sense only in that they depict the formation of 'beliefs' and the production of behaviours as conforming to sense-making patterns. This is pretty much the model in terms of which the dispositionalist who takes the line I described above seeks to explain the explanatory significance of modes of rationalization for *our* beliefs. I have argued that this model is not up to this task, because it does not distinguish cases in which beliefs are formed in accordance with patterns of legitimate inference from cases in which reason-giving relations have a genuinely explanatory role. Cases of the former sort count as cases of believing for a reason only in a sense that is much attenuated.

2. The messiness of rationalization

I have been focusing on a relatively simple case of believing for a reason—one in which the rationalizing turns on a reason-giving relation and the reason-giving relation is grounded in an obvious logical implication. Not all reason-giving relations are so grounded, and not all rationalizing turns so straightforwardly on reason-giving relations. Sometimes reasons for belief fail to be adequate normative reasons because the considerations that constitute them do not stand in a reason-giving relation to what is believed. These are cases that, earlier, I called messy.

Consider a somewhat idealized case of prejudice. Suppose that Charlie believes that people in some population cannot be trusted.

(It does not matter what the population is. It might be a racial group, or a religious group, or a street gang.) As it happens, Charlie thinks that each member of the population that he has encountered or heard about cannot be trusted. On this basis, he believes that nobody in this population can be trusted. The consideration that is the basis for this generalization might or might not be true. Even if it is true, it provides a poor reason for believing the generalization since Charlie has encountered a very limited sample of people in the population. Apart from that, generalizations about character with regard to the population as a whole will almost certainly be ill-founded, since the criteria, such as they are, for membership of the relevant population are unlikely to correlate with character traits. So this is a messy case. Charlie's reason fails to be an adequate normative reason because the considerations that constitute his reason do not stand in a reason-giving relation to what he believes. None the less, his belief admits of a rationalizing explanation—an explanation in terms of his admittedly bad reason. This poses a problem for any theory of rationalizing explanation. I shall call it *the problem of the rationalizing relation*. If rationalizing is not about reason-giving relations, then in what sense is it rationalizing?

This is a problem in its own right. But it brings out further aspects of the problem of explanatory relevance. For one thing, it presents a problem for the dispositionalist approach to vindicating explanatory relevance that I considered earlier in this chapter. That approach is an attempt to deal with the problem of explanatory relevance without invoking the perspective that subjects have on their own reasons and commitments. I argued that it did not do justice to the idea that reason-giving relations can be explanatorily relevant to why beliefs are formed. The messy cases suggest that it also incorporates an overly idealized view of rationalization and, indeed, of our belief-forming dispositions, since the manifestations of our actual dispositions do not always match patterns of legitimate inference. But the problem of the rationalizing relation is also a problem for my attempt to deal with the problem of explanatory relevance. In the favoured example, I take it that I have a (normative) reason to believe that Tom is going to the party. I do so because the considerations in question do stand in a reason-giving relation to the conclusion believed. That is the locus of the explanatory connection between the reason-giving relation and my forming the belief about Tom. The problem of the rationalizing relation shows that it does not provide a template for all cases of rationalizing.

Messy cases should not be conceived as infrequent lapses from generally good practice. Abundant examples of messiness arise in connection with beliefs that have an intimate connection with action. Normative reasons for action often take the form of considerations that show some course of action to be, as I shall say, *a good idea*. They are at once reasons for thinking that the course of action is a good idea, and reasons to take the course of action. Correspondingly, motivating reasons for action are often considerations in the light of which it seemed to the agent that an action would be a good idea. The notion of a good idea is by no means precise and covers a broad spectrum. For instance, something can be a good idea because it serves some valuable end or because it would be fun. I use the notion because it is an everyday way of expressing what we often think about actions.

Consider the sad case of Sally and Harry. Sally's marriage to Harry has turned sour. This is no surprise to her friends, who could never understand why she married Harry in the first place. What kind of explanation might there be for Sally's having done so? Merely alluding to her desire to marry Harry will provide next to no explanatory insight. Let us suppose that Sally offers an explanation: she was in love with Harry, there were various things about him that made him attractive to her as a long-term partner (I'll spare you the details), and, so far as she knew, there were no countervailing facts. A story along these lines is clearly at least a putative rationalizing explanation. It offers an account of Sally's marrying Harry in terms of her reasons for doing so, but her reasons for doing so are the reasons in the light of which marrying him seemed to her, at the time, to be a good idea. If it is indeed the explanation, its power lies in its enabling us in one fell swoop to see why Sally thought that marrying Harry would be a good idea, why she wanted to married him, and why she did so. Rationalizing explanations of action are often best conceived in these sorts of terms. When these reasons concern matters that bring powerful emotions into play, it is not surprising that poor reasons are treated as if they were good ones—that what seemed like a good idea at the time was not. Some factors are given too much weight and others not enough. The idea of rationalizing explanation would not do the job it is meant to if it did not cover this kind of case. To admit this is not to deny that people have many dispositions the upshot of which is that they often reason well. That we have such dispositions is part of the story of why propositional attitudes and rationality are inextricable. It does not follow from this, however, that when beliefs or actions admit of a rationalizing explanation there are always considerations that stand in a reason-giving relation to what is believed.

The issue now is how to extend our account of explanatory relevance to account for messy cases. In some respects the problem is analogous to a problem that arises in connection with perception. Often we believe that something is so because we saw it to be so. I see, and come to believe, that my car is dirty at a particular time. Clearly, the fact that my car *is* dirty is explanatorily relevant to the formation of my belief that it is. Now, I might on some occasion mistakenly think that my car is dirty. Perhaps it seems to be dirty because it is in the garage and the shadows that fall upon it make it look dirty. In this case, the belief is not explained by any fact that the car is dirty, because there is no such fact. None the less, we can see how it could have struck me that the car was dirty, and therefore how I could have come to believe that it was. In thinking that it was dirty I took myself to be faced with the fact that it was dirty, and in the circumstances it is explicable that I should have been misled in this respect. So, although I am mistaken in thinking that the car is dirty, it makes sense that I should think it is because it looked just the way it does when it is dirty.

Our engagements with the rational order are loosely analogous to our perceptual engagements with the world. Prejudiced Charlie takes it that he has reason to believe that no one in the group in question can be trusted. This is not because there is a reason-giving relation between the considerations that constitute his reasons and what he believes, because there is no such relation. None the less, it is explicable that he should have assumed he had a reason. He was thinking inductively. If it were true that all the people in the group that he encountered or heard of could not to be trusted, then he would be relying on confirming instances of the generalization he comes to believe, and would have no knowledge of disconfirming instances. He over-generalizes, because the sample he relies upon does not constitute a suitably varied sample. But it would be explicable that he should have done so if, for whatever reason, he nourished bitterness and resentment against people in the group in question. People in this sort of emotional state are liable to be biased in their thinking about the people they hate.

The example of Sally and Harry also serves to illustrate how an agent's mistakenly believing there is a reason for her to think something could be sustained in the absence of a suitable reason-giving relation. The kind of normative reason that Sally needs in connection with her belief that it would be a good idea to marry Harry is a justifying reason. I am imagining that the considerations she treated in this way did not suffice to justify her thinking this and so did not supply her with a good enough reason for marrying Harry. None the less, at least some ingredients of these considerations would have counted in favour of her doing so. Given her emotional attachment to Harry, it is explicable both that she should have given these considerations inordinate weight and that she should have overlooked or given inadequate weight to indications that Harry might not have been a suitable partner after all.

The cases I have been considering are ones in which an agent displays what, in Chapter 1, Section 3, I called *a semblance of cogency*. The semblance in these cases consists in the following:

(1) the agent treats a set of considerations as being an adequate normative reason to believe a certain conclusion;
(2) these considerations do not constitute an adequate normative reason to believe that conclusion because they do not stand in a reason-giving relation to it; yet
(3) it is explicable that they should have been treated as if they did.

Messy cases of rationalization are ones in which conditions (1)–(3) hold. So why do they count as cases of rationalization? Of course, they are cases of rationalization because they are cases of believing or acting for a reason. To leave the matter there, however, would not address the question how they can be cases of believing or acting *for a reason*. The answer is that, although they are not cases of believing for a good enough reason, they are cases of believing or acting in view of considerations that seemed to the agent to be good enough reasons. So a constraint on believing for a reason is that it should be possible to view the reason-constituting considerations in this light. There are limits to how wrong one can be in those matters. It should be explicable from some point of view that the agent should have taken the considerations in question as good enough reasons. That condition is met in the cases of Sally and Harry and of Charlie.

The discussion thus far has thrown up two types of rationalizing explanation in which the rationalization (for a belief or action) is supplied by beliefs. In one case there is a reason-giving relation that contributes to the explanation of the formation of the belief or the performance of the action. In the other case there is no such reason-giving relation, but even so it is explicable that the agent should have taken it that he or she had (adequate) reason for the belief or action. In the face of this, it might be suggested that we ought to think of these different cases as being of one type rather than two. In both cases, the agent believes or acts in view of considerations *treated as* constituting an adequate normative reason. So why not say that, for some X, such-and-such beliefs rationalize X-ing if only if the agent treats the considerations that make up the contents of these beliefs as adequate reasons to X and on that account Xes? On the first of the cases just mentioned, the fact that there is an appropriate reason-giving relation figures in the explanation of the agent's treating the reason-constituting considerations as providing an adequate reason to X. In the second case there is no such reason-giving relation and therefore no such explanation. None the less, the fact that the beliefs rationalize in the way they do is explanatorily relevant to the formation of the belief or the performance of the action. That is because, had the considerations on which the agent relies not seemed to provide an adequate reason for the belief or action, the agent might well not have formed the belief or performed the action.

Common to the two cases is the fact that the agent treats the considerations in question *as if* they stood in a reason-giving relation to what is believed. This might suggest that rationalizing concerns not actual normative reasons and reason-giving relations, but only what are treated by the agent as normative reasons and reason-giving relations. There are parallels with perception at this point too. A common way of thinking about visual perception is to take it to involve experiences that normally result from causal contact with the physical world, but could be otherwise caused and might misrepresent the way the world is. Thus, even if a given experience of mine representing there to be a glass of water in front of me results from there being an appropriately positioned glass of water in front of me, none the less, it is conceptually, and indeed physically, possible that I should have had that experience, yet not as a result of there being a suitably positioned glass of water in front of me. The merits or otherwise of this view of experience need not concern us. What is of interest is that the view might suggest that, when thinking about the relevance of visual experiences to making sense of why certain beliefs are formed, we may confine ourselves to what is causally downstream from the experiences. Of course, there will usually be a worldly cause of the subject's having the experiences, but, following through the suggestion, that is not to be regarded as being of any special interest to the enterprise of making sense of how a subject responds to perceptual experiences. The problem for such a view is that it underplays the relevance of perceived facts to the sense-making enterprise. It is intelligible that I should come to believe that the coffee in my mug is cold because it is cold and I feel that it is, through handling the mug. It would be odd, and would call for some explanation, if I were to come to believe that the coffee is cold through handling the mug when the coffee is not cold. The explanation in such a case would need to address why the tactual–discriminative capacity that usually enables me to tell when a beverage in a mug has gone cold does not function properly. The point of importance is that the explanation presupposes that I have a fairly reliable tactual–discriminative way of telling whether or not coffee has gone cold. It is only because I have such a capacity that I am in the running for having mistaken beliefs on such matters in response to the handling of mugs. Analogously, we are not in the running for having mistaken beliefs about reason-giving relations unless we have discriminative capacities that, at least in relation to the sorts of subject-matter of which we have a reasonable understanding, reliably lead to correct beliefs about reason-giving relations. It is true that, when beliefs rationalize the formation of some other belief or the performance of some action, the considerations that comprise their contents are, *correctly or otherwise*, treated by the agent as standing in a reason-giving relation to the belief or the action. None the less, to leave the matter there would ignore an important part of an adequate account of rationalization. There are constraints on what can count as *treating such-and-such considerations as a reason for this or that belief or action*. As I have already stressed, if a subject counts as treating certain considerations as a reason for some belief or action when they are not, there must be some explanation for how the considerations could have seemed to the subject to be such a reason. A plausible explanation will presuppose that the agent has appropriate discriminative capacities. People will, of course, vary in their acuteness on such matters, just as they vary in the acuteness of their various modes of perception, but an individual who was incapable of discerning some reason-giving relations would not get as far as making mistakes about reason-giving relations.

What provoked this discussion in the first place was the problem of the rationalizing relation. This is a problem that faces us once we leave behind the cases in which rationalization is provided via an appropriate reason-giving relation. To deal with what rationalizing can amount to when it is not so grounded, we need to advert to what the agent treats as a (normative) reason. The agent's motivating reason for the formation of a belief or the performance of an action is intelligible as such only if it is explicable how the agent could treat the relevant considerations as providing a normative reason for that belief or action. This will be readily explicable if the considerations do constitute such a reason and the agent could be expected to realize this. When the agent is mistaken as to the reason-giving power of the considerations, the mistake may be explicable along the lines recently sketched. The less sense we can make of how the relevant considerations could have been treated as reasons, the less clear it will be to us that we are dealing with belief or action for a reason and the less clear, perhaps, that we have correctly identified the attitudes and actions involved.

In Chapter 1, Section 5, I drew attention to a strategy on which normative considerations are regarded as being explanatorily irrelevant. There is good reason to resist this strategy in connection with the normative considerations relevant to rationalizing explanation. When people take it that considerations stand in a reason-giving relation to some conclusion, they often do so *because* the considerations do stand in such a relation to the conclusion and they understand this to be so. Philosophers are often uncomfortable with such talk, because they are anxious to avoid positing queer connections between queer facts and what people think. This line of thought crops up in connection with moral considerations (Mackie 1977: chapter 1), but it is also a concern of philosophers who have quite self-consciously applied a similar dialectic to wider normative considerations, and, in particular to those that have to do with rationality (Gibbard 1990). Whatever may be the right line to take on moral matters, there is nothing queer about the fact that certain considerations stand in a reason-giving relation to some conclusion. Nor is there anything queer about the fact that subjects can discern that such relations hold, when the subjects have the relevant discriminative capacities, and the relations clearly do hold. To say this is not to deny that there is room for philosophical reflection on the kind of capacities involved and how they operate. What I am concerned to stress is that the existence of the reason-giving relations and of the relevant capacities is not seriously in doubt.

The obtaining of facts concerning reason-giving relations is no less important to understanding our thought and action than is the obtaining of facts that people can and do take in when perceiving the world around them. We understand why people form perceptual beliefs to the effect that certain objects possess certain properties because we think of them as people capable of reliably discriminating cases in which those properties obtain from cases when they do not. It is admittedly a lot easier to be wrong about reason-giving relations than it is to be wrong about perceptible properties in conditions apt for discerning that they are instantiated. Even so, unless people could, with respect to a range of subject-matters, reliably judge that such-and-such considerations stand in a reason-giving relation to such-and-such conclusions, they would not be in the running for making mistakes.

This is reflected in the way we go about understanding people. We make assumptions about what their beliefs and intentions commit them to, and about what there is reason for them to think and do, antecedent to any evidence stemming from them concerning what they think they are committed to. In relation to means–end commitments and implication commitments, for instance, we take it for granted that the subjects in question appreciate that, as we might put it in ordinary parlance, they have to do certain things to carry out their intentions, and that certain conclusions are unavoidable granted certain assumptions. If the view about belief and intention developed in Chapters 4 and 5 is right, then beliefs and intentions in and of themselves incur certain commitments. And if the view developed in Chapter 6 is correct, having certain concepts in and of itself incurs commitments. As in the case of implication commitments and means–end commitments, people may be wrong about these kinds of commitment. But if they have enough grasp of the concepts for it to be plausible that it is *these* concepts they are deploying, then wholesale error on such matters is ruled out.

The thrust of the preceding discussion is towards reinforcing a theme with a long and honourable tradition. It has two parts:

(a) Personal understanding has a distinct subject-matter—it engages with people who are subject to ideals of reason and therefore incur certain commitments.
(b) Personal understanding is distinctive, *qua* understanding, from (natural) scientific understanding because it accords an explanatory role to normative considerations.

The explanatory role of normative considerations is crucial to this picture. But that role is compatible with recognizing that in personal understanding we rely implicitly or explicitly on generalizations. (This picks up a theme from Chapter, 1, Section 4.) For in thinking about why people think or act as they do, and in attempting to anticipate what they will think or do, we rely on assumptions about what people with their attitudes, and therefore their commitments and their reasons, are liable to do under such-and-such conditions. We see what they think and do as an instance of certain patterns of thought and action, but there is a normative dimension to the patterns since they relate thought and action to normative commitments and normative reasons. Dispositionalism, as presented in Chapter 4, is not wrong in representing our concepts of the attitudes as being dispositional. But, because it models the relevant dispositions on the philosophers' paradigm cases, it does not accommodate the normative dimension to the dispositions.

CHAPTER 8

Rationality and Simulation

1. Simulation theory versus the theory-theory

In recent years some have thought that simulation has an indispensable role in personal understanding. One of the aims of this chapter is to examine this idea. Another, related, aim is to consider how viewing people as being rational relates to viewing them as being *like us*.

The debate about simulation is framed in terms of an opposition between *simulation theory* and the *theory-theory*. As the debate has progressed, more and more nuanced positions have emerged. The very nature of the supposed opposition has been as much part of the debate as consideration of which side is right. I shall start off with what looks like a relatively stark contrast. According to the theory-theory, our commonsense thinking about propositional attitudes and actions is informed by a theory. The relevant theory is taken to be a theory in the same sense in which scientific theories are theories. The subject-matter of the theory is human behaviour. The theory posits propositional attitudes of various kinds to explain behaviour and includes generalizations concerning how propositional attitudes relate to each other and to actions. It yields explanations and predictions of human behaviour when applied to particular circumstances.

According to simulation theory, we understand people by simulating them. Here is early statement of the view by Jane Heal:

> The method works like this. Suppose I am interested in predicting someone's action.... What I endeavour to do is to replicate or recreate his thinking. I place myself in what I take to be his initial state by imagining the world as it would appear from his point of view and I then deliberate, reason and reflect to see what decision emerges. (Heal 1986: 137)

Robert Gordon introduces the notion of simulation initially in relation to predicting one's own behaviour in hypothetical situations:

> To simulate the appropriate practical reasoning I can engage in a kind of *pretend-play*: pretend that the indicated conditions *actually obtain*, with all other conditions remaining (so far as is logically possible and physically probable) as they presently stand; then—continuing the make-believe—try to 'make up my mind' what to do given these (modified) conditions. (Gordon 1986: 160)

According to Gordon, we go through a very similar process in predicting the behaviour of others.

> As in the case of hypothetical self-prediction, the methodology essentially involves *deciding what to do*; but, extended to people of 'minds' different from one's own, this is not the same as deciding *what I myself would do*. One tries to make *adjustments for relevant differences*. (Gordon 1986: 162)

The idea, then, is that in understanding or anticipating others' actions and thoughts we imagine being in their shoes and, from that standpoint, consider what to do or think. Where prediction is the aim, the imagined belief or action that is the outcome of the simulation is the belief or action predicted. When explanation is the aim, the point is to see how a given set of attitudes could have led to the belief or action to be explained. What interests me is whether simulation theory points to characteristics of personal understanding that the theory-theory does not accommodate.

The main points of difference between the theory-theorist and the simulation-theorist are disputed. Indeed, doubts have been expressed about whether there is a substantive difference between the stances once these are suitably refined (Davies and Stone 1996). The following is a way of setting out the central claims on which there clearly is a real difference. It is not an attempt to capture every issue arising in the debate.

(a) The theory-theorist thinks

   (i) that, both in ascribing an initial set of attitudes to an agent and in explaining or predicting what agents will think or do given those attitudes, we draw upon a theory concerning how human beings in general are liable to think and act and about how specific individuals are liable to think and act;

(ii) that this body of theory, applied to individuals in particular circumstances, and supplemented by information about their particular habits and traits, suffices for personal understanding; it yields explanations and predictions in terms of their attitudes in essentially the same way that theories in science applied to particular circumstances yield explanations and predictions.

(b) The simulation-theorist thinks

(iii) that an important role is played by simulation both in ascribing propositional attitudes and in explaining and predicting on the basis of attitudes ascribed;

(iv) that, in virtue of the role of simulation, the basis for ascribing attitudes, and for explaining and predicting thought and action in terms of these attitudes, is not as the theory-theory represents it to be.

Clearly, (ii) and (iv) are incompatible. So here at least we have a genuine and potentially interesting difference between theory-theorists and simulation-theorists. Some theorists believe that there are other important points of contrast. For instance, Goldman, advancing a variant of simulation theory, takes issue with (i) on the grounds that there is no reason to think that in trying to understand others we apply a theory (Goldman 1989: section III). Stich and Nichols (1992), by contrast, think that the absence of an explicitly formulated theory leaves open the possibility that our thinking about thought and action is guided by a tacit theory. I shall assume that it is compatible with simulation theory to assume that personal understanding draws upon theory. The central issue is not about whether theory is applied in personal understanding. It is about whether we can account for personal understanding entirely in terms of our applying a theory of a scientific or naive-scientific character. (ii) implies that we can, but if (iv) is right the theory-theory may be part of the story but is not the whole story.

If simulation is indispensable to routine personal understanding, and is not accommodated by the theory-theory, then the theory-theory should be rejected. But what reason is there to think that simulation is at odds with the theory-theory? The answer, I take it, is that if the theory-theory were right there would be no need for simulation. We simulate another when we think what to think or what to do in that person's situation. If the theory-theory is correct, then to understand people all we have to do is to render them explicable in terms of our general theory of human behaviour, and any relevant supplementary assumptions about their own particular habits and traits. There will be no need for simulation. We just ascribe attitudes to people under constraints supplied by our theory and supplementary assumptions, and make inferences about what they will think or do. If simulation is indispensable then this is not the whole story. So the key questions concern whether simulation is indispensable and how it is supposed to be relevant to the ascription of attitudes and the provision of explanations and predictions.

It is not hard to imagine situations in which it might be helpful to pretend that one is in the shoes of another person in order to gain some insight into what he or she might think or do, or might have thought or done. Detectives might usefully do something like this to come up with hypotheses about the next move of whoever is committing a series of crimes. In that kind of situation, the thinking that one would go through from the imagined standpoint of the criminal is explicitly taken as a model or analogue of the criminal's thinking. If that is what simulation has to be, then it is implausible that we routinely engage in simulation when understanding or attempting to understand people. The worry here is phenomenological: there is no sign that we routinely go in for such exercises.

Gordon (1995) has argued that this model-model is not the right way to think about simulation when simulation is taken to have a central role in personal understanding. In particular, we are not to think that simulation produces an outcome—pretend-believing or deciding—such that a belief or decision ascribed to oneself is then transferred to the agent. The idea, rather, is that we transform ourselves in imagination into the agent. '[O]nce a personal *transformation* has been accomplished', Gordon claims, 'there is no remaining task of mentally *transferring* a state from one person [myself] to another' (1995: 56). This is because, as he sees it, the upshot of the transformation is an ascription of a belief or decision using the first person pronoun 'I', *but referring to the person into whom one has imaginatively transformed oneself.* This will deal with the problem only if what the simulation results in is *both* a self-ascription, albeit in imaginary mode, *and* an ascription to the target person. It is hard to see how anything could be that. The upshot of the simulation, where A is the target person, is something like: 'Imagining myself to be A, I ϕ.' What is needed is the ascription, 'A ϕs'. Gordon seems to suggest that there is no remaining task of transference on the grounds that the first-person ascription in imaginary mode just is an ascription to the target person. This looks implausible simply because it is one thing to imagine being A, with the result that one role-plays doing some thing; and it is another to think that A does that thing. There could be a point to the imaginative exercise, but it would be in the context of an explicit simulation, in which the role-play is taken as a model for the thought and action of the target. In such a context there would be an inferential step from the claim that in role-playing mode one has done a certain thing to the claim that the target does that thing. Peter Carruthers has suggested that Gordon's view could be supplemented with the assumption that the person simulating is primitively disposed in such a way that, on arriving at a pretend self-ascription, within the scope of the imaginative exercise, he or she then completes the process by attributing what is self-ascribed to the target.[99] There is a step here from the outcome of the simulation to a claim about the target, but not of a sort that requires the simulator to introspect his own mental processes and on that basis to ascribe a state to the target. That may well be the best way to defend Gordon's theory. As amended it still seems to be open to a phenomenological objection just as serious as the objection to model-model versions of simulation theory. We do sometimes imaginatively put ourselves in the position of a person we are trying to understand and, as if in the position of that person, think what to think or do. But we probably would not go through such a procedure if, for instance, someone were to say to us, 'I am going to see a film tonight.' If you say so to me, I shall believe that you intend to see a film tonight and expect you to do so, subject to the usual provisos. I do not appear to go through a process of simulating uttering (overtly or in imagination) 'I am going to see a film tonight' and then, within the scope of the simulation, ascribe to myself an intention to see a film and a course of action designed to carry out that intention. So if the simulation theory is to be plausible

---

[99] See Carruthers (1996: 33–4). Carruthers does not subscribe to Gordon's view and presents other objections to it.

it has to be seen as a reconstruction of unconscious or tacit thought-processes. That makes it hard to assess its truth. More importantly, it remains unclear why simulation should be taken to be the key notion on which we should focus in giving an account of personal understanding.

Heal (1986: 137; 1994b: 141; 1995; 1998) has argued that we should take simulation theory seriously because it provides the best way to do justice to the fact that, to be able to think about what people think, desire, intend, and so on, we need to be able to think about the subject-matter of their attitudes. There is no disputing that there is such a fact. If I am to think about somebody as intending to hit the bull's eye, I need to have some grasp not only of the concept of intending, but also of what it is, in the relevant context, to hit the bull's eye. Why should this sort of consideration be thought to favour simulation theory?

In the first place, it presents a problem for the theory-theory. Suppose for the sake of argument that we make use in our thinking of relatively high-level generalizations that link attitudes with other attitudes and with actions, but are unspecific about the contents of the relevant attitudes. An example might be that whenever people intend something they are liable, given convenient opportunities, to do what they believe is necessary to carry out that intention. To apply this generalization in a particular case, we need to reckon with the contents of a given belief and intention. Assuming that we know what is intended and what the person believes about necessary means, how is this supposed to provide a basis for explanation and prediction? The theory-theory says that the content and category of an attitude provide an index to the agent's dispositions to thought and action. Knowing the dispositions, we can explain and predict. But, as I noted in Chapter 4, Section 6, it is far from clear *how* content and category are supposed to index dispositions. Carruthers makes a closely related point:

[I]n order to predict what someone who entertains a thought containing a concept such as *cubic* will do or think, I shall have to predict the inferential role of that concept. I *could* do this by deploying a portion of what would be an extensive theory of concepts, whose clauses would severally specify the possession-conditions for the full range of concepts available. But it is immensely implausible that I should ever have had the opportunity to learn such a theory, and even more implausible that it should be innate. (Carruthers 1996: 25)[100]

What then is the alternative? Carruthers adds:

I can *simulate* the role of the concept in the mental life of the other by relying on my grasp of that same concept, inserting thoughts containing it into my reasoning systems, in order to see what I should then be disposed to do or think as a result. (Carruthers 1996: 25)

The important contrast here is between different ways of thinking about how the content of an attitude can steer us to what a person is liable to think or do in the light of that attitude. On one approach, unpacking the content of an attitude takes us first to dispositions of the agent and from there, via assumptions about particular circumstances, to the sought-for conclusions. Those who adopt this approach do not deny that, in understanding people's deployment of a concept, one has to exploit one's own grasp of that concept. What they are advancing is a view about what is involved in exploiting this grasp. On the other approach, we think with the concept as the other does, and attribute to the agent the attitude or action that is the upshot of this thinking. What is crucial is that one exploits one's own grasp of the concept *by thinking with it as the other does*. As Adam Morton succinctly puts it, 'Simulation is understanding others by going through the same thinking as they do' (Morton 2003: 121).

The point I am concerned to stress is that these alternatives are not exhaustive. There is another approach that draws upon the views outlined in Chapters 4, 5, and 6. This focuses on the fact that when we understand people we exploit an ability to make judgements about what it would make sense for them to think or do, given attitudes that they are known to have, or might well have given their circumstances. For instance, I might judge that it would make sense for my son to save money, given that he intends to travel extensively. Accordingly, I expect him to do so, since this is clearly something he has to do to carry out his intention, and his intention is firm. I do not have to imaginatively reproduce his thinking. I just see what he is committed to doing—what he has to do, as I might put

---

[100] Carruthers in the article cited is friendly towards a version of the theory-theory on which it does not imply thesis (ii) in the characterization I gave above.

it—and I expect him to do it. It happens that what I expect him to do in this situation is something I would do in his shoes. So if I were to simulate his thought and action in the light of his intention to travel, the upshot would be that I would, in imagination, save money. But to work out what my son will do I *need not* engage in any such exercise, because I know independently that he is (normatively) committed to saving money, that he is likely to see this, and to act accordingly. The epistemic route to the expectation of action is via the judgement as to what he is committed to doing. I do not need to simulate to make that judgement since, in knowing that he intends to travel extensively and is aware of the financial cost of doing so, I see straight off that he will have to save.

I have been trying to put simulation theory under pressure. Yet in doing so I have come very close to what Heal takes to be at the heart of simulation theory. Consider this passage:

> The other thinks that p_1–p_n and is wondering whether q. I would like to know what she will conclude. Her thoughts (I assume) will follow the connections between things. So I ask myself 'Would the obtaining of p_1–p_n necessitate or make likely the obtaining of q?' To answer this question I must myself think about the state of affairs in question, as the other is also doing, i.e. I must co-cognize with the other. If I come to the answer that a state of affairs in which p_1–p_n would necessitate or make likely that q, then I shall expect the other to arrive at the belief that q. (Heal 1998: 487)

Co-cognition, Heal thinks, is what we should be thinking about when trying to capture the phenomenon that simulation-theorists have been trying to pick out. (She thinks the term 'simulation' is misleading but still aims to capture a mode of understanding which is among those that have been described in terms of simulation; see Heal 1998: 491–2.) However, there is a case for thinking that, if co-cognition is understood in such a way that it is something we routinely do in understanding others, then it is not the case that whenever we have co-cognition we have something properly describable as simulation.

In the schematic case that Heal describes, what *is* clearly relevant to anticipating the thinking of the target subject is that, since she accepts that p_1–p_n, she is committed to accepting that q. In making such a judgement we must, of course, engage with the subject-matter of the assumptions and conclusion in question. Going by the following clarification, this amounts to co-cognition:

Co-cognition is just a fancy name for the everyday notion of thinking about the same subject-matter.... Those who co-cognize exercise the same underlying multifaceted ability to deal with some subject matter. (Heal 1998: 483)

If this is what co-cognition is, then in thinking about the subject matter of p_1–p_n, and q we do indeed co-cognize with the target subject. And there is an obvious sense in which, *if* two people when co-cognizing think through the same thoughts, then each simulates or mimics the other, whether or not he or she is aware of doing so. But the topic is not whether people sometimes mimic one another, but whether simulation is a method whereby we routinely explain or anticipate the thoughts or actions of others. It is one thing for two people to co-cognize, in virtue of exploiting their respective grasps of the same subject-matter, and another for one of them to be engaging in a simulation exercise aimed at explanation or prediction of the other's thought or action. Granted that to explain or predict we need to exercise our grasp of the subject-matter of the other's attitudes, it does not follow that we must be engaging in any such simulative exercise. So it remains unclear why simulation, as opposed to exploiting one's grasp of the relevant subject-matter, is needed in a case in which we see that a certain conclusion follows from assumptions that a person accepts, and infer that she accepts that conclusion. There is co-cognition here because there is thinking about the subject-matter of the assumptions and conclusion that figure in the thinking of the other. For this to be possible we, like the target, must be able to exploit our grasp of the relevant concepts. As Heal notes, this involves, among other things, being able, like the target, to see connections between claims implicating those concepts. We must, therefore, be *able* to do many things that the target can do. But we need not think or act as the target does, or even simulate in imagination the target's thought or action. It is one thing to see connections between claims—to see, for instance, that one is committed to accepting that q by accepting that p_1–p_n; it is another thing to infer that q, and another thing again to simulate in imagination inferring that q. Both actual inferring, analogous to that of the target, and inferring-in-imagination aimed at mimicking the target's thinking, are simulations in a clear enough sense. But there need be nothing that it is natural to call simulation in seeing connections and in the light of these making judgements about actual or possible attitudes and actions of the target.

In response, it might be suggested that we see connections *by* simulating. Perhaps, in reaching the judgement that someone is committed to believing that q by believing that p_1-p_n, we would do so by thinking what we would believe were we to believe that p_1-p_n and the question were to arise whether q. If the suggestion is that we consciously entertain thoughts about what we would believe under the conditions specified, then it is falsified by the phenomenology. Perhaps the idea is that such thoughts would have to figure in a reconstruction showing what justifies a claim about what the target is committed to believing. But now the question is why we should need such thoughts to justify the claim. If we need to back up the claim we can do so in terms of what follows from the assumptions that p_1-p_n. And if called upon to back up what we say about that, we would have to explain the meaning of terms, draw attention to inferential steps, and do whatever else might help to make it clear that the conclusion that q follows from the assumptions.

This is, to some degree, carping. Heal's main concern is to stress the importance for personal understanding of having a capacity to think about the subject-matter of people's beliefs and other attitudes. In working this out she highlights the importance of considerations about rationality. In her earliest essay on the topic, for instance, she writes:

> The difference between psychological explanation and explanation in the natural sciences is that in giving a psychological explanation we render the thought or behaviour of the other intelligible, we exhibit them as having some point, some reasons to be cited in their defence. Another way of putting this truism is to say that we see them as exercises of cognitive competence or rationality. (Heal 1986: 143)

She immediately goes on to say that this feature of psychological explanation is what the replication method, as she then called it, puts centre-stage. While agreeing that it is right to put this feature centre-stage, I doubt that this commits us to the view that personal understanding implicates a method of simulation or replication. On the stance adopted in this book, it is the fact that normative considerations relating to what it would make sense for people to think and do have a crucial and indispensable explanatory role in personal understanding which is at odds with the theory-theory. The theory-theory conceives of theories as natural science conceives of theories. Crudely speaking, theories do their work by representing there to be (non-normatively specifiable) uniformities in nature, and explaining and predicting in terms of these.[101] By contrast, according to the stance that I have been defending, normativity is written into the content of our ascriptions of propositional attitudes and actions (see Chapters 4–6) and normative considerations have an indispensable epistemological and explanatory role in personal understanding. They have an epistemological role because they form part of the basis for ascribing attitudes and actions, and for making judgements about actual and possible connections between attitudes, and between attitudes and actions. They have an explanatory role because, as I have argued in Chapter 7, considerations about what it would make sense for an agent to think or do are relevant to explanations of why a subject forms certain beliefs or performs certain actions.

I have not denied that simulation can be useful. One might wonder whether it becomes important in cases of messy rationalization—cases in which the considerations constituting an agent's reasons do not stand in a reason-giving relation to something they believe or to a course of action (Chapter 7, Section 2). Certainly imagination is required here. Consider, for instance, what philosophically minded historians of ideas do when trying to work out why a philosopher of the past reached some conclusion. This is no easy matter when it not clear that the assumptions apparently relied upon support the conclusion. A natural way of going about the task is to make a conjecture about the shape of the argument, using clues from relevant texts, and then to try to confirm the conjecture by other textual evidence. The aim here is quite explicitly to simulate the reasoning leading to the conclusion. Even then, it is not obvious that simulation will have served as a *method* for arriving at a view about the shape of the argument. If things go well the end result of the exercise will be a

---

[101] This is so no matter how stretched the notion of a (naturalistic) theory becomes. It certainly has been stretched. See Stich and Nichols (1992).

line of thought that is the very line of thought that persuaded the target philosopher of the conclusion in question. It may be that some interpreters would go about this task by imagining themselves accepting the relevant assumptions and thinking about whether the conclusion is true in the light of those assumptions. The aim would be to try to be struck by what might have struck the target philosopher. I take it that this is close to how simulation theorists think of simulation. Yet it looks less like an indispensable method and more like a heuristic that some might find useful. It is not clear either how it is supposed to make due allowance for bad reasoning. It is one thing to come up with missing assumptions, another to work out why given assumptions should have been thought to constitute a reason for thinking something or doing something, when in fact they do not.

Sometimes bad reasoning is due to emotions that colour one's thinking. In a depressed state a person might come to pessimistic conclusions about, for instance, matters of health, career prospects, or relationships with others. Understanding the person involves seeing how the emotions could have contributed to the acceptance of the conclusions in the absence of a good reasons.[102] If one has had the same or similar emotions oneself, and experienced the same or a similar colouring of one's thinking, then one has the materials that, with a bit of imagination, could enable one to see how the pessimistic conclusion could have been reached. It is not that one would be baffled in the absence such experience—it is common knowledge that if you feel bad then things may look worse than they are, and that if you feel good things may look better than they are. But the experience provides something that would not otherwise be available: direct experience of a rich texture of thought interfused with emotion, which can serve as a model for understanding other people. Here, where rationalizations are messy because of emotional colouring, simulation theory is at its best. My critical comments have been directed against the idea that simulation is *routinely* employed in explaining and predicting thought and action.

---

[102] The example of Anna Karenina, discussed in Ch. 5, Sect. 7, is relevant here. Indeed, Tolstoy's novel is replete with examples of thoughts and actions coloured by emotions. How Levin thinks of things when he sees no prospect of happiness following his rejection by Kitty is very different from how he thinks of things just after he has been accepted by her.

The thrust of what I have been arguing is that putting rationality considerations centre-stage in relation to personal understanding does not commit us to putting simulation centre-stage. Some theorists, in contrast to Heal, think that a point in favour of simulation theory is that it does *not* put rationality centre-stage (see Goldman 1989). Others, with no concern to defend simulation theory, play down the significance of rationality considerations. One motivation for being circumspect about rationality considerations is provided by the abundant evidence that we are prone to reason badly. I have already touched upon such matters in Chapter 1. Another motivation is provided by the idea that rationality considerations seem important only because of something else that is the really important thing. I have in mind here a line of thought advanced by Stephen Stich, which I discuss in the next section.

2. Rationality and 'being like us'

Stich accepts that rationality is inextricable from the having of propositional attitudes but thinks this is not very interesting. He argues as follows (Stich 1990: 50–1).

(i) 'In intentional description we characterize cognitive states via their similarity to actual and possible states of our own.' This is 'the principle of intentional chauvinism'. (Compare the principle of humanity in Grandy 1973; related ideas go back to Quine 1960.)
(ii) We are reasonably rational. It follows, given (i), that 'if a cognitive system is intentionally describable then it too must be reasonably rational'.
(iii) Since a cognitive state counts as being a belief only if it admits of an intentional description, it follows, given (i) and (ii), that 'creatures that have beliefs must be reasonably rational'.
(iv) Since '[r]easoning is a process in which beliefs are formed, modified or eliminated', it follows, with the help of (i), (ii), and (iii), that 'creatures that can reason at all must be reasonably rational'.

The key idea is that the principle of intentional chauvinism is a methodological constraint on ascriptions of attitudes. It is because such ascription is necessarily constrained in this way that any well-founded ascriptions of attitudes will make out the creatures in question to be 'reasonably rational'.

Stich then argues that the limits to the irrationality of the intentionally describable 'are uninteresting because they follow the capricious contours of intentional describability' (Stitch 1990: 53). What exactly is capricious about 'the contours of intentional describability'? If beliefs and other attitudes are inextricably linked with rationality, how can that fail to be a deep point about these attitudes? According to Stich, the capriciousness consists in the fact that intentional classification does not mark out 'natural or theoretically interesting kinds[s]' (p. 52). The reason lies in the general conception of cognitive states to which Stich adheres. One way of working out that conception is in terms of the language-of-thought hypothesis, which 'maintains that many mental processes are best viewed as manipulations and transformations of internalized, sentencelike representations' (p. 33). From this standpoint, 'the holding of a propositional attitude like a belief or a desire is identified with having an appropriate mental sentence stored in an appropriate mental location' (p. 33). In the case of belief and desire, we may think of this location as the Belief-Box or Desire-Box, as the case may be. These boxes are, in effect, functionally characterized mechanisms in the brain. Tokenings of mental sentences in these boxes function as, respectively, beliefs and desires. The view opens up an intriguing prospect: that, while all intelligent behaviour is underpinned by cognitive states conceived as tokenings of mental sentences in appropriate locations, the propositional attitude scheme—the modes of intentional description we apply to one another—captures a limited range within the possible range of cognitive states (see Stich 1990: 52–3). The envisaged possibility, it should be noted, is not just that the concepts in terms of which we specify the contents of beliefs, desires, and the like might be a limited range of the possible concepts that could in principle specify attitude contents. It is that a creature could be intelligent, and thus have cognitive states, yet not be intentionally describable at all. Here is how Stich sums up:

Assume that the sort of cognitive architecture presupposed by commonsense psychology is roughly correct and that (iii) and (iv) [above] are not in dispute. Then... there may be people whose cognitive systems exhibit the same general cognitive organization that we do, although the inscriptions in their Belief Boxes don't count as 'real' beliefs, and the processes that manipulate these inscriptions don't count as 'real' reasoning or inference. Still, these systems have 'belieflike' cognitive states and 'inferencelike' cognitive processes, which differ from real beliefs and real inference in ways that are vague, parochial, and of no psychological importance. (Stich 1990: 53)

It is clear that Stich's focus is very different from mine. He is interested in a functional characterization of the machinery that makes cognition and intelligent behaviour possible. The reason why this crops up in a discussion of propositional attitudes and rationality is that Stich thinks that our intentional predicates pick out properties that are specifiable independently of our concepts of propositional attitudes (of believing this, desiring that, and the like). If the language-of-thought hypothesis is correct, they will be specifiable in terms of language-of-thought sentence-types, and locations that determine the functional role and thus the category (belief, desire, or whatever) to which a cognitive state belongs. In some systems there will be locations corresponding to familiar states like believing and desiring. In others there might be locations for categories of state for which we have no names. It is at this level of independent specification that Stich takes the 'natural or theoretically interesting' kinds to be found. From this standpoint the 'contours of intentional describability' are capricious, because they do not mark out distinctions between real kinds of cognitive state, specified below the level of commonsense intentional description. When propositional attitude ascriptions are true, they are made true by something specifiable at the lower (deeper) level, but what is thus specified does not correspond to a kind specifiable at that level. I have adopted what I take to be a commonsense view of propositional attitude ascription that contrasts with Stich's (see Chapter 4, Section 1). According to this view, for a subject to believe that p—to possess the property of believing that p—is nothing other than for that subject to fall under the concept of believing that p. What makes an ascription of such a concept true is not to be found at some other deeper level, so there is no question of there being the kind of mismatch between concepts and real kinds that Stich envisages. It is compatible with my view that there might be intentional psychologies implicating states that are not well described by our propositional attitude concepts. I have taken this possibility seriously at various points at which the issue of non-human animal intentionality has cropped up. My view is also compatible with there being analogies between (a) functionally specifiable systems subserving propositional attitudes as we conceive them, and (b) functionally specifiable systems subserving intentional states of a different kind. Systems linked to sub-doxastic informational states and sub-intentional aims might be examples of the latter. If it is the mechanisms in which you are interested, then you might well not wish to make a song and dance about the differences between (a) and (b). But being interested in the mechanisms is not the only game in town. There are issues about the character of our understanding of one another and of ourselves—the kinds of issues that I have been exploring. Our concepts in general, and our concepts of the attitudes in particular, mark important distinctions because they are the means by which we represent each other to each other and to ourselves.

These remarks relate to Stich's charge that the link between rationality and the attitudes is uninteresting, because intentional description is capricious. There is another feature of arguments (i)–(iv) bearing more directly on issues about simulation. The role given to the principle of intentional chauvinism is such that, on the face of it, assumptions about rationality need have no role in personal understanding. We are to follow the maxim of making out the actual and possible cognitive states of those we seek to understand as being similar to our own. If our ascriptions are well founded, it will turn out that they will be reasonably rational, because we are, but this is accidental to the proceedings. Rationality considerations are not on the epistemic route to the ascriptions. This is grist to the mill of Goldman's (1989) version of simulation theory, which is explicitly canvassed as an alternative to a theory on which understanding is constrained by rationality considerations. I have given reasons for doubting whether simulation has the kind of importance that Goldman and others have ascribed to it. I have also criticized Goldman's downplaying of the role of rationality considerations in personal understanding (Chapter 1, Section 4, under the heading 'Against the rationality assumption'). The point that matters here is that, on the position adopted in this book, it is not similarity considerations that drive attempts at understanding, but normative considerations. If in our attempts at understanding we end up making those we seek to understand like us, that is because they, like us, are subject to ideals of reason and requirements associated with the possession of such-and-such concepts. As creatures with beliefs and intentions, they are subject to the Means–End Ideal and the Implication Ideal, and accordingly incur specific commitments linked to specific beliefs and intentions. As possessors of concepts, they are subject to requirements dictating respect for the conditions of application of the concepts, and must be able to detect empirically the properties that some of those concepts pick out. If we did not find them to be reasonably coherent, reasonably cogent, and reasonably in touch with their surroundings, we could not make any sense of them. But that is not because rationality is a by-product of their being like us, but because being rational is an implication of having propositional attitudes and of possessing concepts.

CHAPTER 9

Limits

1. Taking stock

Throughout this book I have been concerned with propositional attitudes and ascriptions of propositional attitudes. I have paid particular attention to beliefs and intentions because these attitudes play a central role in understanding thought and action and have a distinctive character. They are, as I put it, psychological commitments. As such, their impact on subsequent thought or action is shaped by the normative commitments that they implicate. In thinking or acting as they do, people are routinely responsive to normative commitments and to normative reasons which they know they have. It is via such knowledge that commitments, and reasons generally, come to be explanatorily relevant to the formation of beliefs and the performance of actions. It is compatible with this view that rationalizing explanations are genuine explanations. They provide genuine explanatory insight into why people think or act as they do. Importantly, from my point of view, they represent the formation of the belief or the performance of the action as something that made sense *to the agent*. For in thinking of the agent as having come to think something or do something for a reason, we think of the agent as taking his or her reason to be one in the light of which it makes sense to think that thing or do that thing. But the insight we can acquire in terms of commonsense psychology is limited and the prospects of deeper insight at the level of commonsense psychology and, indeed, any more scientific intentional psychology are limited. In this chapter I briefly consider some of these limitations.

It will help to locate the issues if we take note of two sharply contrasting approaches to the topic of propositional attitudes in the philosophy of mind of the past few decades. On both approaches the theory-theory is accepted. Beliefs, desires, and so forth are regarded as posits of the theory, and the generalizations supposedly making up the theory spell out how attitudes relate to other attitudes, to sensations, to perceptual experiences, and to actions. The difference between the approaches is that one is enthusiastic and the other sceptical about the explanatory and predictive power of the theory. In keeping with this difference, the enthusiasts take the power of the theory to tell in favour of the truth of the generalizations and the reality of the entities posited by the theory. The sceptics, by contrast, think that, despite its usefulness for everyday purposes, the poor performance of the theory is a reason to doubt that it tells us anything deep about human behaviour. Sceptics may go so far as to be eliminativist about the theory. That is to say, they may take seriously the possibility that there will come to be reason to reject the theory, along with its ontology, and replace it with something else.

The enthusiasts are represented by Jerry Fodor, who speaks of the 'extraordinary predictive power' of 'good old commonsense belief/desire psychology' conceived as a theory positing states with causal powers (Fodor 1987: 3). The sceptics are represented by Paul Churchland. In his original eliminativist manifesto, Churchland argued that commonsense psychology is explanatorily weak. He noted that there are phenomena that it does not adequately explain, including 'the nature and dynamics of mental illness, the faculty of creative imagination,...the ground of intelligence differences between individuals', and that there are phenomena it does not even address (Churchland 1981: 73). Among the latter are the functions of sleep, the ability to catch a ball on the run, the variety of perceptual illusions, and 'the miracle of memory'. Then there is the further consideration that commonsense psychology is, in Churchland's words, a 'stagnant or degenerating research program' (p. 75). Whereas in areas in which enquiry is productive and healthy there is development and progress, commonsense psychology has progressed little and has even retreated. There has been retreat, Churchland thinks, because, whereas the ancients thought of the forces of nature in intentional terms—as manifestations of the actions of agents—we, that is, serious naturalists, confine intentional categories to humans and other animals. Churchland concedes that such considerations do not show that the theory is false, but he suggests that 'they do move that prospect well into the range of real possibility, and...show decisively that [it] is *at best* a highly superficial theory, a partial and unpenetrating gloss on a deeper and more complex reality' (p. 74).

I am sympathetic towards Churchland's view that there are serious limitations to commonsense psychology, but I do not think that a good case has been made for eliminativism. As Churchland himself recognizes, the fact that commonsense psychology has explanatory limitations does not show that it is false. No solid case is made for thinking of it as a theory in retreat. If commonsense psychology has not changed much over the centuries, this might show that it is a framework for making judgements nearer to the observational end of the spectrum, and not that it is a theory that has had its day. It is, to say the least, disputable that beliefs, desires, and so forth are properly regarded as hidden states or events that are posited to explain phenomena more directly accessible. That is not the only way to think of them. Believing something, and having a pain in one's foot, are properties of the whole individual. Once we think of the matter in this entirely natural way, it is far from clear that we should think of the properties as being theoretical—invoked to explain behaviour to which we have more direct access. From our early years, we learn to apply concepts of propositional attitudes and of action-types in judgements that are a fairly direct response to what we perceive others to be doing or saying. There is little reason to suppose that our judgement-forming methods in this area reflect adherence to a theory that continues to be accepted because of its explanatory and predictive power. In any case, the main argument for eliminativism about propositional attitudes turns on assumptions about what the physical world would have to be like if there really were propositional attitudes figuring in the causation of behaviour. The strategy is to argue first for a conditional claim to the effect that if the attitudes were ontologically respectable then the physical world would be like *this*, and then to establish that the physical world is not like that. For Churchland, if there really were propositional attitudes then there would be physical categories to which intentional categories were reducible, and thus the world would be as characterized by the theory implicating the reducing categories. Since he thinks, rightly in my view, that the prospects for the required reduction are dim, he concludes that it is unlikely that there are propositional attitudes. A similar approach is taken by Ramsey et al. (1991). They argue that, according to commonsense psychology, 'propositional attitudes are *functionally discrete*, *semantically interpretable* states that play a *causal role* in the production of other propositional attitudes, and ultimately in the production of behaviour' (p. 97). They then argue that connectionist models of cognitive architecture do not accommodate such tokenings and that, accordingly, if these models are right, so is eliminativism about the attitudes. At one level the point about functional discreteness is simply that there may be two distinct attitudes, both of which are potentially relevant to the formation of a belief or the performance of an action but only one of which figures in the relevant causal history. Commonsense psychology does seem to be committed to functional discreteness in this sense, for it acknowledges that an agent might have various desires any one of which could have prompted some action, though in the event only one did. Plausibly, commonsense psychology also has it that the attitudes are *semantically*, and therefore *intentionally*, describable, and enter into the causation of thought and action. It is a further matter, though, whether commonsense psychology represents the attitudes as states comprising representations that are semantically interpretable and tokened in an appropriate location in the cognitive system. Physical structures that are semantically interpretable would possess their semantic contents contingently—it would be by virtue of their contingently possessed causal roles that they have the contents they do. The attitudes, as conceived in commonsense terms, possess their contents essentially. It is a substantial and disputable step to move from functional discreteness as a claim about the attitudes ordinarily conceived, to functional discreteness as a claim about structures identified as beliefs, on some version of cognitive science.[103]

The problem with eliminativist arguments of the sort under consideration is that they rely on the background assumption that the potential of an attitude to affect the subject's thought and action will be closely mirrored by the causal potential of some physical state—a state that, in virtue of its potential, is the physical realization of the

---

[103] Similar criticism may be found in Baker (1995: ch. 3).

attitude. If it then seems implausible that there are physical states with the right kind of causal powers, the conclusion drawn is that there are no such attitudes. But we are not bound to think that propositional attitudes have physical realizations in the required sense, even granted that we are physical creatures. On the conception of the attitudes developed in this book, there are dispositions—albeit normatively specifiable dispositions—that are characteristic of attitudes. But the constraints that the dispositions place on the physical states of subjects are loose. A disposition characteristic of believing P is a disposition to use P as an assumption in one's thinking, when it seems germane to do so, guided by the implication commitments of believing P along with the other things one believes. Having that normatively characterized disposition is compatible with considerable diversity among those believing P at the level of non-normatively characterized dispositions. Of course, there will be diversity owing to differences in the other things believed. (The familiar holism of the mental is not the issue here.) But there will also be diversity among those who believe P, which is not so explicable—diversity that is due, among other things, to differences in logical acumen or in the grasp of relevant concepts.

Consider again the example I discussed in Chapter 7. Suppose that people who believe that Lizzie will go to the party only if Tom is going (C^1), and believe that Lizzie will go (C^2), are disposed in suitable prompting circumstances to make transitions in thought which amount to discharging implication commitments of those beliefs. So they have something like this belief-adjusting disposition: if they were prompted to think about whether Tom is going, they would be liable either to draw the conclusion that Tom is going, or to give up either the belief in C^1 or the belief in C^2. Among those who are so prompted, and therefore who are thus liable, some may be more likely than others either to draw the conclusion about Tom or to give up belief in C^1 or belief in C^2. For some may be more likely than others to put two and two together and see that C^1 and C^2 have implications for whether or not Tom is going. This diversity will be matched by diversity at the level of the neuro-physiological system. No doubt anyone with the belief-adjusting disposition will have some complex physically specifiable disposition, which, in combination with other contingencies, bears on the likelihood of their either drawing the conclusion or giving up belief in one or other of the assumptions. But there is no reason to think that each will have the same such disposition. So there is no reason to expect that each will be in some physical state which is the ground of such a disposition.

In the present context, my focus is in any case not on reasons for rejecting eliminativism, but on the lessons to be learned from the limitations of propositional attitude psychology. I want to take the limitations seriously while preserving the framework of commonsense thinking. That framework, I have argued, incorporates normative assumptions.

Some of the limitations are simply limitations in scope of applicability. It is no serious defect of commonsense propositional attitude psychology that it does not tell us about the functions of sleep or about the ability to catch a ball or to serve an ace at tennis. The limitations on which I shall focus concern the level of insight available into why people think and act as they do. These are limitations of propositional attitude psychology operating in its own proper domain. They suggest that the enthusiasts are overly optimistic, but not that the sceptics are right.

2. Limitations of available explanations

I begin with limitations to the explanatory and predictive power of the sorts of explanations that are available to us. Suppose that I am surfing the web in search of flights to Barcelona. The fact that I intend to take a holiday there and that Barcelona is most conveniently reached by air is a reason for me to be searching for flights. I search for flights for that reason. The fact that a convenient way of doing this is via the web and that I have easy access to the web gives me a reason to search for flights using this facility. I am doing so for that reason. This is a rationalizing explanation of what I am doing. Yet the considerations that constitute my reasons are ones I have known about for some time. My acceptance of them, and my appreciation of their reason-giving force, does not by itself account for why I search for flights when I do. There is a sense in which this is no defect in the explanation. It is one thing to explain why I am searching the web and another to explain why I am doing it now rather than at some other time. The explanation in terms of the reasons specified is of the former sort. As such it may be adequate for ordinary purposes. None the less, what is being explained is a datable event—the performance of an action at a time. Someone seeing what I am doing might ask me why I am doing it. If I were to give my reasons it would be by way of addressing that question—a question about something I am doing now. My answer will be correct so far as it goes only if the considerations cited are those in view of which I am doing what I am doing now. That is to say, my acceptance of those considerations, and my recognition that they give me a reason to surf the web, must figure in a true explanatory account of what led to my now surfing the web. But—and this is the point I am concerned to emphasize—the account in terms of these factors is merely *part* of a wider story about what led to my doing what I am doing now. That is why, though an explanation citing these considerations as my reasons might well be adequate for practical purposes, the insight they supply into why the action was performed is limited. It is important not to infer from this that such an explanation is no real explanation at all. Explanations of occurrences typically provide explanatory insight by alluding to factors relevant to the aetiology of what is being explained. The fact that these factors can be present when something of the sort being explained does not ensue is not in itself an objection to an explanation that refers only to them. What matters is that on the occasion in question, and along with other factors, they should have led to what is to be explained, and that citing them should answer to the relevant interest in explanation. These conditions are met in the case of the rationalizing explanation for my surfing the web. It would be a different matter if I were to leave the table at a dinner party at which I am host to search for flights. In that case my guests are likely to wonder what I am up to and are unlikely to be satisfied by being informed of my reason for searching the web. In such a case what is puzzling is why I should be doing so then and in those circumstances.

When it comes to explaining the formation of beliefs, the limitations are, if anything, even more prominent than in the case of actions. We might wonder why Nick thinks that it would be a good idea for the UK to adopt the single currency of the European Union. We are looking for reasons for this belief. Maybe our interest is dialectical rather than psychological. We want to debate the matter and assess the reasons offered rather than speculate about what led Nick to form his view. But in that case we are not in the business of understanding why he formed his view. If, however, we are interested in what led Nick to form his view, then obviously we are in the domain of psychology. As in the case of action just considered, his reasons provide limited explanatory insight into why he formed his belief. For Nick might have accepted all the considerations that constitute his reasons and yet not formed his belief when he did or not formed it at all. Whether people come to some conclusion on the basis of considerations that they accept depends not just on their acceptance of the considerations, but on their being prompted to bring them into play and draw the conclusion from them.

The sorts of limitations just considered are not of much practical interest. It is easy to think of cases of a more interesting sort. When Sally left Harry (to return to an example from Chapter 7, Section 2) there were, no doubt, various factors of which she and others were aware, which contributed to explaining why she did so. Perhaps there were constant rows and reproaches. Perhaps her interests and Harry's had become, or always had been, too divergent. If these were standing features of their situation, they would not explain why Sally left when she did. But, more interestingly, they are unlikely to tell the whole story about why she wanted to leave. It is a cliché that it is hard to pin down what it is about others that makes them attractive as partners, and that it may be just as hard to pin down what it is about a relationship that makes it seem doomed to one or other party. This does not mean that the factors Sally or her friends might cite to explain her leaving are not genuine explanatory factors. It just means that they may well not provide the full story. They could have been present though Sally did not leave.

3. Limitations to the availability of explanations

When an explanation for forming a belief or performing some action is limited, it will often be the case that a fuller explanation is available at the level of propositional attitudes. Consider again cases in which motivating reasons do not explain why the subject forms a belief or acts some way at a particular time. Perhaps I search for flights when I do because I recalled that I had to do so at a time when it was convenient to conduct such a search. Or perhaps I was thinking about how nice it was going to be to spend time in Barcelona and as a result developed a desire to search for flights right away so as to maximize the options available to me. But just as often there is no commonsense explanation to be had for why people choose to do certain things when they do. When something that needs to be done could as easily have been done at some other time, there need be no rationale for doing it when it is done, other than that it carries out an intention to satisfy an inclination to do it at that time. Why the subject should have such an inclination need have no further explanation in terms of other propositional attitudes. Think of two scenarios in which I intend to visit the library in the afternoon. In one there is a short time for doing so available between meetings; knowing this, I go during that time. In the other I am spending the afternoon reading and choose to go around 3.30. There may be a reason for going just then. Perhaps I intended to have a short break in mid-afternoon. But I might simply have felt like going then. Given this inclination, it is no surprise that I should intend to satisfy it in the absence of any reason not to. But there may be no reason for me to want to go just then and no other explanation for my wanting to go at the level of propositional attitude psychology. Nor, I think, is there any reason *a priori* to suppose that a more refined psychology of propositional attitudes, whatever that might be, would yield an explanation in terms of intentional categories of any kind. There is no more reason to suppose that there must be a commonsense explanation for an inclination to go for a walk, or to resume reading a novel, or to watch television, at a particular time than there is to suppose that there must be such an explanation for feeling hungry at some particular time and thus having an inclination to eat around that time. I do not suggest that this is a startling result. After all, it is generally recognized that there are unmotivated desires. My point is simply that desires that are unmotivated by reasons none the less have explanations. It is just that the explanations may lie outside the domain of commonsense propositional attitude psychology.

Other cases in which the resources of propositional attitude explanation run out have to do not with why the agent does something at a particular time, but with why the agent selects some course of action from among options under consideration. Suppose you are faced with the options of clearing out your garage or reading a novel or going for a walk. There are no very decisive reasons for doing any of these things. There will be other opportunities to clear out the garage, and the heavens won't fall if you never get around to it. The novel is not so gripping that you are desperate to continue reading it. You have no very strong inclination to go for a walk and there is no particular reason why you should. You decide to clear out the garage. There might be an explanation of a limited sort of why you chose to do this. Perhaps it struck you that you had been thinking of doing so for some time, and that you would feel good if it were done or bad if it were not. But even if you had such thoughts, you might have had them and ended up reading the novel. There need be no facts about your beliefs, desires, feelings, and so on, that explain why you chose to clear out the garage rather than do the other things. The thought underlying this example is that you were not psychologically determined to make the choice you did. Given your psychology up to the point of choice, so far as it is captured in terms of propositional attitudes, perceptual experience, and any other elements recognized in commonsense psychology, you were not bound to clear out the garage.[104] There might still be a rationalizing explanation of your clearing out the garage in terms of the consideration that it could be used more effectively if it were cleared out. Such an explanation may be fine so far as it goes. In the light of the consideration it cites—to which you did give some weight—it is at least no great surprise that you should have cleared out the garage. Yet you might so easily have chosen differently. Perhaps in this particular case nothing much is at stake and there would be little interest in knowing what explains the choice. But in other cases in which choices are undetermined by the agent's reasons, there might well be an interest in acquiring further insight into why the choice was made. Think of cases in which people are deciding on which universities to apply for, which subjects to study, which careers to pursue, whether to make a career move, or which houses or apartments to buy. These are

---

[104] It is compatible with the view that such a scenario is possible that you were determined to choose as you did, but that is another matter. Not being psychologically determined is compatible with being determined by the totality of factors accounting for your choice. Compare Wolf (1990: 100–16), who uses a similar example in defence of a type of compatiblism about freedom.

matters on which a great deal can be at stake, yet it may not be very clear how to reach a decision and, when one does decide, not very clear what factors explain the decision. Yet in thinking about our decisions on these matters we, or others, might well aspire to greater understanding than is to be had.

It is not a problem for commonsense psychology that it does not tell us much if anything about mental illness or creative imagination or why some people appear to have a natural talent for playing the violin. In so far as it deals with what people know, believe, desire, intend, feel, and so on, we should not expect it to shed much light on these things. The limits I have just been considering are limits to an understanding to which we sometimes aspire in the domain of propositional attitudes and action. The point I am making is compatible with there being a science dealing with, for instance, mood swings, the ebb and flow of emotions, and their affects on judgement and action. (See Kunda 1999 for a useful review of recent work on cognition and emotion.) Such a science might shed further light on how our thinking about what to believe or do can be influenced by factors of which most of us have little systematic understanding. But to the extent to which it delves below the level of rough generalizations, and the identification of relevant factors, such a science is likely to take us beyond the domain of personal understanding towards matters at the interface between physiology and thought.

In drawing attention to the limits of propositional attitude explanations, I am not expressing a general scepticism about the possibility of self-knowledge or knowledge of others. There is knowledge to be had at the level of propositional attitude psychology. But there are borderlands at which explanatory insight in terms of propositional attitudes tails off. This matters not only because in practice we often aspire to greater insight, but because we can easily think the aspiration is satisfied when it is not. The sorts of cases I have in mind are familiar enough. They are cases in which people put some construction on the behaviour of others that provides a rationale for the adoption of some attitude towards them. Mary makes a passing remark to which Bill takes offence, thinking that it is unjustified criticism directed at him. Or she says something to Bill in a tone of voice that leads Bill to be upset, taking it to be an expression of anger or resentment directed towards him. These are cases in which assumptions are made about what lies behind a remark. We can imagine scenarios for the cases in which the assumptions are ill-founded or inappropriate, reflecting more on the person accepting them than on the person making the remark. In some such cases the assumptions may be straightforward misinterpretation. In other cases the cause of the offending remark or its tone may be obscure, as much to the person making it is as to anyone else. In such cases there is little reason to think that there *must be* a truth of the matter potentially available at the level of propositional attitude psychology. This can be important in a context in which the critical judgements are linked to blame. For blame to be justified, the agent must have failed to do something that he or she ought to have done. The person doing the blaming must therefore assume that it was open to the agent to have acted otherwise. Leaving aside the difficulties in figuring out what that amounts to, the obscurity of the agent's motivation, as much to him- or herself as to others, will often make the assumption suspect.[105] But the attractions of blame as a psychological weapon may provide a strong incentive to the person blaming to imagine that he or she knows more than can be known about the other's motivation.

4. Expectations

In the light of the discussion so far, what should we make of Fodor's optimism about the *predictive* power of commonsense psychology? This is vividly expressed in the following passage:

Commonsense psychology works so well it disappears.... Someone I don't know phones me up at my office in New York from—as it might be—Arizona. 'Would you like to lecture here next Tuesday?' are the words that he utters. 'Yes, thank you. I'll be at your airport on the 3 p.m. flight' are the words that I reply. That's *all* that happens, but its more than enough; the rest of the burden of predicting behaviour—of bridging the gap between utterances and actions—is routinely taken up by theory. And the theory works so well that several days later ... and several thousand miles away, there I am at the airport, and there he is to meet me. Or if I *don't* turn up, it is less likely that the theory has failed than that something went wrong with the airline. It's not possible to say, in quantitative terms, just how successfully commonsense

---

[105] These remarks link up with what Bernard Williams (1995: ch. 3) has called the obscurity of blame.

psychology allows us to coordinate our behaviours. But I have the impression that we manage pretty well with one another; often rather better than we cope with less complex machines. (Fodor 1987: 3)

There is no doubt that we do sometimes make well-founded predictions about what people will do or what they will think. When we do so we take their beliefs and desires into account, or at least presuppose that they have certain beliefs and desires. But considerations about beliefs and desires, and even intentions, are very often only part of the story.

Consider Fodor's example. We are to imagine that all that happens is that two utterances are made over the telephone. The caller asks a question. The recipient of the call replies and makes a statement about where he will be at a certain time. We can easily fill in some of the details. The recipient believes that the caller is inviting him to give a lecture. He says he will and specifies the flight by which he will arrive at the airport in Arizona. He presumes that if he turns up on that flight appropriate arrangements will have been made to receive him. The caller judges that the recipient is saying he will give a lecture and that he will turn up at the airport as he says he will. The result, we may presume, is that each believes that a certain arrangement has been made, each intends to stick to it, and each believes that the other will. When the due time comes things proceed as arranged. How is it that all this happens with such ease? The beliefs formed by each about what the other is saying certainly depend upon an ability to use English, but obviously there is a lot going on beyond identifying what is said.

Because the event is of a familiar sort, the recipient can quickly decide how to respond. If he were being asked by a local radio chat show host to answer listeners' questions about mind, body, and spirit he might have been more circumspect. The nature of the event, and the need to make definite arrangements for it, signal that the invitation is of a relatively formal kind, rather than the come-along-if-you-can-make-it kind. The issuing of the invitation implicates an undertaking to make the arrangements. Acceptance of the invitation is an undertaking to attend as arranged. Both undertakings incur commitments to do the thing undertaken. The caller has reason to expect the recipient to attend, given that he has accepted the invitation, and therefore has incurred a commitment to attending. The recipient has reason to expect that when he arrives as arranged, he will be received accordingly, since the caller has incurred a commitment to receiving him and treating him in the usual way. These expectations are founded on the presumption that, as we might say, there is a way of going about these things. My talk of practices, and of the commitments that participating in them incurs, is a gloss on that ordinary talk. There is, in effect, a practice of arranging for lectures to be given by people from other institutions. It is the fact that such a practice is in play that determines that a relatively formal invitation is being given and accepted. Issuing and responding to such invitations is itself a practice, with rules about what would count as a reasonable excuse for not carrying out the commitments incurred.

There is a standing philosophical temptation to suppose that considerations about normative commitments play no indispensable role in such proceedings except as they figure in the contents of attitudes attributed to people involved. (Recall the discussion of explanatory irrelevance in Chapter 1, Section 5.) In this vein one might suggest that the caller will believe that the recipient will believe that he (the recipient) should proceed as arranged, and the recipient will believe that the caller will believe that he (the caller) should proceed as arranged. If, then, each also believes that the other will want to do what he believes he should do, there is no need to invoke generalizations beyond those comprising what Fodor calls 'good old commonsense belief/desire psychology'. But now we need to consider what reason each would have to suppose that the other will believe he should proceed as arranged. There is no denying that in some cases both caller and recipient might be governed by purely prudential considerations. The caller has prudential reasons not to let the recipient down: it would reflect badly on the caller and his institution, and possibly diminish the chances of attracting good speakers in the future. The recipient has a prudential reason not to let the caller down: it would reflect badly on him and might diminish his chances of being a welcome guest elsewhere. Conceivably, in some exchanges of the general sort under consideration—giving and responding to invitations to lecture or give seminars—one or both of the recipients thinks along those lines and attributes similar thinking to the other. The confidence that each has that the other will proceed as arranged may be grounded in a belief that the other will be motivated by prudential reasons of the sort specified. I suspect that it is fairly rare for academics to think this way. In any case, each of our characters will need some reason to be confident that the other will think along these lines. The important point is that this is not something that can be routinely assumed. There is no need to suppose that it is routinely assumed in order to account for the smoothness of such exchanges, since there is the alternative account that I sketched, relying on the idea that a practice is in play. On this account each participant presumes that there is a way of going about these things—a practice. Each believes that the other believes that this is so, and that the other will take himself to have incurred a commitment to proceeding as arranged. This belief as to what the other believes does not depend on independent information about the normative principles the other happens to accept. It is based on the presumption that a practice is in play and that each is aware of this and has some grasp of what the practice demands. In the absence of a specific reason to be cautious about the matter, each will believe that the other will carry out the commitment unless prevented from doing so or faced with some competing obligation. The fact that the commitment has been incurred, because a practice is in play, is a crucial part of the explanation of why either believes that the other will believe that it has been incurred.

These considerations reflect back on the account in terms of prudential reasons. In the first place, it would be odd for either participant to be confident that the other would be motivated by such reasons, in the absence of specific information about the other's distinctive modes of thinking and action. While there might be cases in which one or both participants are entirely influenced by prudential reasons, there is no reason to think it generally true that people need to believe they have these sorts of reasons if they are to be motivated to keep to arrangements they have made. Many make undertakings and strive not to let people down. So we would need some particular reason to suppose that the other would not be moved but for the prudential reasons. In the second place, even if a participant would not be moved but for prudential reasons, it would be odd if the prudential reasons did not extend to taking account of the consideration that a commitment has been incurred. Part of the reason for thinking so is that the exchange does so obviously involve undertakings and corresponding commitments. Given that it does, not to proceed as arranged, in the absence of a reasonable excuse, would be liable to kindle at least mild resentment. In sum, the very fact that commitments have been incurred affects the kind of prudential reasons there are to stick to the arrangements.

The lesson to be drawn from reflection on such exchanges is that sometimes we are able to form well-grounded expectations about how people will behave because we view them and ourselves as participating in a practice and thus as governed by the rules of the practice. A crucial element in the exchange is the ascription beliefs, intentions, desires, and so forth, but part of the basis for these ascriptions is the presumption that a practice is in play. This is so in very many of the situations in which we form definite expectations about what people will do. Think of routine expectations concerning waiters in restaurants, shop assistants, ticket clerks, bank clerks, postmen, bus drivers, train conductors, people at information desks, receptionists in hotels, ushers in cinemas, and colleagues at work. We form definite expectations about what such people will think or do based on assumptions about their role. Their occupancy of the role is a matter of their participating in the practice and thus being (normatively) committed to carrying out the duties that define the role. We engage with many of them with little if any information about their beliefs and intentions, far less their desires, beyond what we can glean from the role and features of the current situation. If I have just handed over money for a train ticket to a ticket clerk, I will have a definite expectation that an appropriate ticket will be given to me along with any change from the transaction. The expectation is grounded in part in knowledge about what the ticket clerk is supposed to do. I need have no information about the clerk beyond what I gather from my understanding of his job, and my knowledge of what he knows about what I have just done.

The utility of practices is largely due to the fact that they enable us to form expectations about what people will think and do in the absence of specific information deriving from them about their beliefs, desires, and intentions. This is particularly clear in connection with the practices associated with institutional roles. In institutions like firms and armies, people have to be able to form fairly definite expectations concerning people they do not know personally. They can do this if they know what role in the institution the person occupies and the duties attached to the role, and thus the commitments incurred by occupying the role.

Obviously, not all of our definite expectations about people are grounded in knowledge of practices. Many are grounded in knowledge of routines. Members of families have expectations about the behaviour of others in the family based on routines for ferrying children around, having meals, going shopping, and the like. Friends may have routine leisure activities on particular evenings without special arrangements. Each expects that a good number of the others will be there, just on the basis of there being the routine. (Such routines could develop into loose practices, for instance if not turning up without informing others in advance is seen as letting people down.)

I do not take issue with the idea that understanding people and forming expectations about them implicates knowledge of what they are likely to believe, desire, intend, and so on. The point I have been pressing is that we often presuppose that they will have certain beliefs and intentions simply on the basis of the fact that they occupy a role or have a certain routine and are faced with a certain situation. When I expect the ticket clerk to give me the ticket I ask for and the correct change, this is because I know that this is what she is supposed to do. I need not think to myself that, from the fact that she occupies the role of ticket clerk, it is safe to assume that she will believe that she is committed to doing these things, though in regarding her as a ticket clerk I presuppose that she knows what the role requires of her and will act accordingly. Since we are addressing each other, I implicitly assume that she is aware of what is happening in the exchange.

Sometimes we form expectations when neither practices nor routines are elements of the situation and we also lack information, stemming from those we are trying to understand, about their attitudes. This is illustrated by the example used earlier of the young man apparently mugging someone (Chapter 1, Section 5). In that case we have no information stemming from the agent himself about what he is up to and there are no practices or routines knowledge of which would help us out. We have to go on assumptions about what it might make sense for the agent to think, want, and intend in the relevant circumstances, and about what would make sense of his behaviour in those circumstances. In relation to such situations, it is especially clear how much we rely on normative considerations. These considerations have their roots in a framework that we bring to bear on the situation, not on independent information about the normative principles to which the agent subscribes. Their role is therefore analogous to the role played by assumptions about the commitments incurred by participating in practices. In relation to the latter, of course, we are in a position to make the assumptions because we have information about the practices. That is information we are not bound to have. When we are trying to make sense of the behaviour of the young man running, we rely on normative considerations that are implicated in our very grasp of what it is to believe this and intend that.

The enthusiasts about the predictive power of commonsense psychology, conceived as a more or less naive theory, underestimate the extent to which definite expectations depend on knowledge about practices and routines. More importantly, they underplay or entirely overlook the importance of normative considerations 'outside of' the contents of the attitudes of the agents we are trying to understand. It has been a chief aim of this book to highlight the role of these considerations.

Bibliography

Anscombe, G. E. M. (1963). *Intention*, 2nd edn. Oxford: Blackwell.

Antony, L. (1989). 'Anomalous Monism and the Problem of Explanatory Force', *Philosophical Review*, 98: 153–87.

Austin, J. L. (1961). 'Performative Utterances', in Austin's collection of essays, *Philosophical Papers*. Oxford: Clarendon Press: 220–39.

—— (1962). *How to Do Things with Words*. Oxford: Clarendon Press.

Baier, K. (1958). *The Moral Point of View*. Ithaca, NY: Cornell University Press.

Baker, L. R. (1995). *Explaining Attutudes: A Practical Approach to the Mind*. Cambridge: Cambridge University Press.

Bermúdez, J. L. (2000). 'Self-deception, Intentions and Contradictory Beliefs', *Analysis*, 60: 309–19.

—— (2003). *Thinking without Words*. New York: Oxford University Press.

—— and Millar, A. (eds.) (2002). *Reason and Nature: Essays in the Theory of Rationality*. Oxford: Clarendon Press.

Blackburn, S. (1984). 'The Individual Strikes Back', *Synthese*, 58: 325–63. [Page references are to the reprint in Miller (2002).]

Boghossian, P. (1989). 'The Rule-Following Considerations', *Mind*, 98: 547–9.

—— (2002). 'How are Objective Epistemic Reasons Possible?' in Bermúdez and Millar (2002).

Bond, E. J. (1983). *Reason and Value*. Cambridge: Cambridge University Press.

Bradden-Mitchell, B. and Jackson, F. (1996). *Philosophy of Mind and Cognition*. Oxford: Blackwell.

Brandom, R. (1994). *Making It Explicit*. Cambridge, Mass.: Harvard University Press.

—— (1995). 'Knowledge and the Social Articulation of the Space of Reasons', *Philosophy and Phenomenological Research*, 55: 895–908.

Bratman, M. (1987). *Intentions, Plans, and Practical Reason*. Cambridge, Mass.: Harvard University Press.

Brewer, B. (1995). 'Compulsion by Reason', *The Aristotelian Society*, Suppl. Vol., 69: 237–53.

Broome, J. (1997). 'Reasons and Motivation', *The Aristotelian Society*, Suppl. Vol. 71: 131–46.

—— (1999). 'Normative Requirements', *Ratio*, 12: 398–419.
—— (2002). 'Practical Reasoning' in Bermúdez and Millar (2002), 85–111.
Burge, T. (1979). 'Individualism and the Mental', in P. A. French, T. E. Uehling, Jr, and Howard K. Wettstein (eds.), *Midwest Studies in Philosophy*, iv. Minneapolis: University of Minnesota Press: 73–121.
Buss, S. and Overton, L. (eds.) (2002). *Contours of Agency: Essays on Themes from Harry Frankfurt*. Cambridge, Mass.: MIT Press.
Butterfield, J. (ed.) (1986). *Language, Mind and Logic*. Cambridge: Cambridge University Press.
Carroll, L. (1895). 'What the Tortoise said to Achilles', *Mind*, 4: 278–80; reprinted in *Mind*, 104 (1995): 691–93.
Carruthers. P. (1996). 'Simulation and Self-Knowledge', in Carruthers and Smith (1996: 22–38).
—— and Smith, P. K. (eds.) (1996). *Theories of Theories of Mind*. Cambridge: Cambridge University Press.
Churchland, P. M. (1979). *Scientific Realism and the Plasticity of Mind*. Cambridge: Cambridge University Press.
—— (1981). 'Eliminative Materialsm and the Propositional Attitudes', *Journal of Philosophy*, 78: 67–90.
—— (1989). 'Folk Psychology and the Explanation of Human Behaviour', *Philosophical Perspectives*, iii: *Philosophy of Mind and Action Theory*. Oxford: Blackwell, 225–41.
Coltheart, M. and Davies, M. (eds.) (2000). *Pathologies of Belief*. Oxford: Blackwell.
Cullity, G. and Gaut, B. (eds.) (1997). *Ethics and Practical Reason*. Oxford: Clarendon Press.
Dancy, J. (2000). *Practical Reality*. Oxford: Clarendon Press.
Darwall, S. L. (1983). *Impartial Reason*. Ithaca, NY: Cornell University Press.
—— (1997). 'Reasons, Motives and the Demands of Morality: An Introduction', in Darwall *et al.* (1997: 305–12).
—— (1998). *Philosophical Ethics*. Boulder, Colo.: Westview Press.
—— Gibbard, A., and Railton, P. (eds.) (1997). *Moral Discourse and Practice: Some Philosophical Approaches*. New York: Oxford University Press.
Davidson, D. (1963). 'Action, Reasons and Causes', *Journal of Philosophy* 60, 685–700. [Page references are to the reprint in Davidson (1980: 3–19).]
—— (1970). 'Mental Events', in L. Foster and J. W. Swanson (eds.), *Experience and Theory*. London: Duckworth. [Page references are to the reprint in Davidson (1980: 207–27).]

Davidson, D. (1973). 'Freedom to Act', in T. Honderich (ed.) *Essays on Freedom of Action*. London: Routledge & Kegan Paul. [Page references are to the reprint in Davidson (1980: 63–81).]
—— (1974). 'Psychology as Philosophy', in S. C. Brown (ed.), *Philosophy of Psychology*. London: Macmillan. [Page references are to the reprint in Davidson (1980: 229–44).]
—— (1975). 'Thought and Talk', in S. Guttenplan (ed.), *Mind and Language*. Oxford: Clarendon Press. [Page references are to the reprint in Davidson (1984: 155–70).]
—— (1980). *Essays on Actions and Events*. Oxford: Clarendon Press.
—— (1982). 'Rational Animals', *Dialectica*, 36: 317–27. [Page references are to the reprint in Davidson (2001: 95–105).]
—— (1984). *Inquiries into Truth and Interpretation*. Oxford: Clarendon Press.
—— (1985). 'Incoherence and Irrationality', *Dialectica*, 39: 345–54.
—— (1990). 'Representation and Interpretation', in Moyheldin Said *et al.* (1990: 13–26).
—— (1993). 'Thinking Causes', in Heil and Mele (1993: 3–17).
—— (1995). 'Donald Davidson', in Guttenplan (1995: 231–6).
—— (2001). *Subjective, Intersubjective, Objective*. Oxford: Clarendon Press
Davies, M. and Stone, T. (eds.) (1995). *Mental Simulation*. Oxford: Blackwell.
—— and —— (1996). 'The Mental Simulation Debate: A Progress Report', in Carruthers and Smith (1996: 119–37).
Dennett, D. (1978). *Brainstorms*. Brighton, Sussex: Harvester Press.
—— (1981). 'Three Kinds of Intentional Psychology', in R. Healy (ed.), *Reduction, Time and Reality*. Cambridge: Cambridge University Press. [Page references are to the reprint in Dennett (1987: 43–68).]
—— (1984). *Elbow Room: The Varieties of Free Will Worth Wanting*. Oxford: Clarendon Press.
—— (1987). *The Intentional Stance*. Cambridge, Mass.: MIT Press.
Dretske, F. (2000a). 'Norms, History, and the Constitution of the Mental', in Dretske (2000b: 242–58).
—— (2000b). *Perception, Knowledge and Belief: Selected Essays*. Cambridge: Cambridge University Press.
Evans, G. (1982). *The Varieties of Reference*. Oxford: Clarendon Press.
Fodor, J. A. (1987). *Psychosemantics*. Cambridge, Mass.: MIT Press.
—— (1991). 'You Can Fool Some of the People All of the Time, Everything Else Being Equal: Hedged Laws and Psychological Explanation', *Mind*, 100: 19–34.

Foot, P. (1972). 'Morality as a System of Hypothetical Imperatives', *Philosophical Review*, 81: 305–16. [Page references are to the reprint in Foot (1978: 157–73).]
—— (1978). *Virtues and Vices*. Oxford: Blackwell.
Frankfurt, H. G. (1998). *The Importance of What We Care About: Philosophical Essays*. Cambridge: Cambridge University Press.
Gardner, S. (1993). *Irrationality and the Philosophy of Psychoanalysis*. Cambridge: Cambridge University Press.
Gibbard, A. (1990). *Wise Choices, Apt Feelings: A Theory of Normative Judgement*. New York: Oxford University Press.
—— (1994). 'Meaning and Normativity', in Villanueva (1994: 95–115).
—— (2002). 'Normative Explanations: Invoking Rationality to Explain Happenings', in Bermúdez and Millar (2002: 265–82).
Goldman, A. (1989). 'Interpretation Psychologized', *Mind and Language*, 4: 161–85.
Gordon, R. M. (1986). 'Folk Psychology as Simulation', *Mind and Language*, 1: 158–71.
—— (1995). 'Simulation without Introspection or Inference from Me to You', in Davies and Stone (1995: 53–67).
Grandy, R. (1973). 'Reference, Meaning, and Belief', *Journal of Philosophy*, 70: 439–52.
Grim, R. H. and Merrill, D. D. (eds.) (1988). *Contents of Thought*. Tucson: University of Arizona Press.
Guttenplan, S. D. (ed.) (1995). *A Companion to the Philosophy of Mind*. Oxford: Blackwell.
Hale, B. and Wright, C. (eds.) (1997). *A Companion to the Philosophy of Language*. Oxford: Blackwell.
Hampshire, S. (1959). *Thought and Action*. London: Chatto & Windus.
—— (1965). *Freedom of the Individual*. London: Chatto & Windus.
Hare, R. M. (1963). *Freedom and Reason*. Oxford: Clarendon Press.
Harman, G. (1976). 'Practical Reasoning', *Review of Metaphysics*, 79: 431–43.
—— (1977). *Morality: An Introduction*. New York: Oxford University Press.
Heal, J. (1986). 'Replication and Functionalism', in Butterfield (1986: 135–50).
—— (1987/8). 'The Disinterested Search for Truth', *Proceedings of the Aristotelian Society*, 88: 97–108.
—— (1994a). 'Moore's Paradox: A Wittgensteinian Approach', *Mind*, 103: 5–24.

Heal, J. (1994b). 'Simulation vs. Theory-Theory: What is at Issue?', in Peacocke (1994: 129–44).
—— (1995). 'How to Think about Thinking', in Davies and Stone (1995: 33–52).
—— (1998). 'Co-Cognition and Off-Line Simulation: Two Ways of Understanding the Simulation Approach', *Mind and Language*, 13: 477–98.
—— (2002). 'First-Person Authority', *Proceedings of the Aristotelian Society*, 102: 1–19.
Heil, J. and Mele, A. (eds.) (1993). *Mental Causation*. Oxford: Clarendon Press.
Horwich, P. (1998). *Meaning*. Oxford: Clarendon Press.
Hursthouse, R. (1991). 'Arational Actions', *Journal of Philosophy*, 88: 57–68.
Jackson, F. (1995). 'Essentialism, Mental Properties and Causation', *Proceedings of the Aristotelian Society*, 95: 253–68.
—— (1999). 'Non-Cognitivism, Normativity, Belief', *Ratio*, 12: 420–35.
Johnston, M. (1988). 'Self-deception and the Nature of Mind', in B. McLaughlin and A. Rorty (eds.), *Perspectives on Self-deception*. Berkeley: University of California Press, 63–91.
Kim, J. and Sosa, E. (eds.) (1995). *A Companion to Metaphysics*. Oxford: Blackwell.
Kripke, S. A. (1979). 'A Puzzle About Belief', in A. Margalit (ed.), *Meaning and Use*. Dordrecht: Reidel: 239–83.
—— (1982). *Wittgenstein on Rules and Private Language*. Oxford: Blackwell.
Kunda, Z. (1999). *Social Cognition: Making Sense of People*. Cambridge, Mass.: MIT Press.
Lazar, A. (1999). 'Deceiving Oneself or Self-Deceived? On the Formation of Beliefs "Under the Influence"', *Mind*, 108: 265–90.
Lehrer, K. (1990). *Theory of Knowledge*. Boulder, Colo.: Westview Press.
Lennon, K. (1990). *Explaining Human Action*. London: Duckworth.
Levi, I. (2002). 'Commitment and Change of View', in Bermúdez and Millar (2002: 209–32).
Lewis, D. (1972). 'Psychophysical and Theoretical Identifications', *Australasian Journal of Philosophy*, 3: 249–58.
Loar, B. (1981). *Mind and Meaning*. Cambridge: Cambridge University Press.
—— (1988) 'Social Content and Psychological Content', in Grim and Merrill (1988: 99–110).
Loewer, B. (1997) 'A Guide to Naturalizing Semantics', in Hale and Wright (1997: 108–26).

Mackie, J. L. (1977). *Ethics: Inventing Right and Wrong*. Harmonsworth, Middx: Penguin Books.

McCulloch, G. (1995). *The Mind and its World*. London and New York: Routledge.

McDowell, J. (1984). 'Wittgenstein on Following a Rule', *Synthese*, 58: 325–63; reprinted in McDowell (1998a).

——(1985). 'Functionalism and Anomalous Monism', in E. Lepore and B. McLaughlin (eds.), *Actions and Events: Perspectives on the Philosophy of Donald Davidson*. Oxford: Blackwell. [Page references are to the reprint in McDowell (1998b: 325–40).]

——(1994a). 'Knowledge by Hearsay', in B. K. Matilal and A. Chakrabarti (eds.), *Knowing from Words: Western and Indian Philosophical Analysis of Understanding and Testimony*. Dordrecht: Kluwer: 195–224; reprinted in McDowell (1998a: 414–43).

——(1994b). *Mind and World*. Cambridge, Mass.: Harvard University Press.

——(1995). 'Knowledge and the Internal', *Philosophy and Phenomenological Research*, 55: 877–93; reprinted in McDowell (1998a: 395–413).

——(1998a). *Meaning, Knowledge, and Reality*. Cambridge, Mass.: Harvard University Press.

——(1998b). *Mind, Value, and Reality*. Cambridge, Mass.: Harvard University Press.

McGinn, C. (1984). *Wittgenstein on Meaning*. Oxford: Blackwell.

McLaughlin, B. (1995). 'Disposition', in Kim and Sosa (1995: 121–4).

Martin, M. (1998). 'An Eye Directed Outward', in Wright *et al.* (1998: 99–121).

Mele, A. R. (1992). *Springs of Action*. New York: Oxford University Press.

——(1997). 'Real Self-Deception', *Behavioural and Brain Sciences*, 20: 91–104.

Millar, A. (1991). *Reasons and Experience*. Oxford: Clarendon Press.

——(2000). 'The Scope of Perceptual Knowledge', *Philosophy*, 75: 73–88.

Miller, A. (ed.) (2002). *Rule-Following and Meaning*. Chesham, Bucks: Acumen.

Miller, R. (1987). *Fact and Method: Explanation, Confirmation and Reality in the Natural and Social Sciences*. Princeton, NJ: Princeton University Press.

Millikan, R. (1990). 'Truth Rules, Hoverflies, and the Kripke–Wittgenstein Paradox', *Philosophical Review*, 99: 323–53.

——(2000). *On Clear and Confused Ideas: An Essay on Substance Concepts*. Cambridge: Cambridge University Press.

Mohyeldin Said, K., Newton-Smith, W., Viale, R., and Wilkes, K. (eds.) (1990). *Modelling the Mind*. Oxford: Clarendon Press.

Moore, G. E. (1942). 'Reply to my Critics', in P. Schilpp (ed.), *The Philosophy of G. E. Moore*. La Salle, Ill.: Open Court, 535–677.
—— (1944). 'Russell's Theory of Descriptions', in P. Schilpp (ed.), *The Philosophy of Bertrand Russell*. La Salle, Ill.: Open Court.
Moran, R. (1988). 'Making Up your Mind: Self-Interpretation and Self-Constitution'. *Ratio* (n.s.), 1: 135–51.
—— (2001). *Authority and Estrangement*. Princeton, NJ: Princeton University Press.
Morton, A. (2003). *The Importance of Being Understood: Folk Psychology as Ethics*. London: Routledge.
Nagel, E. (1977). 'Teleology Revisited', *Journal of Philosophy*, 74: 261–301.
Nagel, T. (1970). *The Possibility of Altruism*. Oxford: Clarendon Press.
Norman, R. (1995). *Ethics, Killing, and War*. Cambridge: Cambridge University Press.
O'Hear, A. (ed.) (2002). *Logic, Thought and Language*. Cambridge: Cambridge University Press.
O' Shaughnessy, B. (1980). *The Will: A Dual Aspect Theory*. Cambridge: Cambridge University Press.
Owens, D. (2000). *Reason without Freedom: The Problem of Epistemic Normativity*. London: Routledge.
Papineau, D. (1999). 'Normativity and Judgement', *The Aristotelian Society*, Suppl. Vol. 73: 17–43.
Peacocke, C. (1983). *Sense and Content*. Oxford: Clarendon Press.
—— (1992). *A Study of Concepts*. Cambridge, Mass.: MIT Press.
—— (ed.) (1994). *Objectivity, Simulation and the Unity of Consciousness: Current Issues in the Philosophy of Mind*. Oxford: Oxford University Press.
—— (1998). 'Conscious Attitudes and Self-Knowledge', in Wright *et al.* (1998: 63–98).
Pettit, P. (1993). *The Common Mind*. New York: Oxford University Press.
Putnam, H. (1962). 'The Analytic and the Synthetic', in H. Feigl and G. Maxwell (eds.), *Minnesota Studies in the Philosophy of Science*, iii: *Scientific Explanation, Space and Time*. Minneapolis: University of Minnesota Press; reprinted in Putnam (1975b: 33–69).
—— (1975a). 'The Meaning of Meaning' in K. Gunderson (ed.) *Minnesota Studies in the Philosophy of Science*, vii: *Language, Mind and Knowledge*. Minneapolis: University of Minnesota Press; reprinted in Putnam 1975b: 215–71.
—— (1975b). *Mind, Language and Reality: Philosophical Papers*, ii. Cambridge: Cambridge University Press.
Quine, W. V. (1960). *Word and Object*. Cambridge, Mass.: MIT Press.

Railton, P. (1994). 'Truth, Reason, and the Regulation of Belief', in Villanueva (1994: 71–93).

Ramsey, W., Stich, S., and Garon, J. (1991). 'Connectionsim, Eliminativism, and the Future of Folk Psychology', in J. Greenwood (ed.), *The Future of Folk Psychology: Intentionality and Cognitive Science*. Cambridge: Cambridge University Press: 93–119.

Raz, J. (1999). *Engaging Reason*. Oxford: Oxford University Press.

Rey, G. (1997). *Contemporary Philosophy of Mind*. Oxford: Blackwell.

Rosen, G. (1997). 'Who Makes the Rules Around Here?' *Philosophy and Phenomenological Research*, 57: 163–71.

Scanlon, T. M. (1998). *What We Owe to Each Other*. Cambridge, Mass.: Harvard University Press.

Schiffer, S. (1987). *The Remnants of Meaning*. Cambridge, Mass.: MIT Press.

—— (1991). 'Ceterus Paribus Laws', *Mind*, 100: 1–17.

Schueler, G. F. (1993). *Desire, its Role in Practical Reason and the Explanation of Action*. Cambridge, Mass.: MIT Press, 1993.

Searle, J. (1969). *Speech Acts*. Cambridge: Cambridge University Press.

—— (1983). *Intentionality*. Cambridge: Cambridge University Press.

Sellars, W. (1956). 'Empiricism and the Philosophy of Mind', in H. Feigl and G. Maxwell (eds.), *Minnesota Studies in the Philosophy of Science*, i: *Foundations of Science and Concepts of Psychology and Psychoanalysis*. Minneapolis: University of Minnesota Press; reprinted in Sellars (1963b: 127–96).

—— (1963a). 'Some Reflections on Language Games', in Sellars (1963b: 321–58).

—— (1963b). *Science, Perception and Reality*. London: Routledge & Kegan Paul.

Skorupski, J. (1997). 'Reasons and Reason', in Cullity and Gaut (1997: 345–67).

—— (2001). 'Rationality—Instrumental and Other', in R. Bondon, P. Demeulenaere, and R. Viale (eds.), *L' Explication des normes sociales*. Paris: Presses Universitaire de France: 175–86.

Smith, M. (1994). *The Moral Problem*. Oxford: Blackwell.

—— (1997). 'In Defense of *The Moral Problem*: A Reply to Brink, Copp, and Sayre-McCord', *Ethics*, 108: 84–119.

Stein, E. (1996). *Without Good Reason: The Rationality Debate in Philosophy and Cognitive Science*. Oxford: Clarendon Press.

Steward, H. (1997). *The Ontology of Mind: Events, Processes, and States*. Oxford: Clarendon Press.

Stich, S. (1990). *The Fragmentation of Theory*. Cambridge, Mass.: MIT Press.

Stich, S. and Nichols, S. (1992). 'Folk Psychology: Simulation or Tacit Theory?' *Mind and Language*, 7: 35–71.

Stocker, M. (1979). 'Desiring the Bad', *Journal of Philosophy*, 76: 738–53.

Sturgeon, N. (1985). 'Moral Explanations', in D. Copp and D. Zimmerman (eds.), *Morality Reason and Truth*. Totawa, NJ: Rowman & Allanheld, 49–78.

Tennant, N. (1997). *The Taming of the True*. Oxford: Clarendon Press.

Tolstoy, L. (1954). *Anna Karenin*, trans. R. Edmunds. Harmondsworth, Middx: Penguin Books.

Toulmin, S. E. and Baier, K. (1952). 'On Describing', *Mind*, 61: 13–38.

Tversky, A. and Kahneman, D. (1983). 'Extensional versus Intuitive Reasoning: The Conjunction Fallacy in Probability Judgement', *Psychological Review*, 90: 293–315.

Uniacke, S. (1994). *Permissible Killing: The Self-Defence Justification of Homicide*. Cambridge: Cambridge University Press.

Velleman, J. D. (1989). *Practical Reflection*. Princeton, NJ: Princeton University Press.

—— (1992). 'The Guise of the Good', *Nous*, 26: 3–26; reprinted in Velleman (2000b: 99–122).

—— (2000a). 'The Aim of Belief', in Velleman (2000b: 244–81).

—— (2000b). *The Possibility of Practical Reason*. Oxford: Clarendon Press.

Villanueva, V. (1994). *Philosophical Issues*, v: *Truth and Rationality*. Atascadero, Calif.: Ridgeview.

Walsh, D. (ed.) (2001). *Naturalism, Evolution and Mind*. Cambridge: Cambridge University Press.

Watson, G. (1975). 'Free Agency', *Journal of Philosophy*, 72: 205–20.

Wedgwood, R. (2002). 'The Aim of Belief', *Philosophical Perspectives*, xvi, *Language and Mind*. Oxford: Blackwell.

Wikforss, A. M. (2001). 'Semantic Normativity', *Philosophical Studies*, 102: 203–26.

Williams, B. (1970). 'Deciding to Believe' in H. Kiefer and M. Munitz (eds.), *Language, Belief and Metaphysics*. New York: SUNY Press; reprinted in Williams (1973: 136–51).

—— (1973). *Problems of the Self*. Cambridge: Cambridge University Press.

—— (1995). *Making Sense of Humanity, and Other Philosophical Papers*. Cambridge: Cambridge University Press.

Williamson, T. (2000). *Knowledge and its Limits*. Oxford: Oxford University Press.

Wittgenstein, L. (1958). *Philosophical Investigations*, 2nd edn. Oxford: Blackwell.

Wolf, S. (1990). *Freedom within Reason*. New York: Oxford University Press.
Wright, C. (1980). *Wittgenstein and the Foundations of Mathematics*. London: Duckworth.
—— (1984). 'Kripke's Account of the Argument against Private Language', *Journal of Philosophy*, 81: 759–78.
—— Smith, B. C., and Macdonald, C. (eds.) (1998). *Knowing our Own Minds*. Oxford: Clarendon Press.

Index

Achilles and the Tortoise 200–3
Allais's paradox 25 n. 19
animals *see* non-human animals
Anscombe, G. E. M 63–7, 70
Antony, L. 10, 13, 20–1
arational action 70–1
Austin, J. L. 113 n. 64

Baier, K. 11 n. 10, 97 n. 58
Baker, L. R. 101 n. 60, 233 n. 103
Bermúdez, J. L. xii, 157–8
Blackburn, S. 161, 162
Boghossian, P. 35 n. 25, 160, 161 n. 81, 176 n. 86
Bond, E. J. 11 n. 10, 57 n. 39
Braddon-Mitchell, D. 107 n. 62
Brandom, R. v–ix, 14, 184 n. 94
Bratman, M. 80–3, 139, 146 n. 77
Brewer, B. 200 n. 98
Broome, J. 74 n. 47, 75 n. 48, 79 n. 49, 82 n. 52
Burge, T. 164
Buss, S. and Overton, L. 124 n. 68

Carroll, L. 200–1
Carruthers, P. 217, 218–19
character traits 111–13, 116, 118, 124
causal explanation 17–21, 107–8
and generalizations 16–21, 192
Churchland, P. M. 28, 30, 32, 33, 231–2
cogency 6–8, 14, 207
Coltheart, M. 10 n. 8, 28 n. 23

commitments, normative v, ix–x, 23, 39, 40, 42, 72–99, 168, 219–20, 230
and justification 79–83
incurred by beliefs and intentions 72–83, 91–2, 100, 108, 110, 128–9, 131–2, 133, 138, 172, 190–1
incurred through participation in a practice 40, 84–92, 120, 168–78, 242–3, 247
incurred through possession of concepts 184–91
commitments, psychological 100, 120–4, 230
concepts, concept-possession v, 2–9, 178–91, 212, 229
normative 23, 95–6, 100
and conceptions 181–3
and properties 100–3, 229
conceptual principles 118–20
conjecturing 44–7
constitutive aims of belief 43–57, 82, 123–4
constitutive aim of intention 121
constitutive aim of intentional action 57, 63–70, 82
constitutive principles 118–20
correctness in use of concepts 179–85
correctness in use of words, 162–6, 177
rules for 161–2, 165–6, 169–70, 184
Cullity, G. and Gaut, B. 57 n. 39

260 INDEX

Davies, M 10 n. 8, 28 n. 23, 214
Dancy, J. 11 n. 10, 12
Darwall, S. L. 11 n. 10, 15 n. 14, 57 n. 39, 58 n. 40
Davidson, D. 3–8, 10, 13, 18–21, 25–6, 62 n. 43, 96 n. 57, 145
Dean Commitment Principle 119–20
Dennett, D. 4 n. 2, 31–2, 151
dispositional explanation 107, 193–4
dispositionalism 104–31, 190, 193–9, 212
dispositions v, 103–8, 128–9, 138, 190–1, 212, 234–5
  problem of representing the 125–31, 190
Dretske, F. xi, 189

eliminativism 231–5
Evans, G. 191 n. 96
explanatory relevance 21, 192–212
expressivism 24, 34–6

Fodor, J. A. 105, 231, 241–5
Foot, P. 90
Frankfurt, H. G. 124 n. 68

Gardner, S. 153–7
Gibbard, A. 34, 36, 101, 159–60, 168, 176, 211
goal-directedness 52–7, 143, 150, 157, 158
Goldman, A. 6 n. 4, 26–7, 215, 225, 228
Gordon, R. M. 214, 216–18
Grandy, R. 225
guessing 44–5

Hale, B. 161
Hampshire, S. 136 n. 71, 138 n. 72
Hare, R. M. 97 n. 58

Harman, G. 36–7, 131–2, 138 n. 72, 145
Heal, J. 113–15, 125, 167, 213, 218, 220–3, 225
Horwich, P. xi, 161 n. 80, 168, 175–7, 189
Hursthouse, R. 70–1

Implication Commitment Principle 99, 109–10, 117–19, 125
implication commitments 73–8, 123, 129, 212
Implication Ideal 76–8, 92, 123–4, 137, 229
Implication Requirement 77; see also rationality, requirements of
inertia of intentions 146–7
institutions 245–6
Intention Principle 69–71

Jackson, F. 75 n. 48, 107 n. 62
Johnson, M. 157 n. 78

Kant, I. 109
Kripke, S. A. v, xi, 6 n. 3, 159–61, 166, 168, 172, 176
Korsgaard, C. 119 n. 119
Kunda, Z. 240

laws, psychological 18–21, 28–9
Lazar, A. 157
Lehrer, K. 51
Lennon, K. 197
Levi, I. 123 n. 67
Lewis, D. 130, 172, 175
Loar, B. 126 n. 69, 130
Loewer, B. 161 n. 80

Mackie, J. L. 211
Martin, M. 151–2
McCulloch, G. 161 n. 80

McDowell, J. vii, 16–17, 19 n. 18, 49 n. 34, 161, 191 n. 96
McGinn, C. 161, 181 n. 91
McLaughlin, B. 108
meaning x, 39, 159–81
Means–End Commitment Principle 99, 109–10, 117–19, 125
means–end commitments 75–8, 123, 212
Means–End Ideal 76–8, 81, 84, 92, 117, 121, 123–4, 137, 229
Means–End Requirement 77; *see also* rationality, requirements of
Mele, A. R. 139, 140 n. 73, 145, 157
Millar, A. 36 n. 27, 104
Miller, A. 159 n. 79, 161
Miller, R. 3 n. 1
Millikan, R. G. 141 n. 75, 161 n. 80
Moore G. E. 125
Moore's Paradox 125
moral principles 36–8
Moran, R. 112 n. 63, 125
Morton, A. 219
motivational bias 157
Motivation Principle 42, 68–71

Nagel, E. 53 n. 38
Nagel, T. 11 n. 10, 57 n. 39
naturalism 35, 231
Newcomb's puzzle 25 n. 19
Nichols, S. 130, 215, 223 n. 101
non-human animals xi–xii, 32–4, 134–6, 142–3, 150, 191
Norman, R. 109
normative ideals 30
normative import 98–9, 103, 108–25, 136, 170, 175 n. 87
normative statements 92–8, 160
norms 25, 35, 36, 96

O'Shaughnessy, B. 52 n. 37
Owens, D. 44 n. 31, 50–1

Papineau, D. xi, 188–9
Pascal, B. 47 n. 33
particularism 101 n. 61
Peacocke, C. 151, 179 n. 89, 191 n. 96
personal understanding 1–3, 16, 20, 21–4, 34, 39–40, 123, 190, 212, 215, 222–3
Pettit, P. 141 n. 75
practices 40, 84–92, 168–75, 184, 243–7
precarious intentions 139, 146–8
preface, paradox of the 26–7
Promise Commitment Principle 119–20
promises (promising) ix, 84, 120
Putnam, H. 101, 161 n. 80

Quine, W. V. 225

Railton, P. 43 n. 29
radical interpretation 4
Ramsey, W. 233
rational agents (agency) 23, 32–4, 36, 39, 97, 108, 137, 199
rationality xi, 3–9, 16, 24–39, 76–8, 100, 198–9, 222, 225–9
rationality, requirements of 25, 76–8, 92
rationality assumption 4, 7, 16, 23–8, 229
rationality principle 26–8
rationalizing explanation 9–21, 39–40, 41–2, 79, 107–8, 192–212, 223–4, 230–47
rationalizing relation, the problem of the 204–10

Raz, J. 93 n. 54
reasons, motivating (explanatory) 10–14, 68–71, 193, 237
reasons, normative xii, 11–14, 23, 31–3, 38, 41–71, 230
  and justification for belief or action 42–71, 79–80
reflective capacities viii–xii, 14, 32, 34, 123, 133–7, 138 n. 72, 150–1; *see also* reflexivity
reflexivity
  and concept-use 190–1
  of intentions and beliefs 138–51
Rey, G. 30–3
roles (offices) 85, 86, 169, 245–6
Rosen, G. 93 n. 55, 184 n. 94
rule-following 141–3
rules for correct use of words 165–6

Scanlon, T. M. 11 n. 10, 57 n. 39, 63 n. 44, 109–10
Schiffer, S. 105, 130
Schueler, G. F. 11 n. 10, 57 n. 39, 130
Searle, J. 119 n. 65, 138 n. 72, 145
self-deception 151–8
self-referential content of intentions 145–6
Sellars, W. v, 141 n. 75, 196 n. 97
simulation theory 213–25
Skorupski, J. 65, 93 n. 54 and n. 55
Smith, M. 11 n. 10, 57, 59 n. 41
space of reasons viii–xi, 14
Stein, E. 25 n. 20

Steward, H. 101 n. 61
Stich, S. 130 n. 70, 215, 223 n. 101, 225–9,
Stocker, M. 65
Stone, T. 214
Sturgeon, N. 37 n. 28
sub-doxastic states 150, 191, 228
sub-intentional activity 52–7, 143, 150, 158, 191, 228
Sullivan, P. M. 93 n. 55

Tennant, N. 159 n. 79
theory-theory 213–16, 218–19, 223, 231
Tolstoy. L. 154, 224 n. 102
Toulmin, S. E. 97 n. 58
Tversky, A., and Kahneman, D. 27–8

undertaking, practice of 87–9, 242–7
Uniacke, S. 61 n. 42

Velleman, J. D. 43 n. 29, 52, 65, 138 n. 72, 143 n. 76, 145

Watson, G. 65
Wedgwood, R. 43 n. 29
Wikforss, A. M. 167 n. 82 and n. 84
Williams, B. 43 n. 29, 241 n. 105
Williamson, T. 44 n. 30, 49 n. 34, 167 n. 83
Wittgenstein, L. 141 n. 75, 142, 159, 174 n. 86
Wolf, S. 239 n. 104
Wright, C. 161